# REVOLUTION IN MEXICO:

# YEARS OF UPHEAVAL,

## 1910–1940

\*

BORZOI BOOKS ON LATIN AMERICA

*General Editor*

LEWIS HANKE

University of Massachusetts, Amherst

# REVOLUTION IN MEXICO: YEARS OF UPHEAVAL, 1910–1940

Edited with an Introduction by

## James W. Wilkie

University of California, Los Angeles

## Albert L. Michaels

State University of New York at Buffalo

ALFRED · A · KNOPF   New York

# Acknowledgments

———•———

We are grateful to Professor Lewis Hanke for suggesting the need for a study on the "years of upheaval" in the Mexican Revolution; his advice and criticism speeded the completion of this work. Dr. Howard F. Cline generously criticized our conception of this project and offered his usual incisive and valuable comments. George E. Monzón, our research assistant at the Ohio State University, not only transcribed and edited the oral history materials quoted here, but he also aided with several translations. Lyle C. Brown offered editorial counsel, Richard W. Wilkie prepared the map, and John Fuller typed the manuscript. Although we are indebted to the many authors and publishers who have given permission to reprint their works, we are solely responsible for our interpretation of the selections.

JAMES W. WILKIE
ALBERT L. MICHAELS

*Columbus, Ohio*
*Buffalo, New York*
*February 1969*

# Contents

———•———

# REVOLUTION IN MEXICO:

# YEARS OF UPHEAVAL,

1910–1940

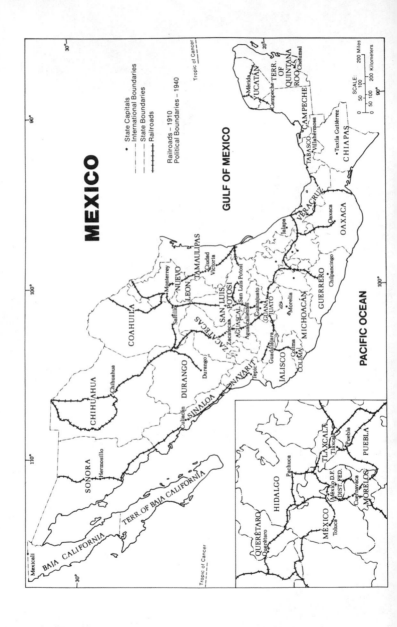

# Introduction

———•———

The Mexican Revolution has a rich and exciting literature, and we have attempted in this volume to sample accounts that will appeal not only to the student of Mexico but also to the general reader. This book may be considered, in a sense, to be a synthesized history of the Revolution during its phase of upheaval. After beginning with selections that provide background to, and an overview of, the period from 1910 to 1940, we follow events chronologically, as seen by different participants or by observers who have summed up periods and events of Mexican revolutionary history from particularly significant points of view. Thus, we have a type of history that unfolds the complexity of the world's first great twentieth-century revolution while presenting a multiplicity of vantage points.[1]

Our goal, in both presenting firsthand accounts and scholarly descriptions, has been to retain the flavor and color of bygone times. The majority of the selections are written by contemporaries of their events and almost half are written by Mexicans. Due to the length of the period under consideration, it is, of course, impossible to include accounts of all the major events. Besides the choice of views on the major historical incidents of the thirty-year period covered in this work, we have also included vignettes, which

[1] See Stanley R. Ross, *Is the Mexican Revolution Dead?* (New York: Knopf, 1966), for a book of readings that takes up a specific historical problem. Dr. Ross does not attempt to offer a narration of events but to examine critically the nature of the Mexican Revolution and its life.

are intended to capture the passions and crises of the times.

The decade from 1910 to 1920 is frequently considered in romantic terms, but in this work we show the unromantic nature of the conflict. The decades of the 1920s and 1930s were also destructive of the old order, in both violent and nonviolent ways. Thus, the really constructive phase of the Revolution (1940 to the present) does not fall within the purview of our book. Consequently, many of the readings may seem to denigrate Mexico's history. In portraying the phase of upheaval that Mexico endured, we do not mean to imply that nothing good was accomplished; instead, we wish to emphasize that such achievements as the Constitution of 1917 were painfully won. A volume on the years since 1940 would offer a totally different picture.[2]

Certainly the gains of the post-1940 era are dependent upon the positive changes wrought by three decades of crisis after 1910. In the following oral history interview, Daniel Cosío Villegas, a leading Mexican scholar, explains how the old order was destroyed and opportunity opened to new generations:

> *Daniel Cosío Villegas:* . . . the destructive force of the Mexican Revolution is being forgotten, and we are accustomed to speak of the Mexican Revolution as if it were the French Revolution—that is to say, as if it were a dead phenomenon of purely historical character. I was present at this tremendous destruction of the old regime by the Mexican Revolution and, though it may seem unbelievable, one of the things that the Mexican Revolution destroyed was the framework of the university professors. I began to serve as a professor . . . as an assistant to Antonio Caso . . . because there were two sociology profes-

[2] Accounts that reflect the growth and optimism of the long-range outcome of the revolutionary process in its constructive phase include, for example, Howard F. Cline, *Mexico: Revolution to Evolution: 1940–1960* (New York: Oxford University Press, 1962); Robert E. Scott, *Mexican Government in Transition* (rev. ed.; Urbana: University of Illinois Press, 1964); and Frank R. Brandenburg, *The Making of Modern Mexico* (Englewood Cliffs, N. J.: Prentice-Hall, 1964).

sors at the Law School: one was Antonio Caso, who
had nothing to do with Huerta's regime [which succeeded the revolutionary government of Francisco I.
Madero in 1913], and the other one was Carlos Pereyra, the historian who was Undersecretary of Education during Huerta's regime. Consequently, when the
Revolution triumphed [in 1914], Carlos Pereyra went
to Spain, where he lived until his death, and only returned to Mexico as a corpse. I filled this post left
vacant by Carlos Pereyra, and I filled it physically
because there was an empty chair and somebody had
to occupy it. . . . I am quite amused when I give a
lecture, especially among North Americans, about the
Mexican Revolution. I ask: "How old do you think I
was when I became a professor at the University of
Mexico?" They do not know what to say, so I tell
them, "seventeen years old." And those who are lis-
tening are astounded.

*James W. Wilkie:* Do you believe that your opportunity came with the Revolution?

*Daniel Cosío Villegas:* Well, partially, yes. If I had
lived in a normal epoch it would have taken me much
work and many years to become a professor. It is
unquestionable that the Mexican Revolution produced
a vacuum that was filled with improvisation, sometimes violent, absurd, and so on, but it was necessary
to carry out vital functions.

*Edna Wilkie:* This experience must have given you
much maturity at an early age, no?

*Daniel Cosío Villegas:* Yes, of course, you can
imagine what it meant to me at that age to examine,
for example, my fellow students, . . . I was sometimes a companion and at others a professor, and that
is rather disconcerting. . . .

*James W. Wilkie:* You lived in Toluca during the
first battles of the Revolution in 1910, didn't you?
Were you aware of the Revolution? Were there many
changes in your life?

*Daniel Cosío Villegas:* That is a good question, and
it has made me think a great deal.

. . .

In 1911, when the commotion caused by the de-

parture of Porfirio Díaz took place, I witnessed, in
Toluca, the departure of the Porfirian Governor of
the state of Mexico. . . . (Fernando González was a
general and a governor at the same time; his children
were my classmates in school, thus, I saw all of them
leave.) However, the physical commotion that took
place was not enough to impress the eyes of a ten-
year-old child.

The people who lived in the province—even in a
province as close to Mexico City as Toluca—were
not aware of the Revolution until 1914. In 1914, the
first revolutionary forces of General Francisco Murguía entered Toluca (the population was 15,000
then), and it was a spectacle to see these men march
through the streets, men from the North whom we
did not know, who did not wear the uniform of the
regular Mexican Army (which was the only one we
knew), who, furthermore, wore Texan-type hats,
which are used in northern Mexico, whose khaki-
colored uniforms were very similar to those of the
American Army, who used American weapons—the
famous 30–30. In sum, people who were entirely different, physically, from the ones we knew. Besides,
these rebel armies came to substitute completely and
totally the former authorities. It was the first time we
ever saw a military government, an authority that presided over the destiny of men's lives and property
without any legal recourse.

Therefore, you may say that not until 1914 did we
have an impression of the Mexican Revolution in
Toluca. Not even in 1913, at the time of the Ten
Tragic Days, for example. In my own case, my eldest
brother was a student in the Military Academy, and
he escorted Madero—as a cadet from the Military
Academy—from Chapultepec to the National Palace;
my father talked to him on the phone that same day
in order to inquire about the situation. But we did
not quite realize what was happening! This is a strange
phenomenon about which I have often thought.

*James W. Wilkie:* Did you know much about the
Ten Tragic Days, the Zapatista movement, and the
movements in the North?

*Daniel Cosío Villegas:* Yes, but we did not have, so to speak, a firsthand impression; we only had newspaper information. Besides, a fourteen-year-old student in those days practically did not read the papers.

*James W. Wilkie:* Did you often travel to Mexico City?

*Daniel Cosío Villegas:* No. The trip from Toluca to Mexico City (we had had a railroad for many years by that time) took from four to five hours. Therefore, during all the years that I spent in Toluca, I never went to Mexico City. Once I came to Mexico City, I never left again. It is strange, isn't it, because today one can go from here to Toluca in thirty minutes, on a broad highway. But in those days, although there was a daily train, even my father came to Mexico City only exceptionally. Neither our mother nor any of us ever came here in five years! This means that the isolation was great. There were telegraph lines, there was mail and rail service. But, nevertheless, Toluca was a world in itself.

*James W. Wilkie:* You lived almost in isolation, and yet only three years later you entered the university to teach sociology. That is quite a change.[3]

Because the Mexican Revolution has now reached a mature phase and massive violence seems to have receded into history, many persons tend to look back and make all men heroes, especially Francisco Madero. If Madero had not been overthrown in 1913, however, perhaps Mexico would have had no real change at all, and not even the apostle of the Revolution of 1910 might have a secure place in history. As General Francisco J. Múgica, a leader in framing the progressive Constitution of 1917, told Frank Tannenbaum:

If Huerta had not destroyed the Madero government, we, the revolutionists, would have had to do so. We, who were really concerned with the social movement, found the Madero government less satisfactory

[3] Translated from James W. Wilkie and Edna Monzón de Wilkie, *Oral History Interviews with Daniel Cosío Villegas,* Mexico City, April 21, 1964. Reprinted by permission.

each day, and it was better for the Revolution that the destruction of Madero came from a reactionary rather than a revolutionary source.[4]

The murder of Madero unleashed a "fiesta of bullets" in which, to the consternation of the United States, armies criss-crossed Mexico in confused battle. President Woodrow Wilson at first tried to keep the United States out of the conflict when he told Congress on August 27, 1913: "It is now our duty to show what true neutrality will do to enable the people of Mexico to set their affairs in order. . . ."[5] By October 27, 1913, however, Wilson was to demand in his Mobile Address that Huerta resign. Then late in November of 1913 Secretary of State William Jennings Bryan outlined the administration's policy in a circular to foreign service officers around the world:

> Usurpations like that of General Huerta menace the peace and development of America as nothing else could. . . .
> It is the purpose of the United States therefore to discredit and defeat such usurpations whenever they occur. The present policy of the Government of the United States is to isolate General Huerta entirely; to cut him off from foreign sympathy and aid and from domestic credit, whether moral or material, and to force him out.
> It hopes and believes that isolation will accomplish this end and shall await the results without irritation or impatience. If General Huerta does not retire by force of circumstances it will become the duty of the United States to use less peaceful means to put him out.[6]

[4] Frank Tannenbaum, *Peace by Revolution: An Interpretation of Mexico* (New York: Columbia University Press, 1933), 150.

[5] U.S. Department of State, *Papers Relating to the Foreign Relations of the United States, 1913* (Washington, D. C.: Government Printing Office, 1920), 822.

[6] U.S. Department of State, *Papers Relating to the Foreign Relations of the United States, 1914* (Washington, D. C.: Government Printing Office, 1921), 443–444.

Woodrow Wilson, in turn, summed up his Mexican policy in a conversation with Sir William Tyrrell of the British Foreign Office:

> "When I go back to England," said the Englishman, "I shall be asked to explain your Mexican policy. Can you tell me what it is?"
>
> President Wilson looked at him earnestly and said, in his most decisive manner:
>
> "I am going to teach the South American republics to elect good men!"
>
> "Yes," replied Sir William, "but, Mr. President, I shall have to explain this to Englishmen, who, as you know, lack imagination. They cannot see what is the difference between Huerta, Carranza, and Villa."
>
> The only answer he could obtain was that Carranza was the best of the three and that Villa was not so bad as he had been painted.[7]

The failure of United States foreign policy in the Mexico of the 1910s is partially developed by Howard F. Cline in Selection 12, and indeed that failure may well stand as an object lesson to overly ambitious United States administrations that do not understand that they cannot reform the world. Mexico had to work out her own destiny in spite of United States policy. Out of confusion came experience, and out of experience came a new society.

Part I presents a background and overview of the Revolution which suggests the political, social, and economic emphasis of this book. Though following portions of the work allude to the cultural changes wrought by the Revolution, we have chosen to quote from such a novelist as Carlos Fuentes, who discusses economic matters, for example, rather than to intrude into our chronology of events with an abstract discussion of the novel of the Mexican Revolution. Nevertheless, the reader should bear in mind that great literature, art, and other cultural developments grew out of the dramatic upheaval in society between 1910

[7] Burton J. Hendrick, *Life and Letters of Walter H. Page* (3 vols.; New York: Doubleday, 1922–1925), I, 204–205.

and 1940, and he will find a brief guide to this activity in our Bibliographic Essay.

In order to understand the events of the 1910s described in Part II, we have asked Lyle C. Brown to write the only commissioned selections in this work. Professor Brown has provided an incisive chronological account of "The Politics of Armed Struggle in the Mexican Revolution, 1913–1915," which will go far in helping the reader to comprehend the confluence of contradictory political and military forces that kept Mexico in constant civil war for three years. He also has provided us with a succinct interpretation of the Constitution of 1917.

Part III takes up "The Northern Dynasty," which governed Mexico from 1920 through 1933. Two men, Alvaro Obregón and Plutarco Elías Calles, dominated the Mexican political scene during that period. The establishment of political order was the keynote of these years in which the military made three major attempts to seize power.

In Part IV, "The Cárdenas Era," we see that with one party in firm command of Mexican affairs, and with relative party harmony prevailing after Calles' expulsion from Mexico in 1936, Lázaro Cárdenas was able to crush the old order during his presidential term, which was from 1934 to 1940. Cárdenas' support of strikes as a political weapon, rapid distribution of land, and expropriation of the foreign-owned oil industry marked the turning point in modern Mexican history. President Cárdenas laid a firm basis for the forging of a new nation in control of its own destiny. Although many have claimed that Mexico experienced rapid social change only under Cárdenas, it is now clear that social change for the poverty-stricken masses has come with greatest impetus under the economic phase of the Revolution, beginning in 1940.[8] Thus, the main con-

---

[8] James W. Wilkie investigates policy and measures social change with a Poverty Index in postulating periods of political (1910), social (1930), economic (1940), and balanced revolution (1960). See *The Mexican Revolution: Federal Expenditure and Social Change Since 1910* (Berkeley and Los Angeles: University of California Press, 1967).

tribution of Cárdenas during his presidential years was his bringing the period of upheaval to a successful conclusion. As Raymond Vernon has written:

> The period from 1910 to 1940, therefore, was an era in which Mexico was developing the essential pre-conditions for the new role of the state. During those thirty years, the state regained physical control over the nation; it began to shape and define a new philosophy for its existence and a new role in the performance of its goals; it manufactured a new set of powers and generated a new crop of institutions; and it began to flex its muscles by attempting new programs and new approaches to the old problems of credit, transportation, water resources, and land tenure in the country.[9]

In choosing 1940 as the closing year for this book, we have intended not only to bring together a series of valuable accounts many of which are no longer in print or readily available to the reader, but also to call attention to the pre-1940 period of the Revolution, which is often glossed over or ignored in the great number of works that have analyzed Mexico in the last twenty years. As historians, we are concerned that the origins of the more recent phases of the Revolution should not be forgotten. Hopefully, we may stimulate the reader to investigate in some depth the three decades after 1910.

[9] Raymond Vernon, *The Dilemma of Mexico's Development; The Roles of the Private and Public Sectors* (Cambridge, Mass.: Harvard University Press, 1963), 59.

# I

# The Revolution: Background and Overview

*In Mexico, the word "revolutionary" has a very special meaning, a very different meaning than it has elsewhere; even more so today, because when people hear the terms "revolution" or "revolutionary" they generally think of them as related to the extreme left or to communism. In Mexico, as you know, by "revolution" we mean not only the social reforms that necessarily had to undergo an initially destructive stage, such as the agrarian reform, but we also consider as revolutionary all those actions that aim to provide the nation with an infrastructure, as it is called nowadays, which will allow industrial, agricultural and cattle-raising development.*

. . .

*The word "Revolution" in Mexico (and we capitalize it to make the point) . . . means that the ideals of the Revolution of 1910 are still the same today, that is, that the ideals that say: "the land belongs to the man who toils on it, the worker has the right to strike, the subsoil wealth belongs to the nation, public services should be nationalized. . . ." The fulfillment of all these ideals are considered revolutionary acts in Mexico!*

Translated from Ramón Beteta, James W. Wilkie and Edna Monzón de Wilkie, *México visto en el siglo XX; Entrevistas de historia oral: Ramón Beteta, Marte R. Gómez, Manuel Gómez Morín, Vicente Lombardo Toledano, Miguel Palomar y Vizcarra, Emilio Portes Gil, Jesús Silva Herzog* (México, D. F.: Instituto Mexicano de Investigaciones Económicas, 1969), 31–32.

*The Mexican Revolution passed through a stage of armed conflict [and] the capture of Zacatecas and the battles of Celaya were a means to achieve a higher end. Peace having been achieved, the victor raised on high a plan which he is putting into practice. . . . There are achievements of the Revolution—rural schools, ejidos, small properties, dams, roads, freedom of expression. . . . There is the Revolution, full of life, abounding with the energies which the new revolutionaries inherited from their elders, from those old combat veterans of the struggle to save the dignity of the country and of our homes.*

Alberto Morales Jiménez, "La Revolución no es Transitoria: Es Permanente," *El Nacional*, January 26, 1942, translated and quoted by Stanley R. Ross, *Is the Mexican Revolution Dead?* (New York: Knopf, 1966), 133.

# CHRONOLOGY OF MEXICO'S PRESIDENTS, 1876-1940

---

| 1876 | *Porfirio Díaz |
|------|----------------|
| 1880 | Manuel González |
| 1884 | *Porfirio Díaz |
| 1911 | Francisco de la Barra |
| 1911 | *Francisco I. Madero |
| 1913 | Pedro Lascuráin |
| 1913 | *Victoriano Huerta |
| 1914 | Francisco S. Carbajal |
| 1914 | *Venustiano Carranza# |
| 1920 | Adolfo de la Huerta |
| 1920 | *Alvaro Obregón |
| 1924 | *Plutarco Elías Calles |
| 1928 | *Emilio Portes Gil |
| 1930 | *Pascual Ortiz Rubio |
| 1932 | *Abelardo Rodríguez |
| 1934 | *Lázaro Cárdenas |
| 1940 | *Manuel Avila Camacho |

* Major presidents.
# Carranza fought successive presidents of the Convention of Aguascalientes (Eulalio Gutiérrez, 1914; Roque González Garza, 1915; and Francisco Lagos Cházaro, 1915).

# 1

# FRANK R. BRANDENBURG

———•———

# CAUSES OF THE
# REVOLUTION *

❧

*The causes of the Mexican Revolution of 1910 have
been heatedly debated: Were they social, economic, or
merely political in nature? Here, Frank R. Brandenburg gives a balanced view. Brandenburg, a member
of the faculty of the School of International Service
of American University in Washington, D.C., taught
for a number of years at the University of the Americas in Mexico. His articles include "Organized Business in Mexico" and "A Contribution to the Theory
of Entrepreneurship and Economic Development:
The Case of Mexico," both of which were published
in* Inter-American Economic Affairs *in vol. 12 (winter 1958), 26–50 and vol. 16 (1962), 3–23 respec-
tively.*

The fourth epoch of Mexican history belongs to one
man: Porfirio Díaz. His "military Díaz-potism" managed
to amputate the cancerous political instability that had been
eating away at the country since 1810. Out of chaos
and civil strife, Díaz brought law and order, though both
largely of his own personal brand. He virtually eliminated

---

* Frank R. Brandenburg, *The Making of Modern Mexico* (Englewood Cliffs, N. J.: Prentice-Hall, 1964), 37–42. Reprinted by permission of the publisher.

banditry and brigandage. Solid material progress ensued in commercial, industrial, and mineral development. Property, at least that of big landholders and foreign holders, became secure. Mexico's credit rating soared in foreign exchanges. Investment capital entered freely and willingly. The new society so impressed diplomats that they placed Díaz on the highest international pedestal. All in all, the outside world credited Don Porfirio with extraordinary wisdom. Mexico was fortunate indeed in having such a great, benevolent leader!

But whatever its international reputation, the Díaz regime ultimately provoked the Mexican Revolution and instilled in the Revolutionary Family a permanent disgust for Díaz himself and for things bearing his stamp. Why, may we ask, is discredit heaped on the one Mexican who succeeded in consolidating the country where others before him had failed?

The revolutionary indictment bears powerful charges on this count. In the political realm, Díaz gave only lip service to the liberal, federalist Constitution of 1857 while building a highly authoritarian, centralist police state. Effective suffrage was a meaningless notion from a disregarded Constitution. The tenure of Díaz and his governors in the states challenges the record of American city bosses such as Crump, Hague, and Curley. Judges, legislators, army men, and local officials did precisely what he ordered, or they lost their posts. His rural police guaranteed the big landholder a cheap labor supply. The peasant had to accept debt peonage and involuntary servitude because his alternative was a beating, imprisonment, or the firing squad. Similarly, industrial peace came to mean government intervention on behalf of ownership; strikes were treason. Freedom of press, assembly, and speech constituted doctrines "unsuited to Mexican political life," as did regionalism, localism, popularism, and judicial review. The political system was a textbook demonstration of despotism. Díaz prevailed, and he was omnipotent.

In the economic realm, the revolutionary indictment

The revolutionaries also indict Díaz for turning over much of the productive machine to foreigners, for making Mexico the "father of foreigners and stepfather of Mexicans." Besides the powerful hold that they held over rural lands, foreigners dominated mining, utilities, industry, and commerce. Americans seized the cement industry. The French monopolized large department stores. The Germans controlled the hardware business. The Spanish took over foodstores and, together with the French, controlled the textile industry. The Canadians, aided by Americans and Englishmen, concentrated on electric power, trolley lines, and water companies. The Belgians, Americans, and English invested heavily in the railroads. And what ultimately shook the roots of revolutionary ideology was the American and British exploitation of minerals, especially oil. Doheny, Guggenheim, Cooke, Cowdray, and other foreigners operated in Mexico within an economic context not much unlike that of the Manifest Destiny and Robber Baron epoch in the United States. Some made great fortunes; others lost millions. Unfortunately for foreign investment, in the early years of the Revolution Mexicans looked upon foreign capital and Díaz's whole undesirable political rule as inextricable twins. Foreign capital as such bothered the nascent Mexican capitalist as much as it did the rank and file.

The latter had still another gripe, which Díaz and foreign companies ignored: Being Mexican precluded them from the better jobs in industry and commerce. Professor [Jesús] Silva Herzog relates an account of an American and Mexican applying during the late years of the Díaz regime for the job of railroad machinist.

| | |
|---|---|
| Supervisor: | "Are you an American?" |
| American: | "Yes, sir." |
| Supervisor: | "Come in and sit down. What are wheels?" |
| American: | "Round things." |
| Supervisor: | "Where is the stove?" |
| American: | "In the caboose." |

| Supervisor: | "Where are the wheels taking the trains?" |
| American: | "Forward." |
| Supervisor: | "Good enough; you can be a machinist." |

| Supervisor: | "What are you?" |
| Mexican: | "Mexican." |
| Supervisor: | "Oh, all the time giving us trouble! Do you understand English?" |
| Mexican: | "No, sir." |
| Supervisor: | "What quantity of fuel will a locomotive burn running twelve leagues per hour and with a pressure of one hundred pounds? How many calories will be developed? What is the consumption of water and oil? What is the friction on the rails? What is the work of the pistons and the number of revolutions of the wheels? What is the amount of steam consumed in a 4 percent decline of two leagues? . . ." |
| Mexican: | "Sir, I do not know because you are asking me many things at the same time." |
| Supervisor: | "Ah! You are a Mexican, you do not know anything. You are very stupid, you still have to ride many miles of track. You will not do as a machinist. You will not do for anything more than a guard with a club on a freight train. You cannot become a machinist because you could not answer my question." |

The peculiarities of life in the cities also militated against social justice. A pseudoaristocratic society prevailed in which the rich, the foreigner, and the select politician denigrated the lower classes. The middle-class professional and intellectual were little better off unless they worked for a foreign concern, where they also felt shackled by a superiority-conscious employer. Ideas incongruous with positivism were not permitted to circulate. To justify racial superiority, Díaz's brain trust infected education and society at large with the doctrine of white supremacy. Indians, claimed the positivists, were inferior because nature willed it! "Salvation lay in transforming Mexico into a white man's country oriented by European values and customs." Díaz handled the proverbial question of Church and state relations inconsistently but realistically. Church properties were confiscated one day, the Church permitted to buy new property the next; anticlerical legislation was enforced by his left hand, retracted by his right. These apparently contradictory actions might be attributed to a desire to conciliate sources of friction. They certainly underscored his own religious predicament, for like thousands of Mexicans before him and since, Díaz was a Freemason married to a devout Catholic.

Some men make their place in history through their actual achievements. Díaz belongs to this group, for he began the material buildup of Mexico. The ends to which he dedicated power may have contradicted man's very nature, but he opened sleepy eyes to what man could erect through physical labor, even in a backward nation. Railroads, electric-power facilities, a steel mill, cement plants, textile mills, and an oil industry became solid realities. By leaving the land to work on the railroads, in the mines, and elsewhere, a few Mexican laborers shook off their provincialism and found a new world unfolding before them, even though social and geographical mobility remained much too low for the dynamic economic development that Mexico required. And although innovation, entrepreneurship, and promotion never became part of the mass vocabulary, they did take root among a select group of foreigners and privileged Mexicans who ran some financial risks, governmental assurances notwithstanding. Excessively feudalistic, exploitative, paternalistic, and foreign-dominated, the material progress introduced by Díaz was not entirely without benefits for Mexico and the Mexican. However harsh the revolutionary indictment of Díaz may be for not implanting in the popular mind the promise of a better life ahead, it cannot justify exclusion of the fact that Mexico really began its economic progress under the aegis of the old autocrat.

2

RAYMOND VERNON

# MEXICO'S ECONOMIC DEVELOPMENT, 1910-1940*

*Was revolutionary upheaval from 1910 to 1940 successful in restructuring the life of Mexico? Raymond Vernon, professor of international trade and investment at the Graduate School of Business Administration, Harvard University, has attempted to answer this question with an important analysis of Mexican economic activity. This overview offers a theme by which the selections that follow in Parts II, III, and IV may be assessed. Vernon has edited* Public Policy and Private Enterprise in Mexico *(Cambridge, Mass.: Harvard University Press, 1964)*.

The striking feature of Mexico's economic performance in the decades which followed Porfirio Díaz's exit was the resumption, after a pause of eight or ten years, of the growth in the economy which had taken place in the Porfirian era. This was more than a simple extension of the growth of the Porfirian era, however. The physical and institutional barriers between the modern and the traditional worlds of divided Mexico were now being rapidly lowered,

---

* Raymond Vernon, *The Dilemma of Mexico's Development; The Roles of the Private and Public Sectors* (Cambridge, Mass.: Harvard University Press, 1963), 78–86. Reprinted by permission of the author and the publisher.

permitting an accelerated flow of labor and capital across the dividing wall. In addition, the public sector was gradually emerging from the relatively passive role which it had exercised before 1920 to one of aggressive participation in the growth process.

Among the many symptoms of economic change in Mexico between 1910 and 1940 was the continued drift of people into the big cities. Although the country's population as a whole was reported as growing only 30 percent in the thirty-year period, the population of the urban areas went up by 56 percent. Guadalajara doubled in the period, Monterrey more than doubled, and Mexico City actually tripled in population; in fact, the 1940 census indicated that nearly half the people then living in Mexico City had been born somewhere else. During this period "middle class" occupations—occupations like clerks, skilled workers, bank and government employees, professionals, and operators of small businesses—grew much faster than the population at large. Illiteracy among the people over ten years old fell from about 70 percent to about 50 percent—a result directly related to the fact that the number of teachers in rural schools rose from practically zero in 1910 to nearly 20,000 in 1940. And the value of assets in manufacturing enterprises, measured in peso terms, grew several times over —considerably more than the general price level.

To get a good sense of what was going on during this thirty-year period, one has to look at the three decades of the period separately. From the available evidence, it appears that the ten years from 1910 to 1920 were lost years for Mexico, at least in terms of current growth. Nobody really knows what happened in detail, but everyone suspects the worst. Official figures suggest—it is possible that they may be reflecting the facts—that although there was not much difference in total agricultural output between the beginning and the end of the decade, the production of corn declined about 40 percent. A barely credible index of manufacturing output suggests that this branch of economic activity may have declined by about a quarter during the decade. The production of minerals, in general, was lower at the end of the decade than at the beginning. The only bright spot in Mexico's economic structure was oil. But the oil economy operated in such an isolated enclave with so limited a use of indigenous manpower and local services, comparatively speaking, that the activity could not have done much to buoy the rest of Mexico's economy. By the same token, when oil production fell dramatically after 1921, the decline probably did less harm to the rest of the economy than the figures might imply.

Between 1920 and 1930 came the first faint signs of economic resurgence. One element in the renewed growth, it is fairly clear, was the resumption of mineral exports as a major activity. Economic expansion in the United States and Western Europe during the 1920s caused an increasing demand for silver, lead, zinc, and copper, with beneficial effects for Mexico's mines. A world boom in henequen also was a factor in Mexico's revival. Besides, during the latter years of the decade there came a swift growth in Mexico's manufacturing industries.

The reasons for the manufacturing spurt are less obvious than the reasons for increased exports. It may be that the modest growth in mining output, which in the aggregate accounted for about one-third of Mexico's total output of goods, contributed to the strong upward trend in manufacturing. Again, part of the growth was probably due to nothing more than the reestablishment of security on the railroads. The group of young industralists that had been brought into existence in the Porfirian period had simply drawn in their horns during the years of revolutionary turmoil and waited again for the day when steel, glass, beer, textiles, and chemicals could be shipped with safety on Mexico's beleaguered railroad lines. When shipments of this sort grew safe in the 1920s, the industrial plants began again to find and exploit the waiting markets in distant parts of Mexico. But the growth of Mexico's industrial production from 1920 to 1930 was not confined to the prerevolutionary industrial plants. Some other vital force seemed to be at work, pushing output upward. Any effort to identify that force is largely conjecture. One particularly plausible line of conjecture, however, relates to the effects of the land seizures and revolutions which went on after 1913. From that date on, there was a wholesale abandonment of haciendas in much of troubled Mexico, and a flight of both capital and labor out of Mexican agriculture.

The flight of capital out of agricultural production and out of rural trade produced the decline of agriculture on which we commented earlier. Of course, most of the capital devoted to agriculture had been frozen on the land in the form of buildings, fences, irrigation works, and other land improvements. But some assets were liquid or could be turned into liquid form, such as bank balances, gold plate, movable crops, trade inventories, and livestock. A part of these assets was exported to the United States and Europe; a part was plundered. But there were also cases here and there in which rural assets were successfully transferred into urban trade, real estate, and industry. As a result, as one traces the lineage of the great names in Mexican industry today, he occasionally comes upon a family whose prominence goes back to the landed estate and the early banking ventures of the Porfirian era.

Meanwhile, the decline of the hacienda system probably weakened the ties which were holding considerable amounts of underemployed agricultural labor on the land. Though the hacienda owner of the Porfirian era may have seen advantages in keeping his labor bound to the land, the incentive of the small private or communal farmer for supporting extra hands on his meager holdings was obviously much weaker. Though there were strong cultural pulls holding family groups together in some localities, the younger sons of many rural families nonetheless were allowed to drift off the land in search of higher pay and better opportunity. The ties of the farmhands to the land were weakened further when hordes of peasant soldiers marched in and out of Mexico's major cities as recruits in the armies of Zapata, Villa, and Carranza. What economists like to call the "demonstration effect" must surely have begun to exert its force on the recruits.

So the big cities, we can assume, began to acquire idle capital and cheap labor during the 1920s. Some of the labor went into construction, just as some of the capital went into private dwellings and apartment houses. But some apparently went into manufacturing. It is hard to say what motivated this movement of capital and human enterprise into manufacturing so soon after the black days of civil war. Persons who lived through the period talk of an unbelievable euphoria which seized many Mexicans of intellect and energy at the time. According to their accounts, the wounds of the Revolution were just beginning to heal and stability was beginning to return to the countryside. José Vasconcelos' teaching missionaries were touring the hinterland; Diego Rivera was adorning Mexico's public buildings with his powerful murals of protest and promise; there was a sense of nation and destiny in the air which had not been felt in Mexico since 1857. A gamble on the concept that Mexico was just beginning to emerge as a modern country may not have been so difficult in such an atmosphere.

The fact that there was a fairly significant flow of investment into the manufacturing industries in the 1920s is suggested not only by the subsequent performance of this sector but also by the comparative importance of capital goods in the total supply of Mexico's goods during that period. According to figures laboriously developed by the Economic Commission for Latin America, capital goods accounted for 10 to 12 percent of the total supply of goods in Mexico during the years from 1925 to 1930. And of these capital goods, the largest category by far was "machinery and general equipment," a term which excludes agricultural and transportation equipment, iron, steel, and cement.

The process of financing the growth of Mexico's cities partly by draining capital and idle facilities off the land could not have gone on forever. The insufficient production of foodstuffs would in the end have proved a bottleneck to further industrial growth. We can see from Chart 1, however, that the 1930s provided the first feeble signs of regeneration in the agricultural sector—enough, at any rate, for

*Chart 1*

*Output of Major Activities of the Mexican Economy (Based on 1950 Prices), 1895–1910, 1921–1940 (Ratio Scale)*

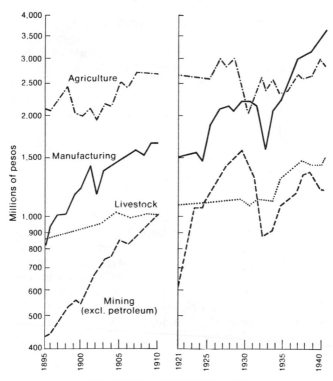

SOURCE: Enrique Pérez López, "El producto nacional," in *México, 50 años de revolución: La economía* (México, D. F.: Fondo de Cultura Económica, 1960), 588–589.

food crops to grow once more roughly at the same rate as the population. The reasons for the beginnings of regeneration seem fairly clear. The land programs of Calles, Portes Gil, Rodríguez, and Cárdenas—but especially Cárdenas—were beginning to reduce the uncertainties about agricultural land ownership all over Mexico. Squatters were beginning to get the assurances they needed about continued possession. Others who had not had the courage to seize some land forcibly were beginning to acquire the land by other means, principally through the expansion of the cooperative and semicooperative agricultural villages. Irrigation was gradually increasing; between 1926 and 1940, the acreage of irrigated land went up by 15 or 20 percent. Despite the fact that the 1926 experiment in agricultural credit had been a fiasco, such credit by the 1930s finally began to get a little easier. Though many areas of agricultural Mexico were overlooked, and some even retrogressed in economic and social terms, the general direction for agricultural Mexico was upward.

Nonetheless, as Chart 1 indicates, manufacturing was the star performer in the Mexican economy during the decade of the 1930s. After a brief depression dip in the first years of the decade, manufacturing expanded at a swift rate. The physical supply of Mexico's investment goods continued to grow, with a sustained heavy emphasis on "machinery and equipment." All types of products were considerably increased, not only such old standbys as textiles, beer, sugar, shoes, soap, and tobacco, but also newer products like cement and iron and steel. Various related indexes grew rapidly as well. The use of energy rose steadily from 1925 to 1940, with gasoline and electric power leading the growth. Measured in kilowatt hour equivalents, the total use of energy rose from 6 billion to 11 billion units during the period. Railroad freight increased from three and a half billion ton-kilometers in 1925 to over five and a half billion in 1940. Clearly, the Mexican economy had already begun to stir.

The basis for the growth of manufacturing was as much

a matter for conjecture in the 1930s as it had been in the 1920s. Certainly it was not exports this time that provided the prime stimulus. Mexico's exports dropped off sharply from 1929 to 1933 as the world demand for metals declined. Despite Mexico's devaluation of the early 1930s, changing the peso's value from about 40 cents to about 28 cents in United States money, the quantity of Mexico's exports in 1940 was barely back to its 1930 level. Neither can one turn to foreign investment as a significant factor in the growth of manufacturing—at least not in this period. Foreign investment in manufacturing was beginning to grow a little, but the growth was still at a quite unimpressive rate, at less than half a million United States dollars a year.

It may be that the process of recovery for manufactures which began in 1933 was stimulated in the first instance by the increased price of imports, a consequence of the drastic devaluation of the peso. Later in the decade, the pickup in the demand for metals and the unprecedented growth of spending from the public sector added to the expansive forces. Beginning in 1935, Cárdenas launched an extensive program of public works, with the usual demand-stimulating effects. By 1940, total investment in public works by the Cárdenas regime came to 1,018 million pesos. Budgetary deficits were recorded each year from 1936 on; and resort to central bank credit was heavy. Not only did this increased public spending stimulate internal demand in Mexico, but it also offered Mexico's comparatively timid young industrialists more frequent opportunities to earn a large riskless profit in the filling of public contracts, thereby stimulating investment in new ventures in the private sector.

But it also seems likely that something more than devaluation and public works spurred the process of growth. The continued trek to the cities, generated partly by the institutional loosening of ties to the land, almost certainly explains part of the process. There, one may conjecture, Mexico began to reorganize its human and capital resources in an environment which used both more effectively. The de-

mand for shelter gave a great lift to the construction industry in the cities. Village handicrafters producing textiles or
shoes were superseded by city factories; home-produced
food and drink were replaced by the output of industrial
plants. Human activity was brought together in clusters,
sufficiently large to justify the installation of electric distribution systems, reliable water supply systems, maintenance
and repair services, and trucking terminals. Self-financing
from profits supplemented the finance capital which may
previously have been drawn out of the agricultural sector.
It may be that the new environment, taken as a whole, was
more congenial to the exercise of latent entrepreneurial
ability. The result was the changing pattern for Mexico's
economic activity which is reflected in Chart 1.

# II

# The Revolution:
# A Fiesta of Bullets

*The Revolution was a sudden immersion of Mexico in
her own being, from which we brought back up, almost
blindly, the essentials of a new kind of state. In addition,
it was a return to the past, a reuniting of ties broken by
the Reform and the Díaz dictatorship, a search for our
own selves, and a return to the maternal womb. Therefore it was also a fiesta: "the fiesta of the bullets," to use
the phrase by Martin Luis Guzmán. Like our popular
fiestas, the Revolution was an excess and a squandering,
a going to extremes, an explosion of joy and hopeless-
ness, a shout of orphanhood and jubilation, of suicide
and life, and all of them mingled together. Our Revolution . . . is the brutal, resplendent face of death and
fiestas, of gossip and gunfire, of celebration and love
(which is rape and pistol shots).*

Octavio Paz, *The Labyrinth of Solitude; Life and Thought in Mexico,* translated by Lysander Kemp (New York: Grove Press, 1961),
148–149.

❀

"Demetrio, please. For God's sake, don't go away! My heart tells me something will happen to you this time."

Again she was wracked with sobs. The child, frightened, cried and screamed. To calm him, she controlled her own great grief.

Gradually the rain stopped, a swallow, with silver breast and wings describing luminous charming curves, fluttered obliquely across the silver threads of the rain, gleaming suddenly in the afternoon sunshine.

"Why do you keep on fighting, Demetrio?"

Demetrio frowned deeply. Picking up a stone absentmindedly, he threw it to the bottom of the canyon. Then he stared pensively into the abyss, watching the arch of its flight.

"Look at that stone; how it keeps on going. . . ."

---

Demetrio's wife in *The Underdogs; A Novel of the Mexican Revolution* by Mariano Azuela, translated by E. Munguía, Jr. (New York: New American Library, 1963), 147.

# CHRONOLOGY OF IMPORTANT
# EVENTS, 1910-1920

1910   Madero calls for revolution with his Plan of San Luis Potosí.

1911   Madero is victorious as President Díaz resigns in May; as president in November, Madero faces revolts led by former followers such as Zapata.

1913   General Victoriano Huerta overthrows Madero, but Venustiano Carranza organizes resistance under his Plan of Guadalupe.

1914   President Woodrow Wilson sends U.S. forces to occupy Veracruz for more than six months; Huerta resigns the presidency in July; Villa and Zapata support Convention of Aguascalientes against Carranza who refuses to surrender the presidency of Mexico.

1915   Villa is defeated by General Obregón at Celaya; U.S. recognizes Carranza as *de facto* president.

1916   Villa raids Columbus, N.M., in retaliation for U.S. recognition of Carranza and successfully eludes General Pershing, who leads U.S. forces in a northern Mexico campaign that lasts nearly a year. President Carranza calls a Constitutional Convention.

1917   Carranza promulgates new Constitution.

1918   The Regional Confederation of Mexican Labor (CROM) is organized.

1919   Zapata is finally killed by government troops; Carranza tries to impose Ignacio Bonillas as president.

1920    Alvaro Obregón leads successful revolt against Carranza, who is killed; Villa accepts amnesty from interim President Adolfo de la Huerta, who turns over his office to President-elect Obregón.

# 3

# FRANCISCO I. MADERO

———•———

## *PLAN OF SAN LUIS POTOSÍ*[*]

❧

*The call for Revolution against Porfirio Díaz was set forth by Francisco I. Madero in October of 1910. Excerpts from Madero's* Plan of San Luis Potosí *reveal the nature of the program that he promised to implement after November 20, the date set for his uprising.*

The elections celebrated in June and July of the current year for President and Vice President of the Republic, magistrates of the Supreme Court of the Nation, and deputies and senators, are hereby nullified.

.    .    .

Abusing the law of vacant lands, numerous small property owners, in the majority Indian, have been dispossessed of their lands by acts of the Ministry of Development or by judgments of the courts of the Republic. It being totally just to restitute arbitrarily dispossessed lands to their former owners, such acts and judgments are declared subject to revision, and those that acquired land by such immoral methods, or their heirs, will be required to return those lands . . . and also to pay an indemnity for damages incurred.

---

[*] Translated from Jesús Silva Herzog, *Breve Historia de la Revolución Mexicana* (2 vols.; México, D. F.: Fondo de Cultura Economica, 1960), I, 133–142. Reprinted by permission of the author.

In addition to the Constitution [of 1857] and laws in force, the principle of NO RE-ELECCIÓN . . . is declared the Supreme Law of the Republic.

. . .

I assume the character of provisional President of the United Mexican States with all necessary powers to fight the usurper government of General Díaz.

. . .

Fellow Citizens: If I call upon you to take arms and to overthrow the government of General Díaz, it is not only as a consequence of the excesses that he committed during the last elections, but also in order to save the nation from the somber future that awaits it if it continues under his dictatorship and under the government of the nefarious oligarchy of *científicos* who are unscrupulously absorbing and destroying the national wealth at great speed. If we allow them to remain in power, they will carry out their plans within a very short term: they will lead the people into ignominy and debasement; they will suck out all their wealth and leave them in the most absolute misery; they will cause the bankruptcy of our weak, impoverished, and handcuffed nation, which will be incapable of defending its borders, its honor, and its institutions.

As far as I am concerned, I have a clear conscience and no one can accuse me of promoting the Revolution for personal gains, for the nation is aware that I did everything possible to arrive at a peaceful settlement, and I was determined even to withdraw my candidacy, provided that General Díaz had let the nation choose at least the Vice President of the Republic. But, dominated by enigmatic pride and incredible arrogance, he refused to listen to the voice of the nation, and he preferred to precipitate Revolution rather than to give an inch, rather than to return to the people a particle of their rights.

. . .

He himself justified the present Revolution when he said [in 1876]: "That citizens may not impose and perpetuate themselves in the exercise of power, and this shall be the last revolution."

If the interests of the nation had weighed more in General Díaz's spirit than his own sordid interests and those of his advisers, he would have prevented this Revolution by making a few concessions to the people.

But, because he did not do so, so much the better! Change will come faster and shall be more radical, because the Mexican people, instead of lamenting like cowards, will accept the challenge like brave men. And because General Díaz intends to rely on brute force to impose an ignominious yoke on the people, they will have to resort to this same force in order to get rid of that yoke, to overthrow that doleful man from power, and to reconquer their liberty.

## 4

## GILDARDO MAGAÑA

———•———

# EMILIANO ZAPATA
# GREETS THE VICTORIOUS
# FRANCISCO MADERO*

❧

*The Revolution of 1910 was victorious within six months, and Díaz left Veracruz for exile on the last day of May in 1911. Although the terms of victory written into the Treaty of Ciudad Juárez, May 21, 1911, compromised Madero's program, and Madero himself issued a manifesto admitting that he had sacrificed the promises of his* Plan of San Luis Potosí *regarding land, these words fell on deaf ears. Madero justified compromise with the old regime as being worthwhile to avoid prolonging the war, and he promised that constitutional means would satisfy legitimate rights concerning the land. But to many Mexicans victory could not be compromised. Although Madero was greeted by huge crowds at every station along the route of his rail journey from Chihuahua to Mexico City and although his entry into Mexico City on June 7 as the apostle of Mexican democracy was a triumphal celebration, an officer in Emiliano Zapata's service, Gildardo Magaña, gives a firsthand view of*

———————————

* Translated from Gildardo Magaña, *Emiliano Zapata y el agrarismo en México* (3 vols.; México, D. F.: various publishers, 1934–1942), 1 (no publisher), 157–161.

*the meeting of Zapata and Madero and recounts their
June 8 confrontation on the land issue.*

On June 6 [1911], General Zapata arrived in Mexico
City with four or five of his principal aides, and accompanied by a small guard, they lodged in a downtown hotel.

In the early hours of the [following] morning, as if nature intended to announce to the metropolitan dwellers the
arrival of the Chief of the triumphant Revolution, they
were awakened by an intense earthquake.

General Zapata, followed by the revolutionaries who
accompanied him, went toward the station . . . hoping to
be one of the first to greet Señor Madero.

Thousands of persons were at the station. The crowd,
wild with enthusiasm and filled with curiosity, wanted to
meet the man who had been the *Caudillo* of the Revolution,
who had defeated the "Hero of Peace," Porfirio Díaz.

General Zapata was one of the first to be greeted by
Señor Madero when he descended from the train. The
Chief of the Revolution invited him to follow and briefly
expressed his desire to see him later in his residence.

.     .     .

Madero continued greeting his admirers and, pushed by
the crowd, was soon out in the street and into a very ele-
gant landau pulled by superb horses. The Zapata brothers,
lost in the crowd, followed the Chief's carriage closely until
they saw him enter the National Palace.

Hours later, General Zapata talked again with Madero at
his home; but because that day was an exceedingly hectic
one, the Chief of the Revolution scheduled a luncheon appointment with him for the next day in order to give due
attention to the affairs of Morelos.

On June 8, after lunch, Madero and the southern Chief
exchanged views on the problems and situation of Morelos . . . :

[*Zapata*]: "What we are interested in is, of course, that
the lands be returned to the people and that the promises
made by the Revolution be fulfilled."

[*Madero*]: "All that will be done, but at its proper time and within the law, because those are delicate matters that cannot and should not be solved with a quick dash of the pen. They will have to be studied, go through judicial process, and be solved by the state authorities. What is convenient at the moment," the Chief of the Revolution added insistently, "is to proceed with the disbandment of the revolutionary forces, because having achieved victory we need not remain in arms."

Then Zapata assured Madero of his readiness to obey all his orders, that he would disband forces as Madero wanted, and that he had absolute confidence that Madero would fulfill all the promises made by the Revolution, above all those relative to the return of the land. But he expressed doubts that the Federal Army would support . . . presidential power:

". . . do you think that because the people overthrew the tyrant these military men are going to change their ways? You can see what is happening with the new Governor, Señor Carreón, who is completely in favor of the *hacendados,* and if this is so now that we are triumphant and bear arms, what will happen to us if we deliver ourselves into the hands of our enemies?"

"No, General," answered Madero, "the time when we needed arms is over; now our battles will have to be waged in another field. If the present government of Morelos does not guarantee revolutionary interests . . . , we shall substitute someone else who will perform his duties; but we must be prudent, and we must not act violently, because if so we would be reproached by our enemies and public opinion. The Revolution needs to guarantee order and show respect for property."

The southern leader stood up and, without leaving his carbine (from which he had not parted even during lunch), he approached Madero and, pointing to the gold chain which the latter wore on his vest, said:

"Say, Señor Madero, if I, taking advantage of the fact that I am armed, should decide to take your watch and keep it, and if as time goes by we should meet again, both of us armed with equal strength, would you have the right to demand its return?"

"I most certainly would, General, and I would also have the right to ask of you an indemnity for the length of time during which you used it illegally!" answered the Chief of the Revolution.

"Well, that is exactly what has happened to us in the state of Morelos," retorted Zapata, "where a few hacendados have seized the lands of the people by force. My soldiers, the armed peasantry, and all the people expect me to tell you, very respectfully, that they wish the restitution of their lands to proceed immediately."

Madero once more assured Zapata that he would fulfill all the promises made, asked him to have faith in him, and said that everything would be settled satisfactorily; that, besides, [the government] would select, among the best organized revolutionary elements from different parts of the country, a few contingents in order to form a certain number of irregular units in the Army.

"We wish, Señor Madero," said Zapata, "that you would visit our state so that you may become aware of our needs so that lands may be returned to the people as soon as possible."

"I offer to go and study the case of Morelos in detail in order to solve it as justly as possible. And in recognition of the services you have rendered the Revolution, I shall see to it that you are conveniently remunerated so that you may acquire a good ranch," said the Caudillo to the Southerner.

Not hiding his displeasure, Zapata stepped back, and hitting the floor heavily with his carbine said, . . . in a respectful manner but with a somewhat louder tone of voice:

"Señor Madero, I did not join the Revolution to become an hacendado; if I am worth anything it is because of the confidence placed in me by the peasants, who have faith in us, for they think we will fulfill what we promised; and if we abandon those who made the Revolution, they would have every right to turn their arms against those who forget their obligations."

Madero, smiling, got up from his chair and said to him:

"No, General Zapata, I want you to understand what I mean: that which was offered shall be fulfilled, and besides, those who have rendered valuable services, such as you and many other chiefs, shall be duly rewarded."

"All we want, Señor Madero, is that our lands, which the *científicos* hacendados stole from us, be returned. . . ."

# 5

# EMILIANO ZAPATA, *et al.*

———•———

## *PLAN OF AYALA**

❧

*The issue between Zapata and Madero over land reform was fully crystallized soon after Madero assumed the office of President on November 8, 1911. From the valley of Morelos the Zapata group proclaimed its* Plan of Ayala *on November 28 and declared open war against the Federal government in nearby Mexico City.*

We, the undersigned, constituted as a Revolutionary Junta, in order to support and fulfill the promises made by the Revolution of November 20, 1910, solemnly proclaim in the face of the civilized world that is judging us . . . the following plan:

. . . we declare the said Francisco I. Madero unfit to realize the promises of the Revolution of which he is the author, because he is a traitor to the principles . . . which enabled him to climb to power . . . and because, in order to please the *científicos, hacendados,* and *caciques* who enslave us, he has crushed with fire and blood those Mexicans who seek liberties.

.    .    .

The Revolutionary Junta of the State of Morelos will not sanction any transactions or compromises until it secures

---

* Translated from Jesús Silva Herzog, *Breve Historia de la Revolución Mexicana* (2 vols.; México, D. F.: Fondo de Cultura Económica, 1960), I, 240–245. Reprinted by permission of the author.

the downfall of the dictatorial elements of Porfirio Díaz and Francisco I. Madero, because the nation is tired of traitors and false liberators who make promises and forget them when they rise to power . . . as tyrants.

As an additional part of the plan that we proclaim, be it known: that the lands, woods, and water usurped by the hacendados, científicos, or caciques, under the cover of tyranny and venal justice, henceforth belong to the towns or citizens in possession of the deeds concerning these properties of which they were despoiled through the devious action of our oppressors. The possession of said properties shall be kept at all costs, arms in hand. The usurpers who think they have a right to said goods may state their claims before special tribunals to be established upon the triumph of the Revolution.

. . . the immense majority of Mexico's villages and citizens own only the ground on which they stand. They suffer the horrors of poverty without being able to better their social status in any respect, or without being able to dedicate themselves to industry or agriculture due to the fact that the lands, woods, and water are monopolized by a few. For this reason, through prior compensation, one-third of such monopolies will be expropriated from their powerful owners in order that the villages and citizens of Mexico may obtain *ejidos,* colonies, town sites, and rural properties for sowing or tilling, and in order that the welfare and prosperity of the Mexican people will be promoted in every way.

The property of those hacendados, científicos, or caciques who directly or indirectly oppose the present plan shall be nationalized, and two-thirds of their remaining property shall be designated for war indemnities—pensions for the widows and orphans of the victims that succumb in the struggle for this plan.

# 6

STANLEY R. ROSS

———————•———————

# THE ARREST OF
# FRANCISCO MADERO
# AND MURDER OF HIS
# BROTHER*

✳

*Madero might well have survived any threat from Zapata, as he had survived other uprisings against his government; but early in 1913 he was toppled from power by his own military commander, General Victoriano Huerta. Thus, Madero's overthrow was the result of betrayal from within his government instead of attack from without. In addition, the golpe de estado was executed by conservative remnants of the Díaz regime rather than by dissident revolutionary elements.*

*In this account of Madero's fall and the murder of his brother, Gustavo, Stanley R. Ross describes the tragic events of February 18, 1913. Professor Ross, Director of Latin American Studies in the University of Texas at Austin, is currently Chairman of the Conference on Latin American History. He has recently*

* Stanley R. Ross, *Francisco I. Madero, Apostle of Mexican Democracy* (New York: Columbia University Press, 1955), 307–313. Reprinted by permission of the author and publisher.

*edited* Is the Mexican Revolution Dead? (*New York: Knopf, 1966*).

It was nearing 1:30 P.M., the normal luncheon hour at the National Palace. General Huerta, Gustavo Madero, and several others had departed for a banquet at the Gambrinus Restaurant. Madero, some of his cabinet officers, and several aides were in a small room adjoining the Salón de Acuerdos conferring about supplies for the government's troops and for the civilian population. The conference was interrupted by the entrance of Lieutenant Colonel Jiménez Riveroll, of the 29th Battalion, who indicated that he had been sent by Huerta to report that General Rivera was arriving from Oaxaca in a rebellious attitude and that Madero should accompany him to a safe place.

The President was in the process of refusing to do so when a commotion was heard in the adjacent salon. Madero and the others hurried into the larger room. There they found Major Izquierdo and twenty-five to thirty soldiers of the 29th Battalion whom a loyal aide had tried unsuccessfully to order to leave. The two files of soldiers in their lead-colored uniforms with rifles tilted, each with two combat belts with shiny banks of cartridges, and each with a mattock hanging from his belt, seemed strangely out of place in the carpeted executive conference room.

The President stood, with his cousin Marcos Hernández (brother of the cabinet officer Rafael Hernández) at his side, facing Riveroll and Izquierdo. Behind the latter were the soldiers while grouped back of the President were his aides, cabinet officers, and others. Discarding all pretense, Riveroll indicated that he had come to arrest Madero on the order of Blanquet in agreement with Huerta. Madero challenged Blanquet's right to order his arrest. When Riveroll sought to seize the President, two of the latter's aides, Captains Gustavo Garmendia and Federico Montes, drew gleaming 38-caliber pistols. Captain Garmendia fired killing Riveroll.

Some of the soldiers, either because they heard Major

Izquierdo order it or as an automatic reaction in the tense situation, discharged their guns. The windows rattled from the multiple explosion, the curtains fluttered, and the room was filled with a cloud of smoke and the acrid smell of burned powder. On the floor were the bodies of Riveroll and Izquierdo and of the mortally wounded Marcos Hernández. Madero, brave to the point of temerity, proceeded to advance toward the confused, leaderless soldiers. Repeating the reassuring "Calm, boys, do not fire," he advanced close enough until he could dash past them to the door which led to another anteroom. While the platoon disbanded, Madero went to the rooms which faced the main plaza. From below, outside the palace, came the cries of *rurales* who had been alarmed by the shots. The President appeared on the balcony and told them not to worry, that the incident was past, and that they should return to their posts.

Although advised to flee to safety, Madero insisted on searching for General Blanquet. The President still could not believe that he had been abandoned by all the military. Accompanied by several aides Madero rode the elevator down to the patio where he encountered General Blanquet. The General stood, pistol in hand, in front of elements of the 29th Battalion. In a strong voice he said, "Surrender, Mr. President." Madero, in a high-pitched, irritated voice replied, "You are a traitor, General Blanquet." Blanquet affirmed, "You are my prisoner."

.     .     .

At the Gambrinus Restaurant, Gustavo Madero was attending a private party honoring the promotion of the President of the Chamber to 'the rank of general. General Huerta was also present. Shortly after 1:30 P.M. Huerta made a telephone call, apparently to confirm that everything had gone according to schedule at the palace, and then excused himself. Twenty minutes later a platoon of soldiers appeared and arrested Gustavo, imprisoning him in a coatroom of the restaurant. General Angeles, who, despite a ceasefire order, continued to fire on the Ciudadela, also was arrested. Sarita [Francisco's wife] and other members of the Madero family took refuge in the Japanese Legation.

General Huerta assumed command and so notified the American Embassy and President Taft. "I have the honor to inform you that I have overthrown this government. The armed forces support me, and from now on peace and prosperity will reign."

.    .    .

Conservative elements in the capital lauded the "patriotic action" of General Huerta. The opposition press jubilantly celebrated the establishment of the new government. *El País* announced that "Maderism has been tumbled noisily and tragically never to be born again." *El Mañana* solemnly affirmed that "it was inevitable, it was fated." And *El Imparcial* sounded the tocsin of vengeance against the deposed governmental leaders for real, rumored, and imagined offenses:

> Fortunately there is no contradiction between political aims and the demands of justice which requires that responsible officials should be punished . . . Those guilty of . . . crimes ought to suffer the legal consequences of their acts. Justice ought to be severe, cold, and inexorable with them.

The followers of Félix Díaz demanded that four prisoners, including Francisco and Gustavo Madero, be turned over to them. However, Francisco Madero and Pino Suárez were essential to Huerta's plan to legalize his position. Therefore, he delivered only Gustavo Madero and Adolfo Bassó, Superintendent of the National Palace, to the Felicistas, as evidence of his good faith. Late on the night of the eighteenth Gustavo was taken by car to the Ciudadela. There, around two in the morning, General Mondragón decreed his death.

The President's brother was forced with blows and pushes to the door leading to the patio. Bleeding, his face distorted by blows, his clothes torn, Gustavo tried to resist that frenzied, drunken mob of nearly one hundred persons.

Holding desperately to the frame of the door he appealed to
that sea of faces reflecting the madness of mob violence.
Referring to his wife, children, and parents, he pleaded
with them not to kill him. His words were greeted by jeers
and laughter. One of the crowd pushed forward and, with
the mattock from his rifle or the point of a sword, picked
out the prisoner's good eye. The blinded Gustavo uttered a
single mournful cry of terror and desperation. After that,
he made no more sounds, but covering his face with his
hands turned toward the wall.

The mob laughed and jeeringly referred to the victim as a
"coward" and a "whiner" and as "Ojo Parado." Prodding
and sticking him with mattock and sword points and dealing
him blows with fists and sticks they forced him to the patio.
Gustavo moved, stumbling, without uttering a word. An
assailant pressed a revolver to his head. The hand holding
the weapon was unsteady and slipped, and the shot tore
Gustavo's jaw away. He was still able to move a short distance, falling, at last, near the statue of Morelos which,
inappropriately, was silent witness to this scene. A volley of
shots was fired into the body. By lantern light it was ascer-
tained that Gustavo Madero was dead. One of the crowd
fired yet another shot into the body explaining drunkenly
that it was the *coup de grace*. The assassins proceeded to
sack the body, and Gustavo's enamel eye was extracted and
circulated from hand to hand.

# 7

ERNEST GRUENING

———•———

# MRS. FRANCISCO MADERO'S ATTEMPT TO SAVE THE LIFE OF HER HUSBAND*

✣

*The United States Ambassador to Mexico Henry Lane Wilson (no relation to Woodrow Wilson) played a major role in the downfall of Madero. Apparently, Ambassador Wilson was worried about the protection of United States property rights after 1910, and he feared that President Madero was unable to contain the destructive forces threatening foreign investment. The Ambassador felt that unless Madero was deposed before William H. Taft turned the United States presidency over to the Democrats under Woodrow Wilson on March 4, 1913, recognition of the Huerta government might not be possible. Ambassador Wilson failed to gain recognition for Huerta before the new administration in Washington called him home in July, perhaps because of the following events narrated by Ernest Gruening. Gruening, later a United States Senator from Alaska, spent eighteen months in Mexico between 1922 and 1927 gathering material for his book on* Mexico and Its

* From *Mexico and Its Heritage* by Ernest Gruening, by permission of Appleton-Century, affiliate of the Meredith Press, and of the author. Copyright, 1928, The Century Company. Copyright renewed, 1956, by Ernest Gruening, 569–573.

Heritage, *a work that is now a classic study of Mexican affairs.*

On February 19, when the murder of Gustavo Madero was spread on the front pages of the Mexico City newspapers, [Henry Lane] Wilson reported the following interview:

> I went to see General Huerta this afternoon to get guarantees of public order and to learn the exact situation. He gave me satisfactory assurances and explained that Gustavo Madero had been killed by soldiers, without orders. General Huerta said that the President and Gustavo Madero had twice tried to assassinate him and had held him a prisoner for one day. He asked my advice as to whether it was best to send the ex-President out of the country or to place him in a lunatic asylum. *I replied that he ought to do that which was best for the peace of the country.*

Not a question about Gustavo Madero's death—not a word of caution lest "soldiers, without orders" also kill Francisco Madero.

Indeed the next day, February 20, the ambassador wired the Department of State that "a wicked despotism [has] fallen." Within two hours he telegraphed again, asking the department "immediately" to instruct "as to the question of recognition of the provisional government, now installed and evidently in secure position." And he added, "It would be well to note that the Provisional Government takes office in accordance with the Constitution and precedents."

An hour later he telegraphed the text of the resignation which had been wrung from Madero and Pino Suárez.

Even before the tragedy that was to transpire, two days later, the Department of State clearly sensed the Ambassador's participation and responsibility. Wired Secretary of State Knox in prompt answer (February 20, 11 P.M.):

> . . . General Huerta's consulting you as to the treatment of Madero tends to give you a certain responsibility in the matter. It moreover goes without

saying that cruel treatment of the ex-President would injure . . . the reputation of Mexican civilization, and this government earnestly . . . hopes to hear that he has been dealt with in a manner consistent with peace and humanity. . . . You may in your discretion make use of these ideas in your conversation with General Huerta."

The next day, February 21, Secretary Knox telegraphed again that "the shooting of Gustavo Madero [had] caused a most unfavorable impression" in Washington, and that "the President [is] gratified to believe that there [is] no prospect of injury to the deposed President or Vice President. . . ."

The Ambassador, however, was apparently more interested in securing recognition than in following either the dictates of humanity or the suggestion of his chief. On February 21 he telegraphed the State Department:

> In the absence of instructions and in view of the extreme urgency, I assembled the diplomatic corps . . . relative to the recognition of the new government. . . . My colleagues . . . agreed that recognition of the new government was imperative, to enable it to impose its authority and establish order. I shall accordingly unite with my colleagues, believing that I am interpreting the desires of the Department, and assisting in the tranquilization. I am sending a circular telegram to all consuls . . . instructing them to do all possible to bring about a general acceptance of the provisional government.

Meanwhile every effort in Mexico was made to get Ambassador Wilson to intercede for the lives of Madero and Pino Suárez. On February 19, the day after Gustavo Madero's murder, the Cuban minister wrote Wilson a definite warning and offered the use of the Cuban cruiser *Cuba,* lying at anchor in Veracruz, to transport the deposed executives. The President's father, Francisco Madero, Sr., and mother, Mercedes G. Madero, distracted by the fate of their son Gustavo, wrote to the diplomatic corps, of which Mr.

Henry Lane Wilson, by virtue of being the only ambassador accredited to Mexico, was the dean, asking for its intercession.

Finally Madero's wife [Sara], stifling her bitterness at what she knew had been the Ambassador's responsibility for her husband's fall, called at the American Embassy. Following is a verbatim account of her interview with Mr. Wilson:

Q. When did you have your interview with the Ambassador?

A. That afternoon, February 20, 1913, Mercedes, my sister-in-law, was with me. The Ambassador was not in when we entered the Embassy. Mrs. Wilson received us, and caused a telephone message to be sent to the Palace (he was with Huerta at the National Palace) notifying the Ambassador that we were there.

Q. What was the manner and appearance of the Ambassador?

A. . . . His manner was brusque. At times Mrs. Wilson tugged at his coat, apparently to try to induce him to speak differently. It was a painful interview. I told the Ambassador that we had come to seek protection for the lives of the President and the Vice President. "Very well, Madam," said he, "What is it you want me to do?"

"I want you to use your influence to protect the lives of my husband and the other prisoners."

"That is a responsibility that I do not care to undertake, either for myself, or my government," replied the Ambassador.

"Will you be good enough then," I asked, "to send this telegram to President Taft?"

I handed him a message addressed to President Taft, which had been written by the President's mother and signed by her. It was through the Ambassador that our only hope lay in obtaining communication with President Taft. We supposed that the cable was in the hands of the government (the Huerta government) and that it was useless to expect that a message of this sort would be allowed to pass.

Q. What was the reply of the Ambassador to your request, after he had read the message?

A. "It is not necessary to send this," he said. But I persisted. "All right," promised the Ambassador. "I shall send it." He put the message in his pocket.

Q. What followed after you had delivered to the Ambassador the message directed to President Taft?

A. The Ambassador said: "I will be frank with you, Madam. Your husband's downfall is due to the fact that he never wanted to consult with me." I could reply nothing to this, for I had gone there to ask a favor, to plead for my husband's life, not to discuss questions of politics, or policies with the Ambassador.

Q. What else did the Ambassador say?

A. The Ambassador continued: "You know, Madam, your husband had peculiar ideas." I said: "Mr. Ambassador, my husband had not peculiar ideas, but high ideals." To this the Ambassador did not reply, and I proceeded to say that I asked the same protection and assurance for the life of Vice President Pino Suárez, as I asked for President Madero. The Ambassador's manner grew very impatient. "Pino Suárez is a very bad man," he said, "I cannot give any assurance for his safety. He is to blame for most of your husband's troubles. That kind of man must disappear. . . ."

Q. What did the Ambassador mean by saying that Vice President Pino Suárez "must disappear"?

A. I inferred that the Ambassador meant that the Vice President's life must be sacrificed. I then represented to him that Mr. Pino Suárez had a wife and six children who would be left in poverty in the event of his death.

Q. What did he say to that?

A. He merely shrugged his shoulders. He told me that General Huerta had asked him what should be done with the prisoners. "What did you tell General Huerta?" I asked. "I told him that he must do

what was best for the interests of the country,"
said the Ambassador. Here my sister-in-law interrupted and said: "Why did you say that? You
know very well what kind of men Huerta and his
people are, and that they are going to kill them!"

Q. What did the Ambassador say?

A. He made no response, but turned to me and said:
"You know that your husband is unpopular; that
the people were not satisfied with him as President." I asked, "Why, then, if this is true, is he
not permitted to go free and proceed to Europe,
where he could do no harm?" The Ambassador
replied, "You need not worry; the person of your
husband will not be harmed. I knew all along that
this was going to happen. That is why I suggested
that your husband should resign." "But if you
knew of this in advance, Mr. Ambassador," I
asked him, "why did you not warn my husband?"
"Oh, no," he replied, "that would not have been
good policy, because then he would have prevented it."

Q. The Ambassador is quoted in an interview in the
New York *Herald* on March 21, 1916, as saying
that you had requested him to ask Huerta to "put
your husband in the penitentiary for safekeeping."
Did you make such a request of the Ambassador?

A. No. We discussed only the personal safety and the
urgency of Huerta being compelled to keep his
promise to allow the President and the other prisoners to leave the country. I spoke of the uncom-
fortable accommodations they had. "He seems to
be getting along all right," said the Ambassador,
"he has slept for five hours without waking."

Q. What was the outcome of the conversation?

A. When the interview was terminated and we went
away, we had gained nothing excepting the Ambassador's assurance that the President would not
suffer bodily harm and his promise to send the
message soliciting the intervention of President
Taft to save the lives of the prisoners.

Q. Was the Ambassador's assurance carried out?

A. Two days later the prisoners were assassinated.

Q. Did you converse with the Ambassador in Spanish or in English?

A. In English.

Q. Is it your opinion that the lives of the President and the Vice President could have been saved by the Ambassador?

A. It is my belief that had properly energetic representations been made by the Ambassador which it was reasonable to expect him to make, in the interest of humanity, not only would the lives of the President and the Vice President been spared, but a responsibility would have been averted from the United States which was thrust upon it by the acts of its then diplomatic representative in Mexico.[1]

On the night of February 22, Francisco Madero and Pino Suárez, shortly before midnight, were taken from the palace. They were told that they were being transferred to the penitentiary for greater comfort. But none of their effects were taken with them. The two men were transported to the rear of the penitentiary. Here the automobiles stopped. The prisoners were asked to step out. As they did so, revolvers were placed to their heads and their brains were blown out. The officer in charge, who personally killed Madero, Cárdenas, was later promoted by Huerta.[2]

. . .

The Government's official version, given out for publication for the next morning's papers, was that a rescue of the

[1] This interview took place August 15, 1916, between Mrs. Madero and an American journalist, Robert Hammond Murray, who, during the Madero and Huerta regimes, and at the time of the interview, was the Mexico correspondent of *The New York World,* and during the World War headed the United States Committee on Public Information in Mexico City. The interview was presented subsequently to Mrs. Madero for her approval as to its correctness, and was sworn to by her before the vice-consul of the United States in Mexico City, April 29, 1927. . . .

[2] With the victory of the Constitutionalists in 1915. [Francisco] Cárdenas fled from Mexico to Guatemala. Subsequently he made a full confession. It was published in *La Nación,* Havana, April 24, 1916.

prisoners had been attempted, that the automobiles had been fired upon, that the prisoners had sought to escape, and that in the firing both had been killed.

.     .     .

Mexico City was shocked with the horror of the crime, especially in view of the conspicuous magnanimity that Madero had shown to rebels against his Government.

The day after the murders, Ambassador Wilson telegraphed the Government's version to the Department of State, and the day following, February 24, telegraphed:

> The tragedy of yesterday evidently produced no effect on the public mind. The city remains perfectly quiet and unofficial telegrams indicate the same situation throughout the Republic, with few exceptions. . . . It is quite evident that the people hail with satisfaction the present regime.

Subsequently, the same day, he telegraphed:

> I am disposed to accept the Government's version of the affair and consider it a closed incident.

# 8

LYLE C. BROWN

———— • ————

# THE POLITICS
# OF ARMED STRUGGLE IN
# THE MEXICAN REVOLUTION,
## 1913-1915[*]

❊

*It is not possible to understand the development of Mexico's Revolution without a clear view of political strife and military attempts to seize power between 1913 and 1915. The apparent confusion in politics during those years has caused many readers to despair of ever making sense out of Mexican affairs, and therefore a concise synthesis of that confused era long has been needed. In order to provide such a study, we asked Professor Lyle C. Brown to write the following article. Brown, a professor of political science at Baylor University, Waco, Texas, has taught at the University of the Americas in Mexico. He has written: "The Mexican Liberals and Their Struggle Against the Díaz Dictatorship: 1900–1906," Antología MCC, 1956 (Mexico City College Press, 1956), 317–362, and "Mexican Church-State Relations, 1933–1940," A Journal of Church and State, 6 (May 1964), 202–222.*

*Published by permission of the author.

On February 18, 1913, Huerta sent telegrams to all state governors notifying them that he had assumed direction of the government and that Madero had been arrested. For the most part the governors did not hesitate to declare their allegiance to the usurper. However, on February 19 Venustiano Carranza, Governor of Coahuila, denounced Huerta's betrayal and issued a circular telegram addressed to all governors and military chiefs calling on them to rally to the support of the constitutional government of Francisco Madero. In Sonora, Governor José María Maytorena was prepared to recognize the Huerta coup, but pro-Madero feeling ran high in that state. Upon hearing of Madero's assassination, some local government leaders publicly proclaimed their opposition to Huerta; and Alvaro Obregón, Benjamín Hill, Juan G. Cabral, and Salvador Alvarado, all of whom were officers in the irregular forces of the state, brought pressure to bear on the Sonora Governor in an effort to force him to denounce Huerta. Finally, on February 26 Maytorena requested that the legislature give him a leave of absence. His request was granted immediately; and on that same day he departed for the United States, leaving the legislature to name Ignacio L. Pesqueira as interim Governor. On March 5 the new Governor promulgated a decree of the Sonora legislature declaring that it did not recognize Huerta as President. The Governor of Chihuahua, Abraham González, was a firm Madero supporter; however, General Antonio Rabago, commander of Federal troops in that state, ordered his arrest as directed by Huerta. On March 7, 1913, González was murdered by his captors; but on the previous day Pancho Villa, accompanied by eight followers, had entered Chihuahua from the United States. Beginning with this small band, Villa built a powerful division that soon numbered several thousand. Other anti-Huerta, or Constitutionalist, forces were also organized in the border states of Nuevo León and Tamaulipas. By midsummer in 1913 much of northern Mexico was no longer under the control of Federal troops; and south of Mexico City, in the state of Morelos, Emiliano Zapata continued to oppose Huerta as he had opposed his predecessors.

Objectives of the Constitutionalist movement were outlined in Carranza's *Plan de Guadalupe,* which was proclaimed on March 26, 1913. It called for the overthrow of Huerta's regime and recognition of Carranza as First Chief of the Constitutionalist Army. Also, the plan provided that with the occupation of Mexico City by Constitutionalist forces, the First Chief would become interim President and would convoke general elections for Federal officials. Subsequently state provisional governors recognized by the First Chief were to call elections for selecting state officials.

Accompanied by Carranza, General Obregón had, by the middle of May in 1914, moved his Army Corps of the Northwest from Sonora southward along the Southern Pacific Railroad to Tepic, bypassing the seaports of Guaymas and Mazatlán, which were strongly defended by Federal troops. On June 10 he began to advance toward Guadalajara, capital of Jalisco and second largest city in the country. After a smashing victory over Federal forces at Orendáin on July 7, Obregón took the city and then moved southwest to occupy Colima on July 19. Meanwhile, Huerta had presented his resignation to the national congress and fled abroad, after placing former Minister of Foreign Affairs Francisco S. Carbajal in charge of the government. When informed of this development, Obregón pushed eastward toward Guanajuato while General Pablo González, commanding the Army Corps of the Northeast, advanced toward the same area from the northeast. A conference between Obregón and González at Querétaro on August 1 was followed by a message that Obregón addressed to Carbajal stating that before beginning his march on the capital he desired to know whether the Federal forces intended to resist or to surrender. In case resistance was planned Carbajal was advised to notify foreign residents, so that they might abandon the city. Alfredo Robles Domínguez, the Constitutionalist agent in Mexico City, urged the Carbajal government to accept Carranza's de-

mand for unconditional surrender. On August 9 he conferred with General José Refugio Velasco, Minister of
War, concerning Obregón's message of the previous day. At
first Velasco insisted that the honor of the Army would not
permit surrender without a fight. However, Robles
Domínguez advised him that American troops (which had
occupied the port of Veracruz since April as a result of
President Woodrow Wilson's reaction to the Tampico incident and his efforts to prevent Huerta from receiving German arms) were prepared to march on the capital if fighting
should result that would endanger the lives of United States
citizens residing in that city. Finally, the Minister of War
agreed to send representatives to Obregón's camp in order
to arrange for the surrender of Mexico City. On August 12,
1914, Carbajal resigned and followed Huerta into exile. On
the following day his representatives met Obregón near
Teoloyucán to sign agreements providing not only for Constitutionalist occupation of the city but also for surrender
of Federal forces throughout the country.

The liquidation of the Huerta regime did not result in
restoration of peace to the war-torn country. From his
stronghold in Morelos, Zapata declared that his movement
under the banner of the *Plan de Ayala* represented the true
revolutionary cause, and he refused to accept the terms of
the *Plan de Guadalupe*. Although Carranza invited Zapata
to meet him at some place along the boundary line between
Morelos and the Federal District, Zapata responded by informing Carranza that he must come to his headquarters at
Yautepec if a conference was desired. Eventually Carranza
did send Luis Cabrera and General Antonio I. Villareal to
confer with Zapata at Cuernavaca, but the results of these
negotiations were negative. On September 4, 1914, Cabrera
and Villareal reported that Zapata was prepared to accept a
peaceful solution to the conflict on the following conditions: (1) submission by Carranza and his generals to the
*Plan de Ayala,* (2) an immediate armistice that would in-
volve the occupation of Xochimilco by Zapata's troops, and

(3) resignation of Carranza as provisional Chief Executive or establishment of a dual executive head consisting of Carranza and a representative of Zapata. Once these three conditions had been fulfilled, Carranza, Zapata, and their generals would hold conferences at Zapata's headquarters in order to determine how the provisions of the *Plan de Ayala* would be implemented. Carranza indicated that he was not opposed to the agrarian reforms called for by Zapata's plan, but declared that he would not consider submitting to his leadership. Thus, as soon as Huerta was defeated, Carranza became involved in a power struggle with Zapata.

Even before Huerta's defeat, however, Carranza was confronted with serious challenges to his leadership in the North. In June 1913 the First Chief had decided that Maytorena should be allowed to resume the governorship of Sonora; however, Obregón's lieutenants in that state could not forgive Maytorena for his unwillingness to denounce Huerta at the time of Madero's overthrow. Also, Villa's Division of the North had scored sensational victories in Chihuahua and Coahuila during the first eight months of the anti-Huerta campaign and had grown increasingly independent. Thus, Carranza feared that the Division of the North might soon drive south and take Mexico City before the forces of Obregón or González could reach the national capital. To prevent such a development, early in May 1914 Carranza ordered Villa to move east from Torreón and take Saltillo. Then the First Chief authorized General Pánfilo Natera to march against Zacatecas, the Federal stronghold on the strategic Mexican Central Railroad leading south to Mexico City. When Natera's force proved inadequate for the operation, Carranza sent Villa a telegram ordering him to send 3,000, and later 5,000, of his men to assist Natera. Villa refused to comply on the grounds that the whole Division of the North would be needed to guarantee the capture of Zacatecas. When Carranza insisted that 5,000 troops would be adequate, Villa offered to resign his command, and Carranza promptly accepted his resignation. Then the First Chief ordered Villa's generals to select his successor. However, they supported their commander, and in defiance of Carranza the entire Division of the North marched against Zacatecas. The city fell on June 23, 1914, but Villa was unable to continue his march toward Mexico City for two reasons: Carranza's forces in northern Coahuila promptly cut off the supply of coal for Villa's locomotives, and other Constitutionalist units in Tamaulipas and Nuevo León prevented supplies from reaching him by way of the port of Tampico. Thus, Villa was halted at Zacatecas and Obregón's Army Corps of the Northwest won the race to the national capital.

At Teoloyucán on August 11, 1914, Carranza received news from Calles that Maytorena, supported by Constitutionalist forces operating in the central and southern parts of Sonora, had denounced the First Chief and had declared himself in open rebellion. Ten days later Obregón departed from Mexico City for Chihuahua with the hope that Villa might be persuaded not to support Maytorena. After traveling to Sonora for a meeting with Maytorena on August 29, Villa and Obregón agreed that Maytorena should continue to serve as governor and commander of all military forces in the state. But within twenty-four hours Obregón deposed Maytorena because of circulation by Maytorena's supporters of a leaflet severely criticizing Obregón. Returning to Chihuahua on September 3, Villa and Obregón decided that General Juan G. Cabral should replace Maytorena as governor and military chief of Sonora. On the same day they drew up a proposal for certain political changes, including the designation of Carranza as interim President, the holding of local, state, and national elections, and the consideration of constitutional reforms.

Obregón returned to Mexico City on September 6 and reported to Carranza immediately. Although the First Chief had little hope that Cabral would be able to bring peace and order to Sonora, he agreed that Cabral should be named governor and military commander of that state. In regard to the Villa-Obregón proposals for political changes, Carranza was less receptive. Finally, he announced that a junta would be convoked in Mexico City on October 1 for the purpose of dealing with such outstanding problems. In an effort to convince Villa and his generals that they should attend this meeting, and with the hope of resolving new problems in Sonora, Obregón returned to Chihuahua on September 16. His mission was a complete failure, and on more than one occasion Villa was determined to have his guest shot; but by September 26 Obregón was safely back in Mexico City. Meanwhile, on September 22 Villa sent Carranza a telegram informing him that he was no longer recognized as First Chief and that the Division of the North would not be represented at the October 1 junta; then on September 25 Villa made public his rebellion in a manifesto addressed to the Mexican people.

In an effort to resolve the conflict between Carranza and Villa, a group of Constitutionalist generals met at General Lucio Blanco's headquarters on September 23, organized a Permanent Peace Commission, and agreed to work for the convoking of a convention of *Villista* and *Carrancista* chiefs. Soon after returning to Mexico City from Chihuahua, Obregón met with the newly formed commission and agreed to serve as a member of a delegation that was commissioned to travel to Zacatecas for the purpose of consulting with Villa's generals concerning the selection of a neutral convention site. Subsequently it was decided that a meeting of leaders to be termed the Revolutionary Convention would convene at Aguascalientes on October 10. Carranza took no part in the organization of the Aguascalientes meeting and continued to insist on holding the Mexico City conference that he had convoked for October 1. Obregón and other members of the Permanent Peace Commission were among the seventy-nine military and civilian Constitutionalist leaders who attended the five-day junta in the national capital. Highlighting the affair was Carranza's offer to resign as First Chief of the Constitutionalist Army and as the provisional Chief Executive; however, Obregón moved that this matter should be referred to the Aguascalientes Convention. Although Carranza did not approve of the Aguascalientes meeting, he was powerless to prevent Obregón and others from attending. At the same time it was obvious that most Constitutionalists were prepared to sacrifice their First Chief if such action would prevent conflict with Villa.

At the opening of the Aguascalientes Convention, the delegates proclaimed it to be a sovereign body. One hundred and two Villistas and Carrancistas attended; and late in October, twenty-six *Zapatista* chiefs joined the meeting. Also attending the convention was General Cabral, who had earlier declared his intention of assuming a neutral position. Carranza was extended a special invitation to participate but refused; however, he did indicate his willingness to retire if Villa and Zapata would do likewise. Subsequently, the convention voted for removal of both Villa and Carranza but took no action in regard to Zapata. Sponsored by Obregón, General Eulalio Gutiérrez was elected as the provisional President to succeed Carranza, and a commission, of which Obregón was a member, was named to inform Carranza of this action. However, when the commission reached Mexico City, Carranza was not to be found. Fearing arrest by Lucio Blanco, who commanded the cavalry forces occupying the capital, Carranza had slipped away on November 1 and had joined General Francisco Coss in Puebla. Shortly thereafter he moved to Córdoba, Veracruz. On November 5 the convention resolved to condemn Carranza as a rebel if he did not surrender his authority to Gutiérrez by six o'clock on the evening of November 10. The First Chief replied by ordering his supporters to withdraw from the Aguascalientes meeting before the deadline that had been set for his resignation. Despite new proposals and counterproposals designed to prevent hostilities by removing both Carranza and Villa, no acceptable plan was presented and the country drifted into civil war once more. On November 11 Obregón pledged his support to Gutiérrez providing that the provisional President should disassociate himself from Villa; however, Gutiérrez had already appointed Villa as commander of the military forces of the convention. Thus, Obregón chose to rally to the defense of Carranza rather than to support a regime that would be dominated by Pancho Villa.

When Obregón took command of the Carrancista forces in Mexico City on November 16, 1914 the Constitutionalist position was far from strong. Villa's army was advancing from the northwest; Zapata's forces were operating on the outskirts of the national capital and threatened to cut off railroad connections with Veracruz; some former pro-Carranza generals had joined Villa; and Lucio Blanco, commander of Obregón's cavalry division, gave indications that he might defect at any time. Under these circumstances Obregón began evacuation of his artillery, machine-gun, and infantry units to Veracruz on November 18. Early on the morning of November 24, Obregón's last train pulled out of Mexico City.

Zapata's forces entered Mexico City on the heels of Obregón's men, but Villa's Division of the North did not reach the Federal District until a week later. Subsequently a meeting between Villa and Zapata took place at Xochimilco on December 4, at which time they agreed that Villa's troops would move on Veracruz, while Zapata's men marched against Puebla. Zapata took the city on December 15, but Villa, instead of undertaking a campaign against Obregón, decided to strike at General Manuel Diéguez in Jalisco. On December 10 Villa left Mexico City and entered Guadalajara a week later, but rumors concerning Gutiérrez's unreliability soon prompted him to return to the capital. When he confronted Gutiérrez with the charge that the provisional President was planning to abandon the Federal District, Gutiérrez explained that there was little purpose in remaining because neither Villa nor Zapata respected his authority. Not only were Gutiérrez's orders disregarded but he was unable to protect members of his government from intimidation and assassination. As directed by Villa, General Guillermo García Aragón, a member of the Permanent Commission of the Convention and Governor of the National Palace under Gutiérrez, had been turned over to Zapata to be shot in satisfaction of a long-standing grudge harbored by the Morelos Chief. Two other leading figures of the Gutiérrez government, David Berlanga and Paulino Martínez, were murdered by Villa's bloody killer, General Rodolfo Fierro. In all, perhaps some one hundred and fifty such assassinations took place during the first two or three weeks following the occupation of Mexico City by Villista and Zapatista forces. Although Villa did renew his promise to respect the provisional President, there was no substantial improvement in the situation; and rumors continued to circulate concerning Gutiérrez's intentions to sever connections with Villa and Zapata. Finally, during the early morning hours of January 16, 1915, the provisional President Guitiérrez and members of his government fled from Mexico City and, accompanied by a small military escort, moved north toward Gutiérrez's native state of San Luis Potosí.

Meanwhile, Constitutionalist forces had been reorganized in Veracruz during the month of December in 1914; and on January 5, 1915, Obregón's army drove Zapata's men out of the city of Puebla. Learning of Gutiérrez's plans to flee from Mexico City, Villa had wired orders for his execution on January 15 and then had headed toward the capital. News of Gutiérrez's flight reached Villa as his train moved south from Aguascalientes. Arriving at Querétaro on January 17, Villa also learned of the defeat of his forces commanded by General Rodolfo Fierro and Calixto Contreras at Guadalajara. Mexico City no longer attracted him. Determined to destroy the Constitutionalist Army in the West, he halted the movement of his units toward the national capital and prepared ,to undertake a campaign in Jalisco. A month later Villa succeeded in defeating Generals Manuel Diéguez and Francisco Murguía at Cuesta de Sayula, but he failed to destroy their force.

As Villa turned his attention to the West, Obregón marched out of Puebla on January 22 and entered Mexico City six days later without a fight. Throughout the month of February he remained in the capital. But early in March, Obregón prepared to move into the Bajío region in order to seek out Villa and to battle the main enemy force. The first major engagement took place at Celaya on April 6 and 7, and a second great conflict was fought at the same place from April 13 to 15. Both battles saw Villa's violent frontal attacks repulsed by Obregón's troops fighting from well-defended positions. Another battle was waged in the region between Silao and León from June 1 to 5 in 1915. Once more the Constitutionalist forces were victorious, but Obregón came close to death on June 3 when he lost an arm at Santa Ana del Conde. Not only did Villa suffer serious reverses in Guanajuato but Diéguez defeated Fierro in Jalisco and General Tomás Urbina was checked at El Ebano after making a determined effort to break into the rich Huasteca oil-producing region of eastern San Luis Potosí, southern Tamaulipas, and northern Veracruz. During the summer of 1915 Obregón's army pushed Villa's main force northward, winning victory after victory. By early September, Villa controlled only the state of Chihuahua, his old stronghold. At this time he called a meeting of his generals and it was decided to place garrison forces in the leading Chihuahua cities and to march the remaining 15,000 troops westward into Sonora where a link-up could be effected with Maytorena's forces.

Arriving in northeastern Sonora late in October in 1915, Villa's first objective was to take the strategic border town of Agua Prieta. Learning of Villa's plans, the Constitutionalist government had made efforts to reinforce General Plutarco Calles' defending forces. It was apparent that without strong reinforcements, Calles' 3,000 men would be unable to withstand Villa's attack; and there was only one possible way that Constitutionalist troops could be rushed to Agua Prieta: via rail through United States territory. Unfortunately, at this time the American government did not recognize the Carranza regime so it appeared that such an arrangement would be impossible. However, the picture changed rapidly on October 19 when Secretary of State

Robert Lansing informed Carranza's representative in Washington that de facto recognition would be granted. At the same time President Wilson imposed an embargo on the shipment of arms to Carranza's opponents.

Taking advantage of the favor he had recently found in the eyes of the Wilson administration, Carranza immediately sought permission to transport troops from Piedras Negras, Coahuila, across the international boundary to Eagle Pass, Texas, and from there by rail through United States territory to Douglas, Arizona, and to Agua Prieta. Permission was granted promptly, and on October 22 Obregón ordered his Chief of Staff, General Francisco Serrano, to rush 4,000 troops and several pieces of artillery to Calles. The first of these reinforcements reached Agua Prieta on October 30 while Villa was preparing to attack, and the last Constitutionalist troop trains arrived on the following night. Thus, when Villa launched his attack on November 1, he found himself opposed by a well-entrenched force numbering over 7,000. Time after time on that afternoon and night, Villa's men charged into the barbed wire entanglements surrounding the town, only to be mowed down by heavy artillery, machine-gun, and rifle fire. A last desperate assault was attempted early on the morning of November 2, but to no avail. Thus, on the following day Villa decided to march westward, leaving Calles in possession of the strategic bordertown.

On November 6 Obregón arrived at Agua Prieta to take personal charge of the Sonora campaign. He found that Villa had split his force, leaving 7,000 troops in the northern part of the state under the command of General José Rodríguez and taking the remaining 5,000 southward to join General Francisco Urbalejo in a campaign against General Diéguez. During the month of October, Diéguez had moved his troops by sea from Mazatlán up the Pacific coast to Cruz de Piedra; and from there he had marched on the port of Guaymas, which was held by some of Maytorena's troops. After taking Guaymas, Diéguez moved north toward Hermosillo, the state capital, which he occupied on

November 6. Obregón decided to strike first against Rodríguez before turning south to assist Diéguez. Under Constitutionalist pressure, Rodríguez was forced to abandon
Naco on November 14, and he withdrew to Cananea and
Nogales. A week later his troops were driven out of Cananea, and on November 26 Constitutionalist cavalry
units commanded by Lázaro Cárdenas captured Nogales
after a brief engagement. While Obregón was preparing to
march south to aid Diéguez, he received the welcome news
that on November 22, after thirty hours of combat, Villa's
forces had been smashed following an unsuccessful attack
against Diéguez at Hermosillo. Thus, with less than 3,000
soldiers remaining in his once powerful Division of the
North, Villa was forced to abandon Sonora in late 1915
and to seek refuge in the familiar mountains and deserts of
Chihuahua.

# 9

# JOHN REED

•

# PANCHO VILLA AND THE RULES OF WAR[*]

❧

*Constitution, laws, elections—these were fine words for the* Plan of Guadalupe, *but they ignored the basic fact that men like Pancho Villa knew nothing of rules—only force and power. Once the struggle to avenge Madero was unleashed, each leader fought his own battle for personal victory. John Reed rode with Villa and out of his experiences came his volume entitled* Insurgent Mexico. *Within a few years, Reed would report on another revolution in* Ten Days That Shook the World (*1919*), *an account of the Bolshevik Revolution of 1917.*

On the field, too, Villa had to invent an entirely original method of warfare, because he never had a chance to learn anything of accepted military strategy. In that he is without the possibility of any doubt the greatest leader Mexico has ever had. His method of fighting is astonishingly like Napoleon's. Secrecy, quickness of movement, the adaptation of his plans to the character of the country and of his soldiers —the value of intimate relations with the rank and file, and

---

[*] John Reed, *Insurgent Mexico* (New York: Appleton, 1914), 140–144. For a new edition of this book, see the Clarion edition (New York: Simon & Schuster, 1969), edited by Albert L. Michaels and James W. Wilkie.

of building up a tradition among the enemy that his army is invincible, and that he himself bears a charmed life—these are his characteristics. He knew nothing of accepted European standards of strategy or of discipline. One of the troubles of the Mexican Federal Army is that its officers are thoroughly saturated with conventional military theory. The Mexican soldier is still mentally at the end of the eighteenth century. He is, above all, a loose, individual, guerrilla fighter. Red tape simply paralyzes the machine. When Villa's army goes into battle he is not hampered by salutes, or rigid respect for officers, or trigonometrical calculations of the trajectories of projectiles, or theories of the percentage of hits in a thousand rounds of rifle fire, or the function of cavalry, infantry, and artillery in any particular position, or rigid obedience to the secret knowledge of its superiors. It reminds one of the ragged Republican Army that Napoleon led into Italy. It is probable that Villa doesn't know much about those things himself. But he does know that guerrilla fighters cannot be driven blindly in platoons around the field in perfect step, that men fighting individually and of their own free will are braver than long volleying rows in the trenches, lashed to it by officers with the flat of their swords. And where the fighting is fiercest—when a ragged mob of fierce brown men with hand bombs and rifles rush the bullet-swept streets of an ambushed town—Villa is among them, like any common soldier.

Up to his day, Mexican armies had always carried with them hundreds of the women and children of the soldiers; Villa was the first man to think of swift forced marches of bodies of cavalry, leaving their women behind. Up to his time no Mexican army had ever abandoned its base; it had always stuck closely to the railroad and the supply trains. But Villa struck terror into the enemy by abandoning his trains and throwing his entire effective army upon the field, as he did at Gómez Palacio. He invented in Mexico that most demoralizing form of battle—the night attack. When, after the fall of Torreón last September, he withdrew his entire army in the face of Orozco's advance from Mexico

City and for five days unsuccessfully attacked Chihuahua, it was a terrible shock to the Federal General when he waked up one morning and found that Villa had sneaked around the city under cover of darkness, captured a freight train at Terrazzas and descended with his entire army upon the comparatively undefended city of Juárez. It wasn't fair! Villa found that he hadn't enough trains to carry all his soldiers, even when he had ambushed and captured a Federal troop train, sent south by General Castro, the Federal commander in Juárez. So he telegraphed that gentleman as follows, signing the name of the colonel in command of the troop train: "Engine broken down at Moctezuma. Send another engine and five cars." The unsuspecting Castro immediately dispatched a new train. Villa then telegraphed him: "Wires cut between here and Chihuahua. Large force of rebels approaching from south. What shall I do?" Castro replied: "Return at once." And Villa obeyed, telegraphing cheering messages at every station along the way. The Federal commander got wind of his coming about an hour before he arrived, and left, without informing his garrison, so that, outside of a small massacre, Villa took Juárez almost without a shot. And with the border so near he managed to smuggle across enough ammunition to equip his almost armless forces and a week later sallied out and routed the pursuing Federal forces with great slaughter at Tierra Blanca.

General Hugh L. Scott, in command of the American troops at Fort Bliss, sent Villa a little pamphlet containing the Rules of War adopted by the Hague Conference. He spent hours poring over it. It interested and amused him hugely. He said: "What is this Hague Conference? Was there a representative of Mexico there? Was there a representative of the Constitutionalists there? It seems to me a funny thing to make rules about war. It's not a game. What is the difference between civilized war and any other kind of war? If you and I are having a fight in a *cantina* we are not going to pull a little book out of our pockets and read over the rules. It says here that you must not use lead [dum-dum] bullets; but I don't see why not. They do the work."

For a long time afterward he went around popping questions at his officers like this: "If an invading army takes a city of the enemy, what must you do with the women and children?"

As far as I could see, the Rules of War didn't make any difference in Villa's original method of fighting. The *colorados* he executed wherever he captured them; because, he said, they were peons like the revolutionists and that no peon would volunteer against the cause of liberty unless he were bad. The Federal officers also he killed, because, he explained, they were educated men and ought to know better. But the Federal common soldiers he set at liberty because most of them were conscripts, and thought that they were fighting for the *Patria*. There is no case on record where he wantonly killed a man. Anyone who did so he promptly executed—except Fierro.

Fierro, the man who killed [William] Benton, was known as "The Butcher" throughout the army. He was a great handsome animal, the best and cruelest rider and fighter, perhaps, in all the revolutionary forces. In his furious lust for blood Fierro used to shoot down a hundred prisoners with his own revolver, only stopping long enough to reload. He killed for the pure joy of it. During two weeks that I was in Chihuahua, Fierro killed fifteen inoffensive citizens in cold blood. But there was always a curious relationship between him and Villa. He was Villa's best friend; and Villa loved him like a son and always pardoned him.

But Villa, although he had never heard of the Rules of War, carried with his army the only field hospital of any effectiveness that any Mexican army has ever carried. It consisted of forty boxcars enameled inside, fitted with operating tables and all the latest appliances of surgery, and manned by more than sixty doctors and nurses. Every day during the battle shuttle trains full of the desperately wounded ran from the front to the base hospitals at Parral, Jiménez, and Chihuahua. He took care of the Federal wounded just as carefully as of his own men. Ahead of his own supply train went another train, carrying two thousand sacks of flour, and also coffee, corn, sugar, and cigarettes to feed the entire starving population of the country around Durango City and Torreón.

# 10

ROBERT E. QUIRK

———•———

# VILLA MEETS ZAPATA*

❉

*With Huerta defeated by mid-1914, the Convention
of Aguascalientes in October saw the break between
the forces of Venustiano Carranza and Alvaro Obregón on one side and Villa and Zapata on the other.
Now, on December 4, Villa and Zapata were to meet
at Xochimilco, famous for its floating gardens on the
edge of the capital city. Until rebels controlled Mexico City, they could not claim real victory no matter
what their other gains. Thus, the meeting of Villa
and Zapata was a festive triumph, and it has been
well described by Professor Robert E. Quirk. Quirk,
professor of history at Indiana University, has written*
An Affair of Honor: Woodrow Wilson and the Occupation of Veracruz (*Lexington: University of Kentucky, 1962*). He is currently serving as managing
editor of the Hispanic American Historical Review.*

It was just at midday that Villa rode into Xochimilco, and a
warm winter sun shone down on the narrow, dusty, cob-
bled streets. The usually quiet town wore an air of festive
expectancy. As the band of *Norteños* headed into the
center of the town, they were greeted by Otilio Montaño.

---

* Robert E. Quirk, *The Mexican Revolution, 1914–1915; The Convention of Aguascalientes* (Bloomington: Indiana University Press,
1960), 135–139. Reprinted by permission of the publisher.

After a short speech of welcome by Montaño and a hearty *abrazo,* Villa was led down the street to be introduced to Emiliano Zapata. In this, their first meeting, was symbolized the union of North and South. Zapata said little, but his sharp hawk's eyes missed nothing. He seemed deeply appreciative of Villa's trust in coming to see him in his own territory with only a small escort. He was now convinced that Villa, first of all the revolutionary leaders, was willing to give him the recognition he felt he deserved.

After the customary abrazos and a few more noncommittal words of courtesy, the two locked arms, and Zapata drew Villa into the municipal school building for their conference. On the second floor in a spacious classroom they took seats at a large oval table. There were few chairs in the room, but it was filled immediately as *Zapatistas* and *Villistas* crowded about the table. It is fortunate that two observers have left detailed accounts of the proceedings: [Leon] Canova, whose journalistic eye caught the color of this gathering; and Gonzalo Atayde, the private secretary of [Roque] González Garza, who took stenographic notes of the conversation.

In Canova's account of the proceedings Villa and Zapata were a study in contrasts. Villa was tall and robust, weighing at least 180 pounds, and with a florid complexion. He wore a tropical helmet after the English style. Though he had given up the nondescript garb he had affected before the battle of Torreón, he still seemed oblivious of the demands high fashion made upon successful revolutionaries. He was clad in a heavy, brown woolen sweater, which was loosely woven, with a large roll collar and buttons down the front, khaki military trousers, army leggings, and heavy riding boots. Zapata, in his physiognomy, was much more the Indian of the two. His skin was very dark, and, in comparison with Villa's, his face was thin with high cheek bones. He wore an immense sombrero, which at times hid his eyes. These, said Canova, were dark, penetrating, and enigmatic. He was much shorter than Villa and slighter. He weighed about 130 pounds. Where Villa was attired in rough, field clothing, Zapata's dress was gaudier and more fastidious. He wore a black coat, a large light blue silk neckerchief, a lavender shirt, and the tight *charro* trousers of the Mexican rural dandy, black with silver buttons down the outer seam of each pant leg. While Villa had no jewelry or ornaments of any kind, Zapata wore two gold rings.

The conference began haltingly as the two chiefs comported themselves like bashful swains. Both were men of action and verbal intercourse left them uneasy. For about half an hour they talked aimlessly. . . . Then the conversation touched on Venustiano Carranza and suddenly, like tinder, burst aflame. They poured out in a torrent of volubility their mutual hatred for the First Chief, and their dialogue was animated for more than an hour. "Carranza," said Villa, "is a man who is very—well, very insolent. . . ." Zapata agreed: "I have always said that . . . that Carranza is a scoundrel."

Villa pronounced his opinion of the middle class revolutionaries who followed Carranza: "Those are men who have always slept on soft pillows. How could they ever be friends of the people, who have spent their whole lives in nothing but suffering." Zapata concurred: "On the contrary, they have always been the scourge of the people." Villa continued: "With those people we shall never have progress, or prosperity, or division of lands. Only a tyranny in the land. . . . Carranza is a person who has come from God knows where, to turn the Republic into an anarchy."

Manuel Palafox leaned across the table to interject an opinion about the Constitutionalist troops: "What they did in Mexico City was without precedent. If barbarians had come in they would have behaved better than those people did." Villa nodded: "It's a barbarity!" Zapata said: "In every town they passed through . . ." His voice trailed off, and Villa picked up the thread: "Yes, they do nothing but massacre and destroy. . . . Those men have no patriotic sentiments." Palafox echoed: "None. No kind of feelings whatever."

Villa complained of his military difficulties with Carranza, asserting that his Division of the North was the only force to fight against Huerta. Pablo González had promised him, he said, in the division's attack on Saltillo, to prevent the passage toward Saltillo of federal troops. But, "he let eleven trains get by!" said Villa. "Luck was running our way, however, and we took care of them and finally took Saltillo and other points." Amid laughter and jests at González's reputed cowardice, Villa added that "if he hadn't been careful, we'd have taken him too!" Villa relished the prospects of his impending war with González, Obregón, and Carranza. His eyes bright with anticipation, he promised to deal with them as the "bulls of Tepehuanes handle the horses up there!"

From the war, the two passed to a matter dear to Zapata: the partition of lands. With the *Carrancistas* there could be no real agrarian reforms, they were agreed. "But now," said Villa, "they will see that it is the people who give orders and that the people will know who their enemies are. . . . Our people have never known justice or liberty. All of the best lands belong to the rich, while the poor naked peasant works from sunup to sundown. I think, however, that hereafter things will be different. And if not, we won't lay down these mausers. I have here close by the capital forty thousand *mauseritos* and some seventy-seven cannons and some. . . ." Zapata was amazed at this catalog of military affluence and he broke in: "Very good!" Villa continued: ". . . sixteen million cartridges and plenty of equipment. When I saw that that man [Carranza] was a bandit, I began to buy ammunition. . . ."

The reference to Carranza brought an outburst from Zapata, who was, now that the ice had been broken, less reserved and much more garrulous. He reviled the Constitutionalists: "Those *cabrones!* As soon as they see a little chance, well, they want to take advantage of it and line their own pockets! Well, to hell with them! I'd have 'broken' all of those cabrones. I never could put up with them. In a minute they've changed and off they go, first with Carranza, and then with some other fellow. They're all a bunch of bastards. I wish I could get my hands on them some other time!"

Villa was increasingly pleased with Zapata. He said: "I am a man who doesn't like to fawn on anybody, but you surely know that I have been thinking about you for a long time." Zapata replied: "And we, too. Those who have gone up north . . . have told me that things looked hopeful for me up there. He is, I said to myself, the only one I can count on. And so let the war go on. I am not going to make deals with anybody. I shall continue to fight, even though they kill me and all of those who follow me."

Zapata then called for someone to bring a bottle of cognac to the table, but Villa asked for a glass of water instead. Partaking of strong liquors was not among his vices. Zapata refused to take Villa seriously and poured two large tumblers full of cognac. Proposing a toast to the fraternal union of the two factions, he thrust the glass at Villa. With all eyes upon him, Villa reluctantly and hesitatingly reached for the cognac. Unable to do otherwise under the circumstances, he grasped the tumbler and gulped down the contents as though it were, in reality, the glass of water. As the spirituous liquor reached his gullet he nearly strangled. His face turned livid and his features became contorted. But he drank the cognac. As he finished the glass, his eyes were swimming and tears ran down his cheeks. In a husky voice Villa called for his glass of water.

When he had recovered his composure, Villa expressed to Zapata his pleasure in knowing the men of the South. "Well, *hombre,*" he said, "I have finally met some fellows who are really men of the people." Zapata returned the compliment: "And I give thanks that I have at last met a man who really knows how to fight." "Do you know how long I have been fighting?" asked Villa. "Nearly twenty-two years." And Zapata replied: "I, too, began to fight at the age of eighteen. . . ." They continued to chat, their conversation leaping from hats to the *cientificos*. . . . Outside a military band struck up a tune and, finding further discourse impracticable, Zapata and Villa left the room, arm in arm.

# 11

# HARRY H. DUNN

———————•———————

# THE CRIMSON JESTER:
# ZAPATA OF MEXICO*

❦

*As the Revolution wore on, many observers began to debate which leaders were the most murderous. Villa and Zapata were obviously in contention for the championship. Harry H. Dunn, a Hearst reporter who rode with Zapata, did much in dispatches to portray Zapata and his "Horde" in a grim light. By Dunn's account, at least, Zapata was a perfect leader for the Death Legion, which operated in the valley of Morelos. In this selection, Dunn describes Zapata's execution of prisoners and the ironic outcome that placed Zapata's opponents in an equally bad light. The scene is Ayala, Morelos, famed for the* Plan of Ayala *in which Zapata set forth his noble goals.*

About two hundred yards from the headquarters building at Villa Ayala a solid clay cliff rises fifty feet or more by about one hundred feet in width at the bottom. When Eufemio and I reached a point whence we could see this cliff, fifty-seven civilian whites and halfbreeds were standing in line in front of it. Before them was Emiliano Zapata. Behind him, half a hundred *guerreros* from the Death Legion

———————————————

* From *Crimson Jester: Zapata of Mexico,* by H. H. Dunn. © 1961 by Crown Publishers, Inc. Used by permission of Crown Publishers, Inc., 267–270.

leaned watchfully on their rifles. Other thousands of the
Horde were scattered over low hills facing the cliff.

Zapata selected every fifth man from the line. The guard
surrounded the remaining forty-six and marched them a
little distance away, where they could see plainly what was
to follow. With his own hands the master of the Horde lined
up the eleven, their backs to the cliff, about two feet apart.
Then he drew one of his silverhandled automatics—the
gifts of John-of-God—from his belt. He shot the first of the
eleven. Then the second, third, and fourth. They fell so
rapidly that each succeeding victim seemed not to realize
what had happened to his predecessor in the line. After the
seventh man, Emiliano tossed his empty pistol to an Indian
to be loaded, and drew the other automatic.

The eighth man collapsed. His knees gave way. He sank
to a sitting posture, resting on his heels. Then he struggled
to his knees, crying for his life. Zapata seized him by the
front of his shirt with his left hand and lifted the wretch to
his feet. Then, as he held him upright, he shot his victim
dead. The ninth man defied and cursed him, laughing in
Emiliano's face. Zapata, calling two *guerreros,* sent him to
be given to the ants.

While all this was going on, the tenth man stood as if
petrified. When Emiliano shot him, he fell forward full
length, like a log. As this shot rang out, the eleventh man,
shouting and screaming, gone stark mad, leaped out and
ran, dodging here and there, along the face of the cliff.
Zapata raised his pistol, then dropped it. From his mouth
came the same cackling laughter I had heard from Villa's
butcher, Fierro, at Escalón.

"Take him alive," he shouted.

Indians caught the mestizo and brought him back, insane, gibbering as monkeys chatter at the scent of a jaguar.
"Keep him safe," Emiliano ordered. "We will send him
back as he is."

He turned to the waiting prisoners.

"This," he said, "will show you the fate of traitors to me,
the Attila of the South. Tomorrow another number of you

shall die. You may think of the manner in which I shall select those for punishment. Until then, go with God!"

Next day every fourth man was selected. On the third day every third man was taken. One went mad overnight, and was kept safe with the other insane fellow. So Zapata killed the prisoners until one remained. This one was given a night alone to consider whether he would be shot the following day. Much to his surprise, however, he was placed on a mule, after having been stripped naked, save for a hat. The two madmen were strapped lengthwise along a packsaddle, on the back of another mule. Then the dead, two by two, were similarly attached to mules, until all fifty-four were provided for, the last mule carrying also what remained of the mestizo on whose body the ants had worked their way.

The sane man's feet were lashed beneath his mule's belly. His left hand was tied securely to the saddle horn. Wet rawhide thongs were used, so that, as they dried and shrunk, they could not be removed except with an edged tool. This man's right hand was left free so that he could guide the mule. Then the other mules were roped together in line, and the lead rope made fast to the saddle in which rode the one sane survivor of the Mexico City *policastros*. A guard of *Zapatistas* took this mule train of death and madness close to Cuernavaca. There the sane man was instructed to report to General Pablo González, again in command in the City of the Cow's Horn, by order of General Venustiano Carranza. This fellow obeyed his instructions to the letter—and was executed on charges of having revealed the whereabouts of the González army to Zapata!

# 12

## HOWARD F. CLINE

———•———

# MORAL IMPERIALISM
# AND UNITED STATES
# INTERVENTION*

৵

*By early 1914 President Woodrow Wilson had lost
his patience with Mexico, and an incident in Tampico
on April 9 furnished an excuse to move against Huerta. Howard F. Cline, Director of the Hispanic
Foundation of the Library of Congress, has provided
a succinct summary of United States diplomatic problems growing out of Wilson's intransigence. Cline has
written* Mexico, Revolution to Evolution: 1940–1960
*(New York: Oxford University Press, 1962). He is
currently Chairman of the Committee on Activities
and Projects of the Conference on Latin American
History.*

Strung along the Panuco River that empties into the Gulf
at Tampico were foreign-owned oil installations—wells,
storage tanks, and a little refining apparatus. The petroleum
colony, chiefly British, were apprehensive that purposely or
accidentally Mexicans might set these strategic properties

* Reprinted by permission of the publishers from Howard F. Cline,
*The United States and Mexico* (Cambridge, Mass.: Harvard Univer-
sity Press, Copyright 1953, '63, by the President and Fellows of
Harvard College), 155–160.

afire in an engagement between Federalists or Constitution-alists. British, French, German, and even Spanish war vessels converged to protect the threatened interests of their nationals.

Since Taft's day, at least, the American Navy had been patrolling Gulf waters. One battleship was permanently at Tampico, while others hung off Veracruz. As Secretary Knox once said, the purpose of the battlewagons was to keep Mexicans "in a salutary equilibrium, between a dangerous and exaggerated apprehension and a proper degree of wholesome fear." Wilson's feelings about the danger of the Mexican situation could be gauged by the number of vessels hovering in Gulf waters. With a major battle for Tampico looming, he had the Navy outnumber and outgun the combined European units there. Admiral Mayo commanded at Tampico, while Admiral Fletcher, with a smaller force, stayed at Veracruz.

Various national naval commanders warned both Constitutionalists and Federalists away from the oil installations. None had qualms about enforcing their warnings with action. With a critical battle going on, Tampico was tense. It was in this atmosphere that a German gasoline salesman rushed aboard Admiral Mayo's flagship and reported that seven American sailors and an officer had been arrested and jailed by Huerta's men.

From a dock that everyone had been forbidden by Huerta's Federalists to use, these Americans had been loading gasoline into a whaleboat flying the American flag. Ordered out of their boat by the government patrol, they had been marched off to the Tampico prison. Immediately Admiral Mayo sent his aide to the *Huertista* commander and demanded the release of the men. Apologetically General Zaragoza explained that his subordinate had made a mistake, and the Americans were released. The whole incident from beginning to end had not occupied an hour.

Admiral Mayo, however, decided that the Mexican explanation was an inadequate recompense for the indignity to the United States Navy. He sent his chief-of-staff (in full uniform) to the commander with an ultimatum: by six o'clock the following evening General Zaragoza was to "hoist the American flag on a prominent position on shore and salute it with twenty-one guns, which salute will be duly returned by this ship." Moreover, the Mexican officer responsible for the "humiliating arrest" of American personnel was to be court-martialed, and a written apology from General Zaragoza was to be sent to Admiral Mayo. Thus spake the Navy for the United States.

Almost simultaneously two other aggravating Mexican incidents occurred. In Veracruz one of Admiral Fletcher's mail orderlies had been arrested and taken to jail by an overzealous Mexican soldier; there had been a Navy reward posted for an AWOL sailor and the optimistic Mexican had hoped that this was the right one. Then, unaccountably, cable messages from Mexico City to the United States were held up for nearly twelve hours by the Mexican censor, just at a time when wires were buzzing to straighten out the Tampico and Veracruz incidents. These matters were lifted from local handling to the hands of the respective national leaders. Huerta faced Wilson.

Huerta was willing to apologize in written form to Mayo and to court-martial the unfortunate officer, but he would not salute the American flag with twenty-one guns, the main issue at stake. It would have been political suicide to do so, since he was buoyed up to a great extent by posing as the stalwart defender of Mexican nationalism; even if he did fire the salute, he was running the risk that the United States might not return it—disastrous to his prestige! With alarming incidents coming so close together, Wilson's mind linked them together as a plot to discredit the United States. He had no realization of the intense antiforeign atmosphere and the normal minor peccadilloes of Mexican life.

On April 13 Wilson spent the whole day studying what he ought to do. He had convinced himself that Huerta was deliberately launching a campaign to lower the dignity of the United States. Wilson delayed his decision until John

Lind returned on April 14. As Lind was a heated proponent of intervention his advice did little to weaken the
President's determination. Here was an issue that warranted
intervention, unsullied by dollars or issues over property.
Nobody could vote against an insult to the flag.

*Intervention.* At his cabinet meeting on April 14 Wilson
announced that he was going to make a strong naval demonstration against Huerta. The whole Atlantic fleet was
then ordered to Tampico, an additional seven battleships
and six smaller vessels to complement the units already
there. The three at Veracruz were to remain. The Navy
warned Wilson that such a concentration might lead to
war. Apparently Wilson was aware of the risk he was running; when he left his cabinet he remarked "If there are any
of you who still believe in prayer, I wish you would think
seriously over this matter between now and our next meeting."

Huerta would be shown that Wilson's bluffing was over
when firepower surrounded him. Yet Wilson did not want
war. The United States naval commanders were told that
the administration wanted no hostilities. This, then, was an
outsize bluff. Until Huerta fired the salute, the Navy would
patrol Mexico and cut off needed supplies, which Huerta
was purchasing in Germany.

Wilson and Bryan then wrote a soft note to Huerta. They
appealed to his "military honor" to fire the salute. The agile
Huerta suggested that the whole matter of the demands be
submitted to the International Court of Arbitration at The
Hague. Wilson remarked to visitors that this was "one of
the humors of the situation." The fleet would reach Tampico about April 22, and Wilson had to inform the country
about the mounting crisis. He had decided that the salute
must be fired, or else. Or else what? No detailed plans were
made beyond that.

On Saturday, April 18, Wilson sent a last ultimatum to
Huerta. The President gave him until noon Sunday to fire
the salute or Wilson would lay the whole matter before
Congress. At the very last minute, Huerta's Minister of

Foreign Affairs—José López Portillo y Rojas—informed the American Chargé d'Affaires that Huerta would fire the salute if the United States would guarantee to return it immediately. The chargé hurried this proposal off to Washington, where Wilson brushed it aside. The hour passed; no salute.

Bryan set about convening a joint session of Congress for Monday afternoon, April 20. The President was in West Virginia, writing his speech and a resolution giving him permission to use the armed forces against Huerta to secure his "recognition of the dignity of the United States." On his return, the President was jaunty, well-rested, and sanguine that his schemes were working well. He told reporters: "I have no enthusiasm for war. I have an enthusiasm for justice and the dignity of the United States, but not for war."

The cabinet meeting on Monday morning modified Wilson's plan. Wilson learned that his projected naval blockade had two serious loopholes: the interdiction of Mexican ports could not, under law of nations, affect third parties— German or British vessels could load or unload their cargoes of munitions at will. Secondly, Huerta was even at that moment receiving a ponderable supply of stores which might tide him over. On Sunday the steamer *México* had unloaded a thousand cases of ammunition. Due soon was the German vessel *Ypiranga* bringing 200 machine guns and 15 million rounds of cartridges. The blockade scheme had to be revised.

The seizure of Veracruz was therefore at this meeting substituted for a naval demonstration off Tampico. The object was capture of Huerta's incoming munitions. The timing of the new operation had to be nice. The only way the Americans could prevent ammunition on the *Ypiranga* from passing into the Mexican President's hands was to seize it on the dock after it had been unloaded, but before it could get transshipped toward Mexico City. Thus at the end of the cabinet meeting on Monday morning all knew that there was going to be a landing at Veracruz. The time of it would be set by the arrival of the *Ypiranga*.

Next on Wilson's tight schedule that crowded day was a conference with Congressional leaders. As a show of bipartisanship in national crisis, Wilson called together the Republicans and Democrats on the House and Senate Foreign Relations and Affairs Committees and read them his speech and resolution. Henry Cabot Lodge, a powerful Republican, objected to both, but with seeming arrogance Wilson silenced him.

In his Congressional message on April 20, 1914, President Wilson rehearsed the three Mexican incidents and asserted that they would lead to an unwanted war if allowed to continue. Even if conflict should come, he stated, it would be only against "General Huerta and those who adhere to him," not against the Mexican people.

After reaffirming his intentions to respect the sovereignty and territorial integrity of Mexico he requested that Congress approve his use of armed force. There was little or no jingoistic talk in Congress, as in 1846. But Wilson's earlier handling of Lodge now bobbed up to plague him. By accident, the Republicans had a temporary majority on the Senate Foreign Relations Committee, which they used to embarrass and harass Wilson.

Lodge refused to allow passage of the resolution as drawn by Wilson. He pointed out that it lacked any references to loss of American life and property, and that the United States could not threaten by name a foreign person, however obnoxious; governments, yes; individuals, no. He wanted all references to Huerta cut out and loss of property and life inserted as the causes of intervention. All Wilson's and Bryan's cloakroom buttonholing could not get the unamended resolution through in time to authorize a landing on April 21, the date the *Ypiranga* was to arrive. When the normal party balances were restored it was passed April 23. But without his resolution, Wilson went ahead with his altered plans, the details of which occupied his attention now.

After his Congressional speech Wilson called a private conference. To advise him, the senior admirals and generals

were present, as were Lind, Bryan, and Daniels. Certain
technical difficulties had appeared. Mayo's units could not
get from Tampico to Veracruz in time to help Fletcher, and
the bulk of the fleet, now deflected toward the southern
harbor, would not arrive until even later. There might be
inadequate forces to take the port. Everyone agreed that it
was to be taken, and that Admiral Fletcher would have to
do the best he could. The civilians, including Wilson, were
convinced that the Mexicans would not fight. When the
definite arrival time was known, Washington would flash
orders to Veracruz to set Admiral Fletcher in motion.
Everyone went to bed for a while.

Later in the evening Bryan got word about the *Ypiranga's* arrival. It would be 10:30 A.M., April 21. Wilson
had Josephus Daniels (later Ambassador to Mexico) order
the Navy to carry out the agreed scheme. About 8:30 A.M.
on April 21 Admiral Fletcher, who had been alerted earlier,
received the fateful orders: Take Veracruz. He immediately
made arrangements with the Huertista commander to turn
over to him unopposed the customhouse and docks. At
11:30 A.M. the United States Navy took the principal
Mexican port.

An hour later the *Ypiranga* hove into port. All sorts of
legal and international difficulties ensued about that ubiqui-
tous Teutonic vessel. She was temporarily impounded and
spent some time evacuating Americans. Finally, with the
once important original munitions still in her hold, she
docked at Puerto México on May 26 and calmly unloaded
them. It turned out that months before and all through the
American military occupation of Veracruz, munitions had
been reaching Huerta through this secondary port.

The actual taking of Veracruz on April 21 seemed to be
moving like clockwork. During the afternoon, however, the
Mexican civilian population, led by 200 Mexican naval cadets of the Veracruz Academy, opened lively fire on the few
American marines and sailors. Admiral Mayo withdrew
them to his two battlewagons for the night and awaited the
arrival of the rest of the fleet. Next day the enlarged force

pulverized the Naval Academy and put an end to fighting by naval gunfire. The casualties of the occupation were 19 American dead, and 71 wounded; the Mexicans lost over 300, including some naval cadets.

When Wilson got news that fighting had actually occurred, with unexpected deaths involved, he was appalled and unnerved. He had not wanted trouble; it could lead to even more serious conflict. Both Huerta and Carranza immediately issued strong statements condemning the occupation and demanding the withdrawal of American personnel. Pancho Villa came to the favorable attention of Americans by stating that the American military forces could remain as long as they liked, just so they did not enter Constitutionalist territory.

In the United States, recruiting offices were jammed, but nobody quite knew whether the United States was at war with Mexico or not. This was the chief end product of moral imperialism. A national sigh of relief went up on April 24, 1914, when the Ambassador of Brazil and the Ministers of Argentina and Chile in Washington jointly offered their good offices to mediate the difficulties between the United States and Mexico. Wilson recovered his nerve, swapped Army occupation for the Navy in Veracruz, and accepted the Latin-American mediation offer. Huerta was still in power in Mexico City, more than a year after the vendetta had gotten under way.

# 13

## VENUSTIANO CARRANZA

———————•———————

# NOTE TO PRESIDENT WILSON CONCERNING THE UNITED STATES OCCUPATION OF VERACRUZ*

❧

*Theoretically General Huerta's loss of Veracruz should have pleased the "First Chief" of the Constitutionalist movement against Huerta, but Carranza sided with Huerta in strongly condemning United States intervention. Mexican honor was at stake in this case, and Wilson found himself to be an unwelcome intruder in Mexico's internal affairs. Carranza's note to Wilson expresses this attitude in no uncertain terms.*

Chihuahua, April 22, 1914

. . . in relation to the unfortunate incident [in Tampico] that occurred between the crew of a launch from the U.S.S. *Dolphin* and the soldiers of the usurper Victoriano Huerta, hostile acts have been undertaken by naval forces

———————————————

* Translated from Jesús Silva Herzog, *Breve Historia de la Revolución Mexicana* (2 vols.; México, D. F.: Fondo de Cultura Económica, 1960), II, 103–105. Reprinted by permission of the author.

under the command of Admiral Fletcher in the port of Veracruz. Faced with this violation of national sovereignty, which the Constitutionalist government did not expect from a government that has expressed its desire to preserve peace with the people of Mexico, I must fulfill a highly patriotic duty in addressing the present note to you in order to exhaust every possible means to prevent two honorable nations from breaking the peaceful relations that still bind us.

.    .    .

The usurped title of President of the Republic cannot invest General Huerta with the powers of either receiving a demand of reparation from the government of the United States, nor of granting a satisfaction if it is required.

Victoriano Huerta is a delinquent who falls under the jurisdiction of the Constitutionalist government, which is the only government—due to abnormal circumstances in the country—that represents national sovereignty in harmony with the spirit of Article 128 of the Mexican political Constitution. All illegal acts committed by the usurper and his accomplices and those that they may yet inflict, whether of an international character—such as those that took place in Tampico—or of a national order, shall be judged and sternly punished within a short time by the tribunals of the Constitutionalist government.

. . . considering also that those acts of hostility that have been consummated exceed equitable demands [for reparation], and because the usurper of Mexico is not the one called to grant reparation, I interpret the feelings of the great majority of the Mexican people . . . and request that you discontinue your acts of hostility, by ordering your forces to evacuate . . . the port of Veracruz, and that you formulate to the Constitutionalist government that I represent . . . your demands arising from the events that took place at the port of Tampico, with the assurance that such demands shall be given due consideration.

# 14

# JOHN REED

———•———

# LA SOLDADERA*

❀

*Diplomatic maneuvers did not change the lives of those who fought. The Mexican soldier of the Revolution traditionally traveled with his* soldadera, *the "soldieress" who loaded his rifle, cooked for him, tended to him, and often carried her latest baby slung in the* rebozo *on her back. The* soldadera *served as more than a modern commissary, she provided the comfort and companionship that kept the soldier on the move for so many terrible years. John Reed tells us of his meeting with Elizabetta in the mountainous deserts of the state of Chihuahua. Reed is introduced to the reader in Selection 9.*

There was nothing remarkable about her. I think I noticed her chiefly because she was one of the few women in that wretched company. She was a very dark-skinned Indian girl, about twenty-five years old, with the squat figure of her drudging race, pleasant features, hair hanging forward over her shoulders in two long plaits, and big, shining teeth when she smiled.

·     ·     ·

Now she was trudging stolidly along in the dust behind Captain Félix Romero's horse—and had trudged so for

———————————

* John Reed, *Insurgent Mexico* (New York: Appleton, 1914), 104–109. For citation of a new edition, edited by Albert L. Michaels and James W. Wilkie, see Selection 9 above.

thirty miles. He never spoke to her, never looked back, but rode on unconcernedly. Sometimes he would get tired of carrying his rifle and hand it back to her to carry, with a careless "Here! Take this!" I found out later that when they returned to La Cadena after the battle to bury the dead he had found her wandering aimlessly in the hacienda, apparently out of her mind; and that, needing a woman, he had ordered her to follow him. Which she did, unquestioningly, after the custom of her sex and country.

Captain Félix let his horse drink. Elizabetta halted, too, knelt, and plunged her face into the water.

"Come on," ordered the Captain. *"Andale!"* She rose without a word and waded through the stream. In the same order they climbed the near bank, and there the Captain dismounted, held out his hand for the rifle she carried, and said, "Get me my supper!" Then he strolled away toward the houses where the rest of the soldiers sat.

Elizabetta fell upon her knees and gathered twigs for her fire. Soon there was a little pile burning. She called a small boy in the harsh, whining voice that all Mexican women have, *"Aie! chamaco!* Fetch me a little water and corn that I may feed my man!" And, rising upon her knees above the red glow of the flames, she shook down her long, straight black hair. She wore a sort of blouse of faded light blue rough cloth. There was dried blood on the breast of it.

"What a battle, señorita!" I said to her.

Her teeth flashed as she smiled, and yet there was a puzzling vacancy about her expression. Indians have masklike faces. Under it I could see that she was desperately tired and even a little hysterical. But she spoke tranquilly enough.

"Perfectly," she said. "Are you the gringo who ran so many miles with the *colorados* after you shooting?" And she laughed—catching her breath in the middle of it as if it hurt.

The *chamaco* shambled up with an earthen jar of water and an armful of corn ears that he tumbled at her feet.

Elizabetta unwound from her shawl the heavy little stone trough that Mexican women carry, and began mechanically husking the corn into it.

"I do not remember seeing you at La Cadena," I said. "Were you there long?"

"Too long," she answered simply, without raising her head. And then suddenly, "Oh, but this war is no game for women!" she cried.

Don Félix loomed up out of the dark, with a cigarette in his mouth.

"My dinner," he growled. "Is it *pronto?*"

"*Luego, luego!*" she answered. He went away again.

"Listen, señor, whoever you are!" said Elizabetta swiftly, looking up to me. "My lover was killed yesterday in the battle. This man is my man, but, by God and all the saints, I can't sleep with him this night. Let me stay then with you!"

There wasn't a trace of coquetry in her voice. This blundering, childish spirit had found itself in a situation it couldn't bear, and had chosen the instinctive way out. I doubt if she even knew herself why the thought of this new man so revolted her, with her lover scarcely cold in the ground. I was nothing to her, nor she to me. That was all that mattered.

I assented, and together we left the fire, the Captain's neglected corn spilling from the stone trough. And then we met him a few feet into the darkness.

"My dinner!" he said impatiently. His voice changed. "Where are you going?"

"I'm going with this señor," Elizabetta answered nervously. "I'm going to stay with him——"

"You——" began Don Félix, gulping. "You are my woman. *Oiga,* señor, this is my woman here!"

"Yes," I said. "She is your woman. I have nothing to do with her. But she is very tired and not well, and I have offered her my bed for the night."

"This is very bad, señor!" exclaimed the Captain, in a

tightening voice. "You are the guest of this *tropa* and the Colonel's friend, but this is my woman and I want her——"

"Oh!" Elizabetta cried out. "Until the next time, señor!" She caught my arm and pulled me on.

We had been living in a nightmare of battle and death—all of us. I think everybody was a little dazed and excited. I know I was.

By this time the peons and soldiers had begun to gather around us, and as we went on the Captain's voice rose as he retailed his injustice to the crowd.

"I shall appeal to the Colonel," he was saying. "I shall tell the Colonel!" He passed us, going toward the Colonel's *cuartel,* with averted, mumbling face.

*"Oiga, mi Coronel!"* he cried. "This gringo has taken away my woman. It is the grossest insult!"

"Well," returned the Colonel calmly, "if they both want to go, I guess there isn't anything we can do about it, eh?"

The news had traveled like light. A throng of small boys followed us close behind, shouting the joyful indelicacies they shout behind rustic wedding parties. We passed the ledge where the soldiers and the wounded sat, grinning and making rough, genial remarks as at a marriage. It was not coarse or suggestive, their banter; it was frank and happy. They were honestly glad for us.

As we approached Don Pedro's house we were aware of many candles within. He and his wife and daughter were busy with brooms, sweeping and resweeping the earthen floor, and sprinkling it with water. They had put new linen on the bed, and lit the rush candle before the table altar of the Virgin. Over the doorway hung a festoon of paper blossoms, faded relics of many a Christmas Eve celebration—for it was winter, and there were no real flowers.

Don Pedro was radiant with smiles. It made no difference who we were, or what our relation was. Here were a man and a maid, and to him it was a bridal.

"May you have a happy night," he said softly, and closed the door. The frugal Elizabetta immediately made the rounds of the room, extinguishing all the candles but one.

And then, outside, we heard music beginning to tune up. Some one had hired the village orchestra to serenade us. Late into the night they played steadily, right outside our door. In the next house we heard them moving chairs and tables out of the way; and just before I went to sleep they began to dance there, economically combining a serenade with a *baile*.

Without the least embarrassment, Elizabetta lay down beside me on the bed. Her hand reached for mine. She snuggled against my body for the comforting human warmth of it, murmured, "Until morning," and went to sleep. And calmly, sweetly, sleep came to me. . . .

When I woke in the morning she was gone. I opened my door and looked out. Morning had come dazzlingly, all blue and gold—a heaven of flame-trimmed big white clouds and windy sky, and the desert brazen and luminous. Under the ashy bare trees the peddlers' morning fire leaped horizontal in the wind. The black women, with wind-folded draperies, crossed the open ground to the river in single file, with red water jars on their heads. Cocks crew, goats clamored for milking, and a hundred horses drummed up the dust as they were driven to water.

Elizabetta was squatted over a little fire near the corner of the house, patting *tortillas* for the Captain's breakfast. She smiled as I came up, and politely asked me if I had slept well. She was quite contented now; you knew from the way she sang over her work.

Presently the Captain came up in a surly manner and nodded briefly to me.

"I hope it's ready now," he grunted, taking the tortillas she gave him. "You take a long time to cook a little breakfast. *Caramba!* Why is there no coffee?" He moved off, munching. "Get ready," he flung back over his shoulder. "We go north in an hour."

"Are you going?" I asked curiously. Elizabetta looked at me with wide-open eyes.

"Of course I am going. *Seguro!* Is he not my man?" She

looked after him admiringly. She was no longer revolted.

"He is my man," she said. "He is very handsome, and very brave. Why, in the battle the other day——"

Elizabetta had forgotten her lover.

# 15

# CARLETON BEALS

———————•———————

# GENERALS*

❧

*If the* soldadera *was swept along by events out of her control, the general who marched his forces across Mexico soon became known for excesses within his control. The generals who lived without any scruples were stereotyped in many a story of greed and immorality, and Carleton Beals put such stereotypes into print. Beals has had a long interest in Mexico, for he was the Principal of the American High School in Mexico City during 1919 and 1920, and he was on President Carranza's personal staff before later becoming a newspaper correspondent in 1923. From 1925 to 1937 he was associate editor of* Mexican Folkways. *Books by Beals include* Mexico, An Interpretation *(New York: Heubsch, 1923)*, *and* Porfirio Díaz, Dictator of Mexico *(Philadelphia: Lippincott, 1932)*.

One of the great chiefs of the land, a General in gold braid, sits in the Don Quixote ballroom of the Regis Hotel in Mexico City. Two . . . prostitutes, in frowsy evening dresses, fondle his fat brown jowls and sip champagne. Suddenly, with bleary eyes, he rises from the table, draws his revolver, and shouts, "Somebody's laughing at me. If

———————

* Carleton Beals, *Mexican Maze* (Philadelphia: Lippincott, 1931), 17–22. Reprinted by permission of the author.

anybody cracks a smile, I'll shoot him dead." The Great Chief turns and blazes away at one of the panels of expensive Don Quixote tiles that line the establishment. They tumble down, crashing in a cloud of plaster.

. . .

A runty policeman slides down the aisle and requests the *caballero* to cease disturbing public order, then returns to his post.

The heavyset man stops his noise, but even in the dark, his creased fat neck glows angrily. Presently he rises, strides to the rear of the theater.

*"Pam, pam."* The runty policeman falls in a pool of blood.

The heavyset man is a GENERAL. No one shall reprimand *him*.

. . .

Meet General "Aspirin" and his aide.

"I have a headache, my General."

"Here is some aspirin," says the General, and blows his aide's brains out.

It is a good joke. Everyone laughs heartily.

. . .

General X enters Uruapan and falls in love with the daughter of a French drygoods man. She repulses him. He arrests her brother. The virtue of the girl is the price of liberation. In this way he seduces not only her, but her younger sister. Then he shoots the brother anyway. The father protests to higher authorities. The General burns his store.

The tables turn. The General . . . is captured and taken toward the cemetery to be shot. On the way, debonairly he tosses his silver-braided sombrero to a passing girl.

Romance knots her heart. She rallies other girls of the town; they rush into the cemetery and interpose themselves before the firing squad. She is the daughter of the leading personage of the community. . . . The General is saved. He marries her—his fourth wife.

.  .  .

Los Altos in Jalisco is declared a combat zone. All the inhabitants are ordered to migrate into concentration centers under penalty of being considered rebels.

"Let me leave ten men on my hacienda to harvest the crop," pleads the owner of the Hacienda Estrella to General F, an officer who has risen with the ideals of the Revolution but now owns an entire block of the most fashionable residence in Guadalajara.

"If a man is there after May first, he'll be shot," announces General F ."Unless, of course——"

"What would be the consideration?" demands the owner.

"You might contribute fifteen thousand pesos to the Social Defense Fund," announces General F, "in cash, delivered to me personally."

"I have no ready cash."

"Too bad," declares General F. As the owner leaves the office, he dictates:

Colonel M. Sixth Regiment—
    Send captain and twenty-five men to harvest crop
Hacienda Estrella, same to be delivered as promptly
as possible ready for shipment at Station Ocotlán.
                                        General F.

.  .  .

Down from Guadalajara to Colima, all day under the hot sun, the train guard rides in an open steel car, sides slit for rifle holes. In the morning, the soldiers build fires on the steel bottom, toast tortillas, and boil coffee, into which they drop a lump of sweet *pinoche*. All day they ride, stretching red sarapes for shade, playing with Spanish cards for cartridges, thrumming guitars, telling yarns.

With them, as mascot, goes an eleven-year-old boy, cartridge belt criss-crossed over his chest, rifle in his hand, straw sombrero tilted cockily over one ear, his black, tousled hair hanging into his perky eyes.

The train swings through a rocky pass. "Man the rifle holes!" cries the Captain.

A withering fire whips down from behind a cropping of rock. The mascot gives a cry. His sombrero flies into the air. His teeth smash against the sprawling feet of a machine gun.

The train rolls on without being stopped.

"Where do the sonnabiches get their ammunition?" complains the Captain, handing his smoking rifle to a soldier to be cleaned and reoiled.

Two other soldiers dump the boy's body over the edge into the abyss. "We aren't supposed to have his kind along. It would look bad," declares the Captain.

A pock-faced soldier puckers up his thick-lipped mouth, rips a flower from the cord of his visor and tosses it after the body.

# 16

# ROBERT E. QUIRK

————•————

# BATTLE OF CELAYA*

✣

*The battle of Celaya, fought in the state of Guana-
juato on April 4 to 7 and April 13 to 15, 1915,
marked the turning point of the struggle between the
Carranza-Obregón forces and the troops of Villa. Due
to the superior tactics of Obregón, Villa was defeated.
Robert E. Quirk has described this battle and analyzed
its meaning. Professor Quirk was introduced to the
reader in Selection 10.*

Celaya was a small city in 1915 with a population of
approximately twenty-five thousand, known in Mexico
principally for its candied fruits, the *dulces de Celaya.* Once
Villa had initiated his attack several of Obregón's subordinates importuned their commanding general to pull back to
Querétaro. But he saw correctly that Villa's superior cavalry and greater numbers in infantry would inflict severe
punishment on the withdrawing Constitutionalist troops.
Moreover, Celaya possessed in its many canals and drain-
age ditches an excellent terrain for defense. During the next
ten days the events at Celaya made the twin battles there
the turning point in the Revolution, and for those few days
it was the most important site in all of Mexico.

Between April 4 and 6 Villa concentrated his troops in

———————————

* Robert E. Quirk, *The Mexican Revolution, 1914–1915; The Convention of Aguascalientes* (Bloomington: Indiana University Press,
1960), 221–225. Reprinted by permission of the publisher.

Irapuato. His battle plans were twofold: to defeat Obregón at Celaya and to come to the aid of the *Villistas* in Jalisco. But Villa underestimated Obregón as an enemy, for he remained in Irapuato instead of advancing with his division. His troops were committed piecemeal by their individual commanders as they arrived at the line of fire. The battle took shape in a helter-skelter fashion, growing from a small fire fight between the advance guards into a full-scale battle without Villa's maintaining reserves or taking the other normal precautions of an attacking commander. Villa and his subordinates continued to show their predilection for massed cavalry and infantry attacks, regardless of their own losses, in the hope of driving the enemy back by sheer weight. It was to be a costly and ruinous tactic.

At about 10 A.M. on April 6, Villa's scouts, probing forward from Irapuato, reached Guaje and engaged the Constitutionalist advance guard of Fortunato Maycotte. As more Villistas appeared, Maycotte's cavalry, offering little resistance, fell back precipitously toward Celaya. Through the day the buildup of the Division of the North continued before Celaya. As attack followed attacking wave against the Constitutionalist positions, Obregón's well-entrenched riflemen and his machine guns took a high toll of lives. Nevertheless, the fighting raged unabated through the night of the sixth and into the morning of the seventh. Despite the withering fire of Benjamín Hill's infantry, a single Villista charge in the early morning hours carried troops of the division into the center of Celaya. They jubilantly mounted into a church tower to ring out on the bells the news of Obregón's defeat. But this was but a premature and empty boast. The invaders were ejected, and during the day Villa's initial superiority turned into a Constitutionalist advantage.

Obregón seized the opportunity of a lull in the fighting to throw the full weight of Cesareo Castro's cavalry on Villa's flank to drive back the now dispirited soldiers of the North. Villa's division had been too reckless in its expenditure of men and, perhaps even more, of ammunition. By the evening of April 7 the Villistas were back in Irapuato, licking their wounds. The Constitutionalist Army was itself too spent to exploit its victory, and the issue between Villa and Obregón was still to be decided.

.   .   .

A week's respite following the first enounter at Celaya gave both sides the opportunity to regroup and reorganize their forces. Villa was now deadly intent upon victory at any cost, and he put aside notions of launching a simultaneous attack on the enemy in Jalisco, drawing together his strongest forces in Irapuato. Obregón wisely remained on the defensive in Celaya and reinforced his entrenchments. Fortune smiled upon the Constitutionalists as a shipment of one million cartridges arrived from Veracruz in time to be used in the battle. Villa again scorned to take the defensive, hoping to retrieve victory by the same means which had brought him success against the Federals at Torreón and Zacatecas.

.   .   .

On April 11 Villa asked four consular officers in the city of Irapuato to pass through the enemy lines under a flag of truce, bearing a message for Obregón. It was a plea, coupled with a threat, that Obregón come into the open to fight, or Villa would bombard the city "within two or three days" with sixty pieces of artillery. He asked the Constitutionalist commander to consider the inhabitants of Celaya and to save the town itself from destruction. Obregón was not to be drawn from his prepared positions, however, on a humanitarian ruse. He had learned from the European war what Villa seemingly had not—massed attacks could not succeed against trenches, machine guns, and barbed wire. He spurned Villa's challenge to meet his division in the open, knowing that the Northern cavalry and infantry would cut his numerically weaker forces to shreds.

As he promised, Villa opened his attack upon the Constitutionalist positions at 6 A.M. on the thirteenth. His artillery, 75 and 80 mm. guns, boomed out its support for the charges of the division's infantry and horsemen. To belie his boast of two days earlier, Villa evidently could count on no more than thirty guns for this engagement. Obregón's troops were in their trenches in readiness, the infantry under Hill and the artillery under the charge of a German officer, Maximilian Kloss. Obregón stationed Castro's cavalry brigade and a force of infantrymen well behind Celaya in reserve. The Constitutionalist lines were now in a broad semicircle, embracing the western outskirts of Celaya. For more than twenty-four hours, as the men of Villa and Obregón fought each other with unabated fury, the flower of Mexico's revolutionary armies was despoiled. Villa mounted attack upon attack, determined to ram through the enemy lines. But the trenches held, and this time there was no penetration. In the end, Obregón picked the psychological instant of an exhausted Villista charge to order his reserve cavalry against the division's left flank. It was the same tactic which had won the first engagement. As the cavalry charged, the infantry reserve enclosed the enemy's right flank and the Northerners wavered, then fell back in a general, disastrous, pell-mell retreat. The heavy guns were abandoned, and the foot soldiers flung aside their weapons and other encumbrances in their mad scramble to save their own lives.

.    .    .

J. R. Ambrosins, an American who passed through the area immediately following the second defeat of Villa, has left a vivid account of the destruction wreaked on the Division of the North. In a telegram to a friend in Mexico City he called the battlefield "a terrible sight." Dead bodies, he said, "were strewn on both sides of the track as far as the eye could reach." Ambrosins asserted that he had personally seen five thousand Villista prisoners entering Celaya and that there must have been at least four thousand killed. Obregón claimed to have captured eight thousand enemy soldiers and at the same time minimized his own losses. He fixed his casualties at five hundred killed and wounded, probably far too low an estimate, however, even for an entrenched army. Villa admitted to George Carothers after the battle that he had lost six thousand men at Celaya. In any event, it was a crippling blow to Villa, one from which he never recovered.

# 17

LYLE C. BROWN

MEXICO'S CONSTITUTION

OF 1917[*]

*With Constitutionalist forces generally victorious, Carranza called a Constitutional Convention to meet on December 1, 1916, in Querétaro, the capital of the state of Querétaro. In December 1914 Carranza had issued a manifesto entitled* Additions to the Plan of Guadalupe, *because military necessity demanded promises to the Mexican people in order to gain support for his regime based in Veracruz. The* Additions *promised social, economic, and political reforms, and on January 6, 1915, Carranza decreed the "Law of Restoration and Dotation of* Ejidos," *which began to implement one of the reforms. Once back in Mexico City, Carranza believed it necessary to commemorate his triumph by distinguishing his Constitutionalist movement from the Constitution of 1857. Also he needed to legalize the* Additions *in order to gain support for his shaky regime. On October 22, 1916, elections of representatives to the convention were held in territories occupied by Carranza and Obregón; this was the nearest that the Constitution ever came to popular ratification. Although loyal Carrancistas gathered in Querétaro in late 1916 under the radical direction of Francisco J. Múgica, they rejected major*

[*] Published by permission of the author.

*portions of Carranza's draft to write their own docu-*
*ment, completed in early 1917. Carranza accepted the*
*new Constitution, but he never really attempted to put*
*it into effect. The Constitution served as a guide and*
*was not implemented to any great extent until the era*
*of Lázaro Cárdenas. Implementation has been gradual*
*indeed, and a provision for profit sharing between em-*
*ployers and employees has only been in effect since*
*1962.*

*The provisions of the Constitution of 1917 are sum-*
*marized in this selection by Lyle C. Brown. Professor*
*Brown is introduced to the reader in Selection 8.*

During 1916 the Constitutionalist regime prepared to consolidate its military triumph while at the same time continuing to combat remnant rebel elements that continued
guerrilla war against the Carranza government. On September 19, 1916, Carranza issued a decree calling for elections
to be held on October 22 for the purpose of selecting delegates to a national constitutional convention. This convention opened at Querétaro on December 1, and at that time
the First Chief delivered an address outlining the principal
features of the draft constitution that he placed before the
delegates. Essentially, Carranza's plan was simply a modified version of the Constitution of 1857, which incorpo-
rated various reforms that had been decreed by the First
Chief during the struggle with Villa. This draft was referred
to a committee headed by Francisco J. Múgica, one of the
delegates from Michoacán. Although formerly a close associate of Carranza, Múgica felt that the First Chief's plan
was too limited, particularly in regard to such socioeco-
nomic matters as public education, land distribution, labor
guarantees, and regulation of religious organizations. A majority of the delegates concurred with Múgica; thus, the
Constitution of 1917, which was proclaimed on February
5, contained more genuinely revolutionary provisions than
had been recommended by Carranza.

Nationalism, secularism, anticlericalism, agrarianism,
and social consciousness are manifested in the revolution-

ary features of the Constitution of 1917. Article 27 stipulates that aliens may acquire land only on the condition that they consider themselves to be Mexican nationals and promise not to seek protection of such property by their own government. However, under no circumstance is an alien to own land within zones one hundred kilometers in width along international borders or within zones fifty kilometers wide along coasts. According to Article 32, under equal circumstances Mexicans are to enjoy preference over aliens for all concessions, government positions, offices, or commissions. Also, only Mexican nationals may serve in the country's Army, Navy, or Merchant Marine. Other evidence of nationalism and antiforeign sentiment is found in Article 33, which declares that aliens may be banished from the country without judicial process merely on orders from the President.

Article 3 declares that instruction in all public educational institutions shall be free and secular; also, it specifies that private primary schools must impart secular instruction and may be established only subject to official supervision. Further, no religious corporation or member of the clergy may establish or direct a primary school. Monastic orders are prohibited by Article 5, and Article 24 provides for government supervision of public worship. Other anticlerical provisions are found in Article 130, which prohibits establishment of a state religion, establishes marriage as a civil contract, and bans religious oaths. This article authorizes each state legislature to determine the number of clergy allowed to function within its territory, specifies that only native Mexicans may practice the religious profession, and prohibits members of the clergy from holding public office, voting, assembling for political purposes, or criticizing the Constitution. Also, it prevents construction of new churches without government consent; and under the terms of Article 27, religious institutions are prevented from owning land. Further, all places of public worship, together with other properties used for religious purposes, are declared to belong to the nation.

In answer to demands of the rural masses for land reform, Article 27 empowers the federal government to divide large landed estates, to develop small landholdings, and "to establish new centers of rural population with such lands and waters as may be indispensable to them." As for rural population centers that are totally lacking in lands or water, or that are in need of additional quantities of these resources, Article 27 establishes their "right to be provided with them from the adjoining properties, always having due regard for small landholdings."

Various rights of labor are recognized in Article 123. This article guarantees the right of workers to organize unions, establishes a normal workday of eight hours, provides for double pay for overtime work, limits night work to seven hours, bars boys under sixteen and all women from late night work and all unhealthful or dangerous employment, prohibits employment of children under twelve, gives mothers special protection through provision for a three-month vacation with pay before the birth of a child and an additional month of paid vacation after the birth, provides for profit sharing and minimum wage protection, specifies equal pay for equal work by male and female workers, and requires payment of wages in cash.

18

## EMILIANO ZAPATA

# OPEN LETTER TO CARRANZA*

*The Year: 1919! Zapata was still at war with the federal government in Mexico City. The Constitution was now over two years old but had been ignored since promulgation on February 5, 1917. Zapata spelled out the failure of the Revolution and of the Carranza government in an open letter to the President dated March 17, 1919. Less than a month later, April 10, Zapata was killed in a treacherous move by one of Carranza's officers, Colonel Jesús M. Guajardo. Carranza's victory was a short-lived one, however, for he was murdered a year later. Zapata had served as the unalterable conscience of the Revolution and his open letter to Carranza left a final political testament to the close of a troubled decade, which has been described in the following terms.*

I am not addressing the President of the Republic, whom I do not know, nor the politician, whom I distrust. I speak to the Mexican, to the man of feelings and reason, whom I find impossible to conceive as a man not capable of being stirred sometime (even for an instant) by the anguish of mothers, the suffering of orphans, the anxieties and desires of the nation.

* Translated from Julio Cuadros Caldas, *Mexico Soviet* (Puebla: Santiago Loyo, 1926), 193–199.

I shall say bitter truths; but I shall not express to you anything that is not true, just, and honestly said.

From the moment that the idea of making revolution, first against Madero and then against Huerta, germinated in your brain, . . . the first thing you thought of was to further yourself, and for that purpose you set yourself to use the Revolution for your own improvement and that of a small group of friends or opportunists who helped you to rise and who are ready to help you to enjoy the booty: wealth, honor, business, banquets, sumptuous parties, bacchanals of pleasure, satiating orgies of ambition, power, and blood.

It never occurred to you that the Revolution should be beneficial to the great masses, to that immense legion of oppressed whom you attempted to sway with your speeches.

　　　·　　　·　　　·

Nevertheless, in order to triumph you had to proclaim great ideals and principles and to announce reforms.

But in order to prevent popular commotion (a dangerous, double-edged weapon) from turning against he who used it and in order to restrain the semifree people, . . . a tyranny was created to which the novel name of "revolutionary dictatorship" was given.

　　　·　　　·　　　·

In order to win the vindicating goals of the Revolution, a dictator was necessary—it was then said. Autocratic proceedings were inevitable in order to impose new principles on an obstinate society.

In other words, the formula for the so-called Constitutionalist policy was this: "To establish liberty one must use despotism."

It was on these sophisms that your authority, absolutism, and omnipotence were founded.

How have you used those exhorbitant powers that were to bring about triumph for the principles of the Revolution?

It is necessary here—in order not to commit the sin of rashness—to analyze calmly and to review retrospectively the events that developed during your long-lasting rule.

On the economic terrain, actions could not have been more doleful: robbed banks; forced issue of paper money once, twice, three times, disavowing the emitted bills later —with loss of public faith; the disorganization of commerce caused by these monetary fluctuations; industry and all sorts of enterprises in agony under the weight of exhorbitant and almost confiscatory contributions; agriculture and mining dying for lack of guarantees and lack of safety in communications; the humble and the working people reduced to misery, hunger, and deprivations of all kinds because of the paralysis of work, the high cost of food products, and the unbearable rise of living costs.

In agrarian matters, the haciendas have been given or rented to favorite generals; the old *latifundistas* of the high bourgeoisie have been replaced—in not a few cases—by modern gun-toting landowners who strut about in military attire; the people's hopes have been deceived.

Neither have the *ejidos* been returned to the people— who continue to be despoiled—nor are lands being distributed among the working class or the poor and needy peasants.

In labor matters, with the aid of intrigue, bribes, . . . and by appealing to the corruption of leaders, the disorganization and effective death of unions has been achieved.

Most of the unions exist in name only: their members have lost faith in their former leaders, and the most conscientious ones . . . have dispersed in dismay. . . . We have just seen labor meetings presided over and "sponsored" (!) by a provincial governor, well known as one of your most unconditional servants.

And . . . let us look into the political terrain in which you have displayed all your art, all your will, and all your experience:

Do free elections take place? What a lie! In most, not to say in all, of the states, the governors have been imposed by the central government; federal deputies and senators are creatures of the President; scandals in municipal elections have exceeded the limits of toleration and credibility.

In electoral matters you have imitated with mastery, and in many cases you have surpassed your old Chief, Porfirio Díaz.

But what am I saying? In some states it has not even seemed necessary to take the trouble to carry out elections. The military governors are still reigning there, imposed by the federal Executive that you represent, and the horrors, abuses, unheard of crimes, and outrages of the preconstitutional period continue.

· · ·

You called the movement that emanated from the *Plan of Guadalupe* a Constitutionalist Revolution, even though in your purpose and conscience you were to violate the Constitution step by step, systematically.

There cannot be, in effect, anything more anticonstitutional than your government: in its origin, in its background, in its details, in its tendencies.

You govern by trespassing the limits fixed for the Executive by the Constitution. You do not need to have budgets approved by Congress. You establish and abolish taxes and tariffs. . . . You name deputies and senators, and you refuse to give information to Congress. You protect pretorianism and from the beginning of the Constitutional era you have restored a hybrid mixture of a military and civil government, which is civil in name only.

The so-called Constitutionalist soldiery has become a whip for the people of the countryside. According to a confession made by one of your highest chiefs (no less than the Secretary of War, Jesús Agustín Castro), the Revolution is extending and new rebels appear every day, in part due to excesses and misbehavior of your military leaders without honor who lack scruples of any kind and who, forgetting their role as guardians of the peace, are the first to upset it with their crimes and their acts of vandalism.

That same soldiery steals seeds, cattle, and beasts of burden in the countryside. In the small villages they burn or sack humble dwellings, and in the big cities they speculate on a large scale with stolen grain. . . . They murder in broad daylight; they assault automobiles and commit crimes in the streets during busy hours on the main avenues; and they carry their boldness to the point of organizing dreadful gangs of offenders who break into the rich dwellings, seize jewelry and precious objects, and organize the craft of robbery in a high style.

.     .     .

Nobody believes in you or your ability to pacify anymore, nor in your greatness as a politician or governor.

It is time for you to retire, it is time to leave your post to more honorable and honest men. It would be a crime to prolong the situation of undeniable moral, economic, and political bankruptcy.

Your remaining in power is an obstacle to union and reconstruction.

.     .     .

# III

# The Northern Dynasty

*. . . dual government is characterized by a* de facto *authority, without constitutional limitations or political responsibility . . . in which the Chief only wears the constitutional garments but does not rule or govern. Power resides in the strong man who usually makes his appearance in the periods of crisis and who counts on the backing of public opinion, because he is the symbol of public tranquility and the only one capable of guaranteeing the normal economic development of the nation. . . . [Such] circumstances were propitious to mark Calles as the strong man of Mexico.*

---

Translated from Francisco Javier Gaxiola, Jr., *El Presidente Rodríguez (1932–1934)* (México, D. F.: Editorial Cultura, 1938), 111–113.

*No one doubts anymore—not even the conservative elements—that it is obvious that capitalism is falling to*

*pieces; its system has placed us in such a situation [world depression] that while millions of individuals die of starvation, wheat is used for combustion and coffee is being dumped into the ocean. Nations and peoples are becoming isolated from each other by their customs barriers, and cooperation between the nations of the world becomes increasingly more difficult.*

---

Translated from Samuel Velázquez G., *El Nacional,* February 21, 1933.

# CHRONOLOGY OF
# THE NORTHERN DYNASTY

———————•———————

1923    President Obregón designates Plutarco Elías Calles as his successor and suppresses Adolfo de la Huerta's revolt.

1924    Under new President Calles, much power is wielded by Luis Morones, head of the CROM.

1925    A Church-state struggle begins which leads to the Cristero religious war against the Mexican Revolution, 1926–1929.

1927    U.S.-Mexico diplomatic argument over rights of U.S. oil companies under Mexican law sees climax of hostility as Ambassador James Sheffield is replaced by Dwight Morrow.

1928    Under Morrow's influence Calles backs down on oil dispute, slows land reform, and reaches agreement on foreign debt; Generals Gómez and Serrano oppose Obregón's return to the presidency but are killed. President-elect Obregón is assassinated by a Catholic fanatic before he can take office. Emilio Portes Gil becomes interim president.

1929    Portes Gil brings an end to the Cristero War; Calles founds the National Revolutionary Party (PNR) to institutionalize the Mexican political system; Pascual Ortiz Rubio is elected president over José Vasconcelos; military rebellion headed by General Escobar fails.

1932    Confronted with problems of economic depression and political confusion, Ortiz Rubio resigns and Abelardo Rodríguez assumes the presidency.

1933   The PNR meets in Querétaro to adopt a radical program and select Lázaro Cárdenas as its presidential candidate.

1934   Cárdenas is elected president; Congress prepares legislation to implement program of Socialist Education.

# 19

# HOWARD F. CLINE

———————•———————

# THE NEO-BOURBONS*

❈

*With the death of Venustiano Carranza in 1920, the men of Sonora dominated politics for the next thirteen years. Alvaro Obregón selected Plutarco Elías Calles to succeed him in the presidency in 1924, and Calles hand-picked three men to fill out unexpired portions of the new six-year term beginning in 1928. Obregón had an important measure of influence during Calles' term and planned to become President again in 1928, but he was assassinated. Calles ran a full-fledged "dual government" in which he had all of the influence after 1929, but all of his political calculations were upset by the world depression, which hit Mexico in the early 1930s. Although Obregón and Calles had frightened the United States Department of State with talk of radical social and economic action during the early 1920s, they had shifted to a more capitalistic-oriented stance by the late 1920s, just at a time when Wall Street's solutions to economic development problems were coming into discredit.*

*Howard F. Cline has characterized the "Sonora Gang" as "Neo-Bourbons," and his term gives meaning to the era of the Northern Dynasty. Information on Cline is given in Selection 12.*

---

\* Reprinted by permission of the publishers from Howard F. Cline, *The United States and Mexico* (Cambridge, Mass.: Harvard University Press, Copyright, 1953, '63, by the President and Fellows of Harvard College), 192–194.

The task of consolidating the Revolution and setting up the proper political equipment fell to the Northern Dynasty, headed by Alvaro Obregón. His court was composed of an interlocking directorate of military men, intellectuals, labor leaders, and agrarians. From 1920 through 1933 these leaders hacked away at the roots of Mexican difficulties; slowly and painfully they wrestled with the undramatic chores of reconstruction and rehabilitation. By historical accident national leadership for the Revolution had come primarily from the North; this circumstance goes far to explain the peculiar cast, the emphasis, and the goals of their programs. The general tone of the golden twenties everywhere in the world provided the atmosphere in which they toiled.

The North, it may be remembered, was the chief Mexican heir of the Spanish Bourbon traditions. Until the Madero Revolution of 1910, no Northerner, or group of Northerners, had directed Mexican destinies. With the success of Venustiano Carranza over the opposing factions in 1916, Northern hegemony was provisionally established. Obregón was assisted in his displacement of the "First Chief" by a great many people, the most notable of whom were Luis N. Morones, a labor leader . . . , and northern henchmen of Obregón, Plutarco Elías Calles and Adolfo de la Huerta. By Obregón's victory in 1920 the Northern Dynasty was firmly seated. In almost apostolic succession the ruling power was transmitted by a line of leaders who chose their own successors: de la Huerta (1920), Obregón (1920–1924), Calles (1924–1928); Obregón (1928), and Calles' puppets (1928–1933).

*Neo-Bourbons.* Strikingly alike in many respects were the means and ends of the Bourbon Dynasty and their remote offspring, this Northern Oligarchy. The Bourbon Renaissance of the late eighteenth century was paralleled by a Mexican Renaissance which burst forth in the 1920s and astounded the world by its performances in many spheres.

Like their Spanish prototypes, the Northern clique were

benevolent despots—everything for the people, little by the people. The sanction for their absolutism was not Divine Right but the Constitution of 1917 and their demonstrated ability to mobilize and direct the political and military power generated by the masses of Mexicans who had fought the Revolution under their leadership. With the earlier Bourbons, they shared innumerable features. The principal ones were their insistent drives for material improvements; their reliance on a talented middle class bureaucracy recently elevated to consideration; their determination to build a yeoman agricultural society; their sponsorship of cultural reforms in aesthetics and education; and a manifest anticlericalism which broadened to include attacks on corporate activities of all sorts.

So near in outlook and methods, so distant in time and immediate backgrounds, these two ruling groups who transformed Mexico differed from each other in fundamental ways and purposes. The Bourbons had been interested in bettering Mexico for dynastic reasons, oriented toward a wholly European situation. The Northern Oligarchy was strongly Mexican and its being was integrated around a program of "Mexico for the Mexicans."

# 20

HUDSON STRODE

———•———

# ALVARO OBREGÓN:
# THE HAPPY MAN WITH
# ONE ARM*

❧

*The Neo-Bourbon policy of "Mexico for the Mexicans" frightened the government of the United States, and President Obregón's term was preoccupied with achieving recognition from President Warren G. Harding. This problem caused Hudson Strode to introduce his sketch of Obrégon with a quote by Porfirio Díaz: "Poor Mexico—so far from God and so near to the United States." Professor Strode wrote:*

Though the Harding administration looked upon him as a bolshevik of deepest crimson, Obregón was not even a socialist. He refused to make too wide a breach in the hacienda system. He did not believe land redistribution should come with a wrenching violent enough to disrupt the national economy. In his term of office he distributed 3,000,000 acres among 624 villages—not much, perhaps, but almost seven times Carranza's record. But he did not intend to risk crop shortages by giving too much land to Indians who might not work for themselves after they had it. Many would raise barely enough for their own fam-

---

* From *Timeless Mexico,* copyright 1944, by Hudson Strode. Reprinted by permission of Harcourt, Brace & World, Inc., 263–272.

ilies, and felt no responsibility as farmers to help feed the rest of the nation. Some who received twenty or thirty acres of land would cultivate one acre for themselves and let the rest go to weeds. Even in Morelos, where the peasants, shortly after Zapata's death, had got the land they had fought for, there was discontent. Among the new small freeholders, who had not yet the skill to manage for themselves, many pleaded openly for the return of the hacienda.

Though Obregón supported the labor unions and strongly urged labor to organize so that industrial wages would rise, he had no patience when labor troubles disrupted production. While giving protection to workers, Obregón astutely fostered native capitalism. He tried to instill some constructive energy into his people, and he saw the creation of native industries as a step towards the gradual supplanting of foreign capital.

*Obregón was a colorful figure in Mexican history and the arm he lost in combat in June 1915 was a source of constant comment. According to Strode, he once joked with Blasco Ibáñez: "All of us are thieves, more or less, however, the point is that I have only one hand, while the others have two. That's why people prefer me."*

*For a decade after 1934 Professor Strode took frequent leave from the Department of English at the University of Alabama to pursue research in Mexican history. In 1941 he published* Now In Mexico *(New York: Harcourt, Brace, 1947).*

A born leader, as engaging as shrewd, he was also an able organizer and executive. His sense of balance made him know when to compromise. He was never in danger of an ideal swaying him too far. Though a forceful and persuasive speaker, he was too earthy ever to become lyrical in his thinking. He found life an exciting adventure, and in his last years he warmed his one hand at its metaphorical fires with more satisfying ardor than most men could with twice their two hands. He took his drinks neat and plentiful, but he never had hangovers. His easy familiarity of manner was the same to men of every class. Little children adored him. Dogs instinctively trusted him. His smile was frank and warming, with sometimes a soupçon of amiable mockery. Even after he became President he was still careless of his dress, wearing unpressed suits and a weatherstained old panama. This was not affectation; he felt more comfortable that way. His conversation was as unconventional and casual as his clothes. His trick of always saying the unpredictable made him pungently entertaining and a "natural" for front-page copy. As a wisecracker he was unsurpassed among his fellows.

Though there was plenty of fun in this ruddy-faced, chubby new President, there was no more nonsense than there was illusion. He had a remarkably clear picture of the needs of the people of the time. He allowed the Mexicans just as much liberty as he thought good for them. He was determined not to let the peace be broken if he could help it. Unlike Madero, he knew they wanted bread more than freedom. He believed that the uplift of the masses must come by gradual evolution. To illiterate Indians could not be given middle class responsibilities overnight. Economic welfare came next in importance after peace, and then as large doses of agrarian justice and elementary education as the country could afford.

· · ·

For education he did far more than had ever been done by any preceding president. The famous José Vasconcelos, Obregón's Minister of Education, is really the father of popular education in Mexico. But it was Obregón who chose Vasconcelos to do the job, and he gave his minister vital encouragement and as much of the state funds as he could possibly allot at the time. Almost a thousand rural schools were built under the Obregón administration. Vasconcelos not only built schools and created libraries, but he tried to make the schools cultural centers of the villages, and he sometimes even fed warm breakfasts to the smaller children.

· · ·

Vasconcelos had the zeal of a redeemer. He decided the people should read and read the best, and he had vast editions of the classics printed to distribute among them. Verna Carleton Millán gives perhaps the most authentic version of a much-told story which casts a revealing light on the basic situation in Mexico:

Once, when Obregón and Vasconcelos had escaped from the presidential train which they were warned was to be attacked by rebels, they became lost in wild, unfamiliar territory. On horseback they pushed on for hours, and finally came upon a lone hut. The old Indian standing by the door was astounded to see strangers in his remote domain.

Obregón called to him with that friendly common-denominator manner that men rarely failed to respond to: "Friend, can you tell me where we are?"

The man shook his head.

"But what place is this?"

The man shrugged.

"What town are we near?"

"Who knows?"

"Were you born here?"

"Yes."

"And your wife, too?"

"Yes."

Obregón carefully enunciated his last question. "You and your wife were both born here—you've always lived here—yet you still do not know where you are?"

"No," the old man reaffirmed with unperturbed indifference.

The President turned to his Minister of Education and said, with amused irony, "Make a note of this man, José, so that you can send him copies of the classics you have just edited."

Though Obregón kept the peace, though Mexico was more prosperous than she had been for more than a decade, though patently he represented the great majority of the population, the United States under the Republican President Harding withheld recognition. Harding was hand-inglove with the oil men who were still boiling with fury because the Mexicans had reaffirmed in the Constitution of 1917 the ancient Spanish and Mexican legal principle that the nation's subsoil wealth belongs to the state. At the very time that a group of American oil men was hoping to possess eternally the oil of Mexico, this same group was trying to sell the United States oil reserve that belonged to the Navy. The notorious Teapot Dome scandal which cost President Harding his reputation and perhaps his life was just brewing.

From the beginning, Obregón had insisted that Article 27 should not be retroactive. But the Harding government refused to recognize the government of Obregón unless the President signed a treaty to that effect, which would guarantee American property rights acquired in Mexico before May first, 1917. The United States administration considered the reform program in Mexico a threat to American vested interests, and demanded "adequate safeguards" in the form of a treaty. Secretary of State Hughes drew up a pact called a "Treaty of Amity and Commerce," which was presented to Obregón on May twenty-seventh, 1921, less than three months after Harding took office.

.     .     .

Diplomatic assurances were not deemed sufficient. The United States government demanded a treaty. Obregón refused to accept recognition on such high-handed conditions. He considered it humiliating to the national dignity to do so. Besides, no matter how he may have felt about the increased business that would come to Mexico with official recognition, he had to be wary not to make obeisance to Wall Street in the sight of his own people. The spirit of nationalism had been waxing ever since the Pershing chase after Villa.

.     .     .

It is believed that Secretary Hughes felt a bit ashamed of his course. At any rate, since Hughes saw that Obregón would not be coerced into signing the treaty, [in 1923] he changed his methods and sent two commissioners to Mexico to negotiate for recognition. Certainly, public opinion in the United States was against the Harding and Hughes attitude to Mexico, and many businessmen and bankers were clamoring for recognition.

From May fourteenth to August fifteenth, the two American commissioners conferred with two Mexican commissioners. At length they arrived at what passed for a satisfactory mutual agreement. But the impasse was really broken only because of Obregón's cleverness in playing the American bankers off against the oil men, in causing the bankers to press for recognition so that they could begin collecting interest on loans. To insure a peaceful presidential succession, Obregón had felt that United States recognition would be worth whatever compromise he might make from the standpoint of expediency. He made some slight concessions, agreed to pay compensation for the Revolution's damages to American property, and reaffirmed that Article 27 would not be interpreted as retroactive. A storm of protest from a portion of the Mexican public greeted the announcement of the terms. Obregón's enemies found excuse to accuse him of selling out to the United States. On September third, 1923, after Obregón had been President for almost three years, the United States recognized his government.

The belated recognition helped avert a complete overthrow, but it did not circumvent a revolt. With his astute judgment, Obregón had chosen Plutarco Elías Calles, his Secretary of Interior, for his successor. Calles was recognized as a man of uncommon ability, but he was not generally popular, because he refused to waste energy in winning friends. And because he professed socialism, the generals with a passion for loot, as well as estate owners, the Catholic Church, and the British oil companies, straightway created an opposition and backed Adolfo de la Huerta, Obregón's long-time friend and the incumbent Minister of the Treasury, a former radical who had become progressively more conservative. Soon another counter-Revolution was in full blast. It took three bloody months to squash it.

Again there flared the traditional betrayals and flagrant displays of callous opportunism. In Obregón, however, there was none of Madero's chicken-hearted compassion for troublemakers. He ordered every captured rebel officer above the rank of major to be shot.

"But you can't shoot me," cried a young reactionary attorney, Francisco Treviño, who had been caught with the de la Huerta forces. "I am not even a soldier. The penal code does not prescribe the death penalty for insurrection." Obregón's bluff Minister of War, Francisco Serrano, with tragicomic grace immediately signed an order appointing Lawyer Treviño a "General in the Mexican Army." At the bottom of the page he added a mordant postscript: "Shoot General and Lawyer Francisco Treviño."

Adolfo de la Huerta was more fortunate; he escaped to California and became a singing teacher. His little flair of self-gratification as a tool of the reactionaries had cost his hard-up nation sixty million pesos. A vast deal of Obregón's constructive work had been sabotaged by the unworthy rebellion.

# THE NEW YORK TIMES

———•———

# BOLSHEVIST MEXICO?*

❧

*Often U.S. Department of State hostility to Calles'
program was not only irrational, it was frequently
based upon a deliberate attempt to mislead the American public. In the new year 1927 Secretary of State
Frank B. Kellogg was busy trying to convince the
Senate Foreign Relations Committee that United
States intervention in Nicaragua was necessary to prevent all of Latin America from falling into Communist hands. Explaining this early version of the
"domino theory," which still dominates United States
foreign policy, the Secretary of State set out to confuse
his critics in the Senate, especially Chairman of the
Foreign Reations Committee William E. Borah, with
information gathered from privileged sources. Kellogg's information justified his Nicaraguan policy by
shifting blame for intervention from the United States
to Mexico. Thus, the Secretary of State tried to turn
the attention of administration critics from the real
issue of intervention to a false issue of Mexico's alleged attempt to establish a Bolshevist government
in Nicaragua. The Secretary of State did not even try
to prove that Mexico was Bolshevist—he simply
stated that because Mexico was aiding the United
States enemy in Nicaragua, it must be trying to establish a Bolshevist government in that country. The*

———————————

*Mexicans could not understand how anyone could be confused by the erroneous logic developed by President Calvin Coolidge and his Secretary of State.*

*Thursday, January 13, 1927:* The New York Times *headlined two stories that have appeared many times with different names, dates, and places since the Russian Revolution of 1917. In the first dispatch Richard V. Oulahan reported from Washington, D. C. on Kellogg's statements revealing a Communist plot to the Senate Foreign Relations Committee. In the second dispatch Mexican arguments with the United States government logic were presented by quoting an editorial from the Mexico City daily newspaper* Excelsior.

## Dispatch by Oulahan

WASHINGTON, Jan. 12—For several hours today the Senate Committee on Foreign Relations listened to Frank B. Kellogg, Secretary of State, set forth the reasons that induced President Coolidge to adopt his present policy toward Nicaragua's disturbance. It was a story full of interesting and illuminating detail.

For the first time the administration, with Mr. Kellogg as its authoritative spokesman, furnished the evidence upon which is based its contention, never voiced officially before, that the Calles government of Mexico is seeking to establish in Nicaragua a Bolshevist regime, hostile to the United States. He offered the testimony of photographs and written reports to prove that all the ships which carried munitions of war to the forces of Juan Sacasa, who is seeking to overthrow the Díaz government in Nicaragua, flew the Mexican flag and that, with one exception, they came from Mexican ports. Documentary evidence was offered to show that the Mexican government directed the shipment of arms and munitions to Sacasa.

### BOLSHEVIST ACTIVITIES SUMMARIZED

The administration's allegations concerning Bolshevist activities with reference to Nicaragua was summarized in a statement prepared at the State Department and left with the committee. By agreement between the committee and Secretary Kellogg the text of this statement was furnished to the newspapers. It is a long recital of steps taken by the Red International of the Communist Party to overthrow American rule in the Philippines and Puerto Rico and establish governments hostile to the United States in Cuba, Mexico, Haiti, and Central and South America.

Documents quoted told of the formation of the All-American Anti-Imperialistic League, under instructions from Moscow, the object of the league being to organize Latin America against the United States, one of the purposes of the league, according to Mr. Kellogg, being to "actively support Latin-American strikes against American concerns."

In this statement there was no conclusive evidence to show that the present Mexican government had entered into any agreement with the Bolsheviki to overthrow the influence of the United States in Nicaragua, but the statement contained an extract from a resolution of the Central Executive Committee of the Workers' Party of the United States, that is, the Communist Party, adopted Nov. 12, 1926, reading as follows:

> "We cite particularly the present attitude of the Calles government in Mexico—its general Latin-Americanism, its policy in Central America, its tendency toward cooperation with the All-American Anti-Imperialistic League, and the decision of Mr. Calles to send a personal representative to the Brussels World Conference Against Imperialism."

### KELLOGG HEARD WITHOUT HECKLING

Secretary Kellogg stated his case behind closed doors. Contrary to some predictions he was not heckled or questioned in a hostile manner by any of the committeemen. No clashes took place between him and Senator Borah, Chairman of the Committee and the foremost critic of the administration's Nicaraguan policy. Mr. Borah took little part in the examination of the Secretary of State. For most of the considerable period the committee had Mr. Kellogg before it Senator Borah stood behind his chair at the head of the long committee table and gave close attention to the administration spokesman.

From what could be gathered from members of the committee Mr. Kellogg, broadly speaking, made a good impression. He established a better case for the President's course in Nicaragua than some of the committeemen expected.

## *Quote from* Excelsior's *editorial:*

"What Coolidge did not deny and cannot deny is that through the resignation of Solorzano the presidency belonged to Vice President Sacasa. Chamorro deliberately stole the post and afterward his tool, Díaz, was put in by the United States. In spite of any constitutional form the fact remains that Dr. Sacasa was robbed of the post which belonged to him.

"Sacasa still has rights even though American arms help to back Díaz.

"In the whole world there will remain a conviction that the fraud and violence used in this case would never have been consummated without the help of the President of the United States. Moreover, in spite of the American marines guarding the capital of Nicaragua and watching the shores the situation of Adolfo Díaz is perilous and he can only be saved by prompt and efficient help of the White House.

"The fact is that we have clear proofs, states Mr. Coolidge, that arms and ammunition have been sent to Nicaragua since August, and on various occasions in great quantities. The ships that transported this armament, he adds, were equipped in Mexican ports and some arms indicate that they were owned by the Mexican government.

"Such is the tremendous charge which the government of the United States makes. Let us suppose it is true that the revolutionary movement of Dr. Sacasa was prepared in Mexico and that from Mexico the rebels received armaments which have been used in the Revolution with the consent and cooperation of the Mexican government.

"For Mexico Sacasa is the legitimate President of Nicaragua and has been recognized with all the customary forms. In view of this, what is there immoral in that our government helps its friends with arms, ammunition, and money to defend him against the other faction? Is it true that only the United States can legitimately give aid to the government of another nation and Mexico is forbidden to do a similar thing?

"Such is the morality of the President of the United States covered with a disguise of hypocrisy or puritanical rectitude."

# 22

# DWIGHT W. MORROW

———•———

# CALLES AND THE
# MEXICAN OIL CONTROVERSY*

❀

*In late 1927 Dwight W. Morrow presented his creden-
tials as Ambassador to Mexico and soon made diplomatic history. Morrow realized immediately that Calles was not a Bolshevik in any sense of the word, and
he reversed the policy of hostility that former Ambassador James R. Sheffield had developed to bring
United States–Mexican relations close to a complete
break. Calles-Morrow "ham and egg" breakfasts were
famous for amicable discussion (although the breakfasts were misnamed because Calles ate popcorn
lightly powdered with chocolate). In this selection
Morrow writes to Secretary of State Kellogg on November 8, 1927, to report on his solution of the oil
problem. American oil companies claimed that the
Petroleum Law of December 26, 1925, was confiscatory in that it required all companies to exchange perpetual rights for a fifty-year concession, regardless
of the fact that many companies held permits that
antedated the constitutional provisions of 1917 on national ownership of subsoil wealth. The companies
concerned took their cases to the Mexican Supreme*

---

* Dwight W. Morrow to Secretary of State Kellogg, November 8,
1927, U. S. Department of State, *Papers Relating to the Foreign
Relations of the United States* (3 vols.; Washington, D. C.: Government Printing Office, 1942), III, 190–192.

*Court, arguing that they should not be subjected to retroactive legislation. The government's case, of course, was that the state's rights were inalienable and that Díaz did not have the power to grant permanent concessions of subsoil wealth. Morrow was apparently shocked at the ease with which the matter was settled in conversation with Calles, but he soon rationalized the whole matter.*

*Morrow was a partner in the Wall Street firm of J. P. Morgan before being appointed to the Mexican ambassadorship. His biography is presented in Harold Nicolson,* Dwight Morrow (*New York: Harcourt, Brace, 1935*).

The President opened the conversation this morning by asking me directly what solution I thought could be found for the oil controversy. I told him that I thought an almost necessary preliminary to any solution would be a clear decision of the Supreme Court. . . . He then rather startled me by saying that such a decision could be expected in two months. I said to the President that it was important that during the time the cases are pending before the court no overt act which could be called confiscation should take place; that if difficulties were not to increase, pending a decision by the courts, there should be no change in the *status quo*.

I think it proper to say that there was nothing in the President's conversation to indicate that he intended to direct the courts to make a decision. In fact, he would doubtless assert that he had no such power. His words were entirely consistent with the fact that he had knowledge of what the courts already had in mind. At the same time it must be remembered that it is generally believed in this country that the courts are not independent of the Executive. While this may seem quite shocking to those trained in American jurisprudence and English jurisprudence, it is not an essentially different situation than has existed in all early governments and is substantially the same situation that existed in England two or three hundred years ago. The King's Bench was originally more than the name of the court; it was the bench that belonged to the King, and administered justice for him.

[Calles stated] that the government of Mexico had never wanted to confiscate any property. Least of all did they want to confiscate the oil properties; that they needed the revenues, and obviously "they did not want to commit suicide"; that the act of 1925 was a most necessary piece of legislation at the time because the country was in considerable disorder and there was an extreme radical wing whose wishes had to be met in that legislation; that he had thought the grant of the fifty-year right as good as a perpetual right to take out the oil, and that such a grant would satisfy every practical purpose, but that the oil companies had not cooperated with him at all, but in fact their representatives had boasted all over Mexico that they did not need to obey the laws of Mexico.

.    .    .

I returned from the President's castle to the embassy. A half hour later Mr. Robinson called upon me and told me that the President was very anxious that none of the oil people should know at all about our conference, that his greatest difficulty in dealing with the oil question in a proper way had been the oil people themselves, and that if they knew that a Supreme Court decision was likely to come down within a short time they would again begin to intrigue.

# 23

# FRANK R. BRANDENBURG

———•———

# THE ACHIEVEMENTS
# OF CALLES*

❧

*The realism that Calles expressed in his economic de-
velopment resulted in a number of achievements,
which have been summed up by Professor Frank
Brandenburg. Brandenburg was introduced to the
reader in Selection 1.*

These are some of Calles' more important achievements:
(1) direction of the national fiscal and monetary system was
put firmly in the hands of the state, which gave birth to the
central Bank of Mexico, to efforts to resolve the differences
outstanding on Mexico's external debt and reparations
claims, to sounder taxation, and to the establishment of a
general controller's office for overseeing national budgetary
matters; (2) for the first time since Díaz, Mexico achieved
the semblance of financial stability; (3) public road construction was undertaken in earnest and placed under the
direction of a new agency, the National Road Commission;
(4) the desire of Mexican farmers for irrigation found real
hope of fulfillment for the first time in Mexican history
when Calles established a National Irrigation Commission;

* Frank R. Brandenburg, *The Making of Modern Mexico* (Englewood Cliffs, N. J.: Prentice-Hall, 1964), 74–75. Reprinted by permission of the publisher.

(5) public ownership of subsoil rights was reasserted in the promulgation of a new Law on Petroleum; (6) the electric power industry became subject to strict governmental regulations with the passage of the National Electricity Code; (7) cognizance of the urgent need to help in the financing of agriculture led to the founding of a National Bank of Agricultural Credit; and (8) the first real steps were taken to professionalize the Army and reduce its numbers to sensible proportions, under the able direction of Gen. Joaquín Amaro, Calles' Secretary of War. Besides these revolutionary innovations, . . . financial interests, industrialists, real estate developers, and mining groups had enough confidence in Calles and his "new economic policy" to invest in revolutionary Mexico. Calles had behind him trade unionists and agrarians, plus a stockpile of anxious local entrepreneurs prepared to develop the nation's business. He had grasped the urgent need for pushing forward with the expansion of the economy's infrastructure.

# 24

ERNEST GRUENING

———•———

# PUBLIC HEALTH IN MEXICO*

❧

*Despite Calles' realism and constructive efforts to build a new Mexico, the public health problem had not been resolved by the time he left office. Ernest Gruening, whose book* Mexico and Its Heritage *appeared the same year that Calles left office, had a special interest in examining the state of public health almost twenty years after the Revolution began. Obviously revolution must be measured in part by improvement in living standards, and to Gruening public health was a vital interest. Gruening, introduced in Selection 7, received an M.D. degree in 1912 but never practiced medicine; instead, he became a journalist for the* Boston American, *and during the early 1920s he was editor of the* Nation. *Thus, when he went to Mexico he wanted to see how the people lived for political as well as medical reasons. Gruening found the terrible state of public health to be an age-old problem beyond the ability of any one man to solve and, although we may note that after over three more decades of Mexico's continuing Revolution conditions are much improved, public health gains do not compare with economic gains. When in 1960, for example, 71.5 percent of Mexico's population lived with-*

*out sewage disposal, 68.4 percent lived without water
within their dwelling, 51.2 percent lived in only one
room, and 24.1 percent did not regularly eat meat,
fish, milk, or eggs, then it is clear that the country's
next big breakthrough must come in public health.
Gruening's observation that health problems in rural
Mexico were as bad if not worse than those of urban
areas should offer a sobering interpretation to those
who still believe that the peasant's communion with
nature and "spiritual peace" make country life pref-
erable to city life.*

The unhealthiness of the Mexican people is due to a variety
of causes which in this day may be reduced to the heading
of "social":

Under the caste system, little modified in four centuries,
its serfs, living often literally no better than animals, could
scarcely cope with disease. But aside from sheer destitution,
a definite heritage of bad habits nullified available assets for
good health.

Conspicuous is ignorance of ventilation. The houses of
Mexican poor on the plateau have always been built without windows and chimneys. The door alone serves as every
kind of aperture, and the benefit of pure air is destroyed in
an enclosed atmosphere vitiated by hours of human and
animal exhalation.

This ignorance extends to the aristocracy. I have seen
houses on Yucatecan haciendas, built by the *hacendado* for
his peons, which lacked even the advantage in airiness of
the permeable bamboo lattice huts, and whose only opening
was the doorway.

The houses of the well-to-do are, relatively, little more
healthful. The type of construction of palace, hotel, and
*casa de vecindad* is of rooms around a courtyard, cubicles
in which the door into the patio is the only entry for air and
light. Within these cul-de-sacs the air is dead and sunlight
cannot penetrate. Cold, damp, and cheerless in wet
weather, they are breathless in hot. A window opposite the

doorway in each of these rooms would transform them, but that, until most recently, was undreamed of.

Servants' quarters even in palatial residences are generally damp basement cells without light, air, or heat. The janitor's family in many an office building cowers in the darkness under the stairway. "That is what they are accustomed to," is the almost invariable answer from master or landlord. Precisely this attitude characterized the opposition to model tenements in New York only a generation ago.

Fresh air is commonly held to be dangerous—an idea still prevalent on the European continent. A deep-seated fear of night air causes the widespread and irrational practice of muffling the mouth and nostrils, and leads also to tight shutting of the doorway when darkness falls. Within, among the poor, in a single room, which has served as a workshop by day, human beings of all ages and both sexes share quarters in terrible congestion and inevitable filth amid workshop odors, the smoke of a smouldering *brasero,* the smell of cooking, the emanation of fetid breaths, the foulness of unwashed bodies, and the stench of excrement. In one block in the Colonia de la Bolsa in Mexico City in 1927, I found an average of two families per room and one animal per person. In one case eight persons and fifteen animals—a dog, a cat, two pigs, and eleven chickens—huddled in a room twelve feet square. This condition is not exceptional. I found it elsewhere in the capital, in Veracruz, Toluca, and Guanajuato. It exists to only a slightly lesser extent in rural communities, where ample space and building materials are available. Pigs, donkeys, and chickens make themselves at home around the family hearth. Ignorance as much as economic pressure has made for such housing. In 1923 the stevedore mayor of Veracruz, Rafael García, showed me his living quarters of two rooms in one of which seven persons slept. As evidence of political honesty, it was gratifying, and contrary to the not uncommon blossoming out in luxury of new officeholders. But as a revelation of lack of knowledge of the elementals of living in the city's chief executive, it was lamentable.

Propinquity with animals makes for the chronic residence of parasites on the human body: The varieties of lice—cephalic, corporal, and pubic—bedbugs, ticks, *pinolaria,* and other regional pests, in addition to the bacterial diseases they transmit, are the constant source of skin irritation brought about by the incessant scratching of dirty nails. Pediculosis is widespread. Dr. Roberto Medellín, secretary of the Department of Health, is authority for the statement to me that in the "disinsectization" practiced on army recruits *three grams* of pediculi were removed from one individual.

Beds are unknown among the humbler dwellers of city and country. A straw *petate* stretched on earthen floor and the blanket, used by day as a coat, serve as bedding. Such covering is insufficient during the cold winter nights on the mesa. The *campesinos* lie huddled together sleeplessly: Small wonder that in the warmth of the morrow's sun they gratefully stretch out their cramped limbs and drowsiness overcomes them.

In the warmer regions, vertical bamboo slats, an inch or two apart, and a leaky thatch form an inadequate shelter when a *Norte* blows the chill rain in gusty cascades. It would seem simple to fill up the interstices in the walls, and to make the roofing watertight. But it has never (with rare exceptions) been done and is therefore (with rare exceptions) not now done.

Paralleling the proscription of air are taboos about water. Bathing was a frequent practice among the Aztecs, and probably no cleanlier race exists on earth today than the Maya.

.    .    .

Aztec practice survives on the mesa in the *temazcalli* or steam bath, but the pre-Conquest bathing in lakes, rivers, and ponds of which the earlier Spanish chroniclers spoke with a certain astonishment, has disappeared.

Today Mexican workers are being re-educated away

from the belief that bathing is dangerous to health. Wrote Lumholtz a quarter of a century ago:

> A custom universal among Mexican working men, amounting almost to superstition, is to avoid contact with water when warm from their labor. I could never induce them to wash their hands under such circumstances, as they were afraid of catching cold, or getting influenza or pneumonia.

But apart from such inhibitory beliefs in regions where water may be plentiful, a large proportion of Mexicans encounter in the extreme aridity of the plateau a constant obstacle to cleanliness. Failure to exploit subsoil water courses, to sink artesian wells, and to provide adequate storage for rain water, has left a scant supply for ablutionary uses. And for drinking purposes, the water has often become so contaminated as to be highly noxious.

A common water supply for the mesa village is a stagnant pool. Sometimes it is a mere accumulation of rain water holding over from one rainy season to the next, and growing steadily fouler. Sometimes it is a tiny pond fed by springs. Occasionally it is a meagerly trickling stream expanding into a shallow reservoir. Often this water is literally invisible for the covering of green algal scum. Yet man and beast drink it, and it serves for cooking and washing. Of course, natives have through the generations developed a high degree of immunity to water which would be lethal to a stranger, and every drop of which is a microscopic aquarium. Nevertheless, the polluted water kills many babies.

Shortly after my first arrival in Mexico, in company with a group of Americans and Mexicans bent on an ascent of Popocatepetl, I spent the night in Amecameca, lying picturesquely at the volcano's base. During supper at the village inn, I inquired whether the water, standing in caraffes on the table, was "good."

"Look here," spoke up an old-time American resident. "If you're going to be happy in Mexico, don't ask whether the water is 'good,' or where it came from. It's the best water they have. It's fine, drink it."

Thus encouraged I did so. In front of the hotel after supper gazing upward at the great snow mass turned crimson in the sunset, I glanced up and down the village street, crudely paved with small round stones. In a central gutter water trickled. Occasionally from some habitation an Indian housewife would empty the contents of a jar or bucket into the street. Presently the hotel *mesero* emerged and filled up from the same stream the water caraffes which were then set back on the table. I experienced no physical ill effects—doubtless the melted snow water entered the village more than ordinarily pure. But subsequently I saw natives in town and village drawing their water from gutters much farther removed from the source.

Even where the water is potable, its scarcity dominates life. In the capital the municipal supply is "turned off" at night, and in quarters fortunate enough to be connected with it, the householder, before 7 P.M., prepares for eventualities by filling basins, pitchers, or bathtub—if he has one. Elsewhere ideal sanitary arrangements are next to impossible. One cannot flush without water. A sewerage system is known to but a few Mexican cities, and not wholly to any, and the disposal of human excrement is fraught with constant peril. In many towns the drain debouches into the street. The dry air of the mesa checks putrefaction. But the microbic contents desiccate and blow about as dust. Attempts to combat this menace are singularly ineffective. Street sweeping is seldom other than dust raising with brooms that are mere handfuls of untied straws, and so short that the sweeper bends double to do his work. A large part of Mexican labor is carrying water, picturesque when borne by native women with a graceful *olla* on shoulder or head; less so when gasoline tins balance on a yoke.

The water shortage makes for greater consumption of alcohol.

Total abstinence in Mexico is practically unknown.

Many children are accustomed to drink from infancy. Some kind of stimulant is considered an essential part of the meal in almost every home, high or low. In the lowlands the intoxicant, made from sugar cane, is *aguardiente* (literally "fiery water," which recalls the "firewater," the name applied by the North American Indian to the spirits of the "paleface").

On the Mesa Central, the most densely populated section of Mexico, *pulque*—"the national beverage"—is the fermented juice of the maguey, which includes several varieties of the agave. Stretching in endless rows, or growing haphazard, these crowns of heavy bluish-green leaves, each tapering upward into a needle point, often taller than a man, are the most characteristic vegetation of central Mexico.

The destructive effects of pulque derive largely from its peculiar elaboration and the quantity of its consumption. The magueyes are grown from suckers that spring up about the parent plant, are transplanted into rows when two or three years old, and reach maturity after about eight years. Normally the plant would flower into a stalk from twelve to twenty feet tall. To make the plant productive, it is not allowed to blossom. The heart is cut out in such a way as to leave a cavity, which then fills with from one to two quarts daily of sweetish *aguamiel* for as long as six months.

This unfermented juice, the slight nutritive qualities of which reside in its sugar content, is not palatable to many Mexicans. Fermentation is induced before the withdrawal of the liquid by introducing wood shavings into the plant cavity. Inadequate covering of the aperture likewise gives access to dust and insects. The liquid is tapped every day or two through a long gourd, called *acocote*. The *tlachiquero* sucks it with his lips, creating a siphon. The liquid filling the tube exerts a corresponding suction, into which the tlachiquero's saliva is often drawn, thus adding a variety of bacteria. The liquid is then transferred to a pigskin container in which the pulque is transported on burro back to the *tinacal*. There it is poured into vats made of beef hides, hung on wooden frames. No other containers, is the belief, will give the proper "body." Here fermentation is stimulated by adding various impurities, but generally this process takes place after the pulque has reached the city and passed through the pulque exchange. What milk trains are to a modern American city, pulque trains are to Mexico City. From the nearer pulque haciendas, burros and carts carry a part to suburban *pulquerías*.

Among the adulterants that are poured into the pulque are *tequesquite,* a chalky rock; *xixi,* a native plant that contains lye; vegetable parings; and sometimes even *caninilla,* or dog excrement, to increase the fermentation. Almost any dirty objects, such as rags or old rope, have somewhere served to "improve the flavor" of this popular beverage— for the complaints most apt to be voiced by the customer are that the pulque is too "fresh," "sweet," or "pure." In one of the beef hide tubs of the tinacal the so-called seed is made, in which a limited quantity of highly fermented liquid is kept, which serves to hasten the fermentation of the fresher liquid in other tubs.

Pulque is never bottled. It is ladled out in the pulquerías from barrels which are seldom fully emptied and to which the newer pulque is incessantly added. Though its alcoholic content is not high—approximately 5 to 7 percent—the beverage continues its fermentation with the gastrointestinal tract of the consumer, causing the putrefaction of its contents, impeding digestion, and creating a toxemia diagnosable through a symptomatic stupor. Pulque is in varying degrees a *bacterial culture.* It may transmit almost every microbic disease known to man.

Despite general recognition of pulque's harmfulness, its abolition encounters virtually insuperable obstacles; religion, habit, addiction, and economic reasons make for its perpetuation.

The origin of pulque is immemorial. Tradition ascribes to it the decline and fall of the Toltecs. While the Aztecs restricted its use, it was also an element in their religious festivals.

.     .     .

It is not surprising therefore that habits of intoxication have become rooted in the Mexican people. Mothers in their ignorance, and in the absence of milk, wean their children on the whitish pulque. Starr, in the nineties, repeatedly found villages whose inhabitants were all intoxicated. Drinking as an accomplishment of religious festivals has been preserved.

So general is this habit that the incapacity of workers on Monday and their high percentage of absenteeism from the effects of Sabbath inebriety has given the first work day of the week the cognomen of *San Lunes*—"Holy Monday." The Mexican factory hand's output is lowest on Monday, and rises steadily through the week, the reverse of the American worker, who shows the effect of fatigue increasingly with each consecutive day of labor. It takes some Mexican workers six days to recover fully from their Sunday carousal.

In mesa villages in the late afternoon I have repeatedly encountered loquaciousness and good nature indicative of a general mulling with *licor divino,* the result often, I am convinced, not so much of deliberate imbibing, for its effects, as of a repeated allaying of thirst brought about by labor in the meridian sun. Under its burning rays one must quench one's thirst or die, and pulque, white, foamy, and cool, is always accessible. And when one contemplates the conditions under which the natives of the mesa live, one inclines with Flandrau, to marvel "not, like the tourist of a week, that they are dirty, but that under the circumstances they are as clean as they are; not that so many of them are continually sick, but that any of them are ever well; not that they love to get drunk, but that they can bear to remain sober."

In the economic field pulque is strongly intrenched. This mammoth industry occupies nearly a million acres of agricultural land. Much of it at present useless for other crops, gives employment to a million and a half people, and pays not less than ten million pesos in taxes. Its sudden abolition would profoundly affect administration, national and state, agriculturist, laborer, retailer, consumer—and produce an economic cataclysm. Since each plant, costing 2.00 pesos up to maturity, gives some 300 liters of juice, an acre, which holds about 400 plants, yields to the hacendado 2400 pesos of gross income. The juice is valued on the farms at about two centavos a liter and is sold in the cities for from twelve to fifteen. A hacienda which produces sixty barrels daily employs not less than sixty tlachiqueros, ninety peons, and forty others engaged in specific tasks—or approximately three persons per barrel. In addition are those who transport the pulque, and the employees in pulquerías, *cantinas,* and *fondas,* the poor man's restaurants, of which there are more than 2000 in Mexico City alone.

·　　·　　·

In other ways the Mexican diet is deleterious. Poverty, first, makes it inadequate [and] examination of the budgets of Mexican laborers shows that the caloric content of the food they could afford to buy barely furnished the energy required by an individual "at absolute rest." The insufficiency falls most heavily on the children, who, with few exceptions, are noticeably undernourished and enter adult life handicapped beyond repair. Ignorance is largely responsible. The poorer mother suckles her child as long as she can, and it is common for two and even three children of different ages to seek their nourishment at her breast. When she weans the child it is on adult foods—*tortillas, frijoles,* bananas, and even *chiles.* Clean cow's milk is not available for the majority of Mexicans, and its use is undeveloped. Even in well-to-do families children of three and four often drink black coffee and are allowed to gorge themselves on meats and sweets. The transitional alimentation for the infant in the shape of cereals and well-cooked green vegetables is almost unknown. The large infant mortality may be ascribed first and foremost to diet.

The most detrimental factor in that diet is the caustic chile—whose almost universal use is also a direct heritage from pre-Conquest days. Mexicans of course develop a tolerance and craving for highly spiced foods, but that they pay the price in ill-health and death is evidenced by the extraordinary preponderance of gastrointestinal ailments. Of the deaths from all causes in Mexico City in the nine years 1904–1912, 32.1 percent were due to diseases of the digestive tract. The enormity of these figures may be judged from the fact that in the United States in 1924 the corresponding diseases accounted for but 6.6 percent of all deaths. It is the relative *proportions* that are significant.

In addition to the character of the food is its quality. Refrigeration is not a factor in Mexico. The masses never secure its benefits. The meat hangs in butcher shops exposed to dust and flies—a less serious condition in the dry air of the mesa than in the lowlands. Food in markets has only now begun—in the capital—to be covered, in consequence of the vigorous methods of the Department of Health. Outside the capital, and still to a considerable extent in it, the danger of contamination is constant. Rotten fruit and decayed food are still offered for sale, and their lower prices attract purchasers. Much of the food for the masses is prepared by unwashed hands within a few inches of the sidewalk or germ-laden soil. And the manner in which Mexicans of the middle class, of adequate means, will not hesitate to buy hunks of boiled fowl, *enchiladas,* and other victuals exposed at the railway stations after no one knows how much handling by unclean fingers, shows that disregard of elementary precepts of hygiene is not confined to the poorer classes.

Much Mexican ill health is due to venereal disease. The comparison of 8.3 deaths per 100,000 from syphilis in the United States in 1924, with 59.1 in Mexico City in 1926 is suggestive, merely. Neither of the above figures includes locomotor ataxia and general paresis of the insane, which are derivatives of syphilis. But the testimony of Mexican authorities is conclusive.

The social background that makes for the prevalence of

venereal disease was thus depicted by the historian Francisco Bulnes:

> According to the civil register of Mexico City, 70 percent of the births were of natural (illegitimate) children. Violation of the women of the humble classes was an established and respectable custom. According to the calculation of Dr. Domínguez, 60 percent of the population suffered with chronic alcoholism. In 1919 the medical service of the Department of Education declared that the majority of the children attending school were afflicted with hereditary syphilis. The lower classes, in order to become still lower, smoked tobacco with or without *marihuana,* in the superior classes *nirvana* was sought . . . by means of opium and its alkaloids and cocaine.

The picture while florid is not exaggerated. It is confirmed by other less rhetorical observers. Writing early in the last Díaz decade, Julio Guerreo, jurist and publicist, calls attention to the fact that in the previous year 666 *new* prostitutes had been inscribed in the Inspección de Sanidad. Dr. Luis Lara Pardo, physician and student of Mexican social problems, toward the close of the Díaz régime found that 12 percent of all the women in Mexico City between the ages of fifteen and thirty were *inscribed* as prostitutes, a proportion approximately ten times greater than in Paris. The actual number in Mexico, obviously unrecorded, he considered very much greater.

The consequences to the physical and mental health of Mexico's population he sums up in these words:

> Venereal disease is so common that to reach adult life without having contracted it may be considered exceptional. . . .
> Today venereal disease has become so widespread that only an infinitesimal group of individuals who appear nearly immune to infection, may be said to be exempt. We may assert without fear of exaggeration that these diseases cannot spread further, because the population is already saturated with them.

Again Mexico is paying the price of ignorance, for as Dr. Pardo asserts, "in Mexico venereal diseases are considered as trivial as measles or whooping cough, as illnesses to which every man must some time in his life pay tribute."

# 25

# JAMES W. WILKIE

———•———

# THE MEANING OF THE CRISTERO RELIGIOUS WAR*

❧

*The Mexican hierarchy resisted the Mexican Revolution, which constitutionally deprived the Church of its traditional privileged position in society; and to prevent social upheaval by the masses the hierarchy tended to ignore the poverty and poor living conditions that the Revolution insisted upon changing. In 1921, for example, Archbishop Francisco Orozco y Jiménez had issued a Pastoral Letter that asked:*

What poor are they upon whom God looks with compassion?

Certainly not those poor who are discontented with their fate, envious of the fortunes of others, who rebel against work and who wish to enjoy the present life without the necessity of earning their bread in the sweat of their brows.

Much less are they the poor who envy the rich only because they are rich, and only await the time when they can fling themselves against them with lighted torch or fratricidal dagger in hand, with the vehement desire for an unjust distribution of riches.

---

* James W. Wilkie, "The Meaning of the Cristero Religious War Against the Mexican Revolution." Reprinted from *A Journal of Church and State,* Vol. VIII (Spring 1966), 214–233, by permission of the publisher.

The Savior loves the poor who are resigned and submissive, long suffering and patient;—who have not put their desires in the things of this world but who try to lay up treasure in heaven.

*The Archbishop's solution to poverty was an exhortation:*

Rich: Love the poor, extend to him your hand and look upon him as your brother, in order that the hate in his heart may be extinguished.

Poor: Love your humble condition and your work; put your hopes in heaven; there are the real riches.

One thing only I ask:
Of the rich, love
Of the poor, resignation.
And with this, society will be saved.[1]

*After 1921 the Obregón and Calles governments became increasingly involved with frequent and serious conflicts with the Church hierarchy and lay leadership. When in 1925 the Episcopacy objected to President Calles' covert support of an Orthodox Catholic Apostolic Mexican Church with a Mexican patriarch linked to Mexican nationalism, and when in 1926 Archbishop José Mora y del Río reaffirmed the hierarchy's refusal to accept Articles 3, 5, 27, and 130 of the Constitution of 1917, Calles acted to implement the Constitution. He secularized all primary education, began the deportation of foreign-born clericals, and required the registration of all clergymen with the government in order to regulate their "professional conduct." Seventy-three convents were closed within a few months. Lay Catholic leaders, including Miguel Palomar y Vizcarra, organized the National Religious Defense League to reconquer religious liberty by taking up arms. Reputedly, the League was able to mobilize 25,000 rebels between 1926 and 1929 in order to fight in the name of "Christ the King." The meaning of the* Cristero *rebellion has never been well understood because scholars*

[1] Quoted by Marjorie Ruth Clark, *Organized Labor in Mexico* (Chapel Hill: University of North Carolina Press, 1934), 95–96.

*have generally considered the Roman Catholic
Church and the Mexican government as monoliths.*

According to Palomar y Vizcarra, as spontaneous armed
movements spread to the states of Guanajuato and Durango, the League mobilized its organization to unite these
small movements into a unified struggle for the reconquest
of religious liberty. The goal of this movement which cen-
tered in the western states—particularly Jalisco, Michoacán, and Colima—was not to overthrow the government,
but to win recognition of the "essential religious liberties."
Theoretically, once religious liberty were won, the war
would be over. The League proudly adopted the name
"Cristeros" which the government disrespectfully applied to
the rebels, and it set out to develop ideologically its position
as defender of the faith.

The League presented a memorial to the Mexican hierarchy on November 26, 1926, asking for the Episcopate to
approve armed defense and to enable priests to serve canon-
ically as military men. The League was especially interested
in Episcopal action on the latter request in order that Mexican clergy who were not willing to back guerrilla war
would be persuaded to act outside the canonical norm and
support armed defense of religious liberty. The Episcopate
did not respond in writing; but within a few days [Leo-
poldo] Ruiz y Flores and [Pascual] Díaz, who was Secretary of the Episcopal Committee, orally informed the
League that the Episcopate (including the Primate of Mexico, Archbishop Mora y del Río) approved of the memorial
with the reservation that the committee could not authorize
priests to function as military men but would give permission for the clergy to minister to military detachments.

Church moderate Pascual Díaz, who later became the
Archbishop of Mexico and who ended the Cristero War in
1929, subsequently affirmed that the League solicited hier-
archial support; but he maintained that though the Episcopate did not stop the movement, neither did it give its ap-

proval to the war. Díaz noted that the hierarchy had no reason to interfere in the League's affairs since it was free to defend its rights in its own manner.

This defense of Episcopal action by Díaz was a major factor in the split that was to emerge between militant lay Catholics and the hierarchy under Archbishop Díaz in 1929, for as the leader of the League, Palomar y Vizcarra, has cogently pointed out:

> If the Episcopate did not feel that it could interfere with the commencement of a war, why did it sign a truce with the government to end the war on June 21, 1929? If it were not the province of the hierarchy to sanction the League's struggle, why did it step in and cut the ideological ground from under the League after over two years of bloody struggle?

Change in the Church's official stance may be traced to the death of Archbishop Mora y del Río. The Primate of Mexico died in exile in San Antonio, Texas, on April 23, 1928. His death at the age of seventy-five brought to end a nineteen-year control of the Mexican Church and eliminated the prerevolutionary generation from hierarchical command. Apparently Mora y del Río had been chosen at the express wishes of the old dictator, Porfirio Díaz, to become Archbishop of Mexico in 1909. Fifty-six years of age in that year, Mora y del Río was young enough to adapt to new times once the Revolution got under way. He became known as a liberal churchman. For example, he was famous for giving in to the government to prevent clashes, as when he instructed the clergy not to perform the marriage ceremony unless the civil ceremony had been carried out as required by law. In the 1920s when Church-state tensions increased Mora y del Río was in his seventies; he must have felt by then that his conciliatory policy had not been successful and that the Church might gain from a stronger stand. At any rate, under his leadership the hierarchy which supported militant action was in control of Church policy and a truce with the government was not possible.

The passing of Mora y del Río allowed Church moderates under Bishops Díaz and Ruiz y Flores to come to power. Díaz had played an important role in attempting to negotiate a settlement with the government as early as August 21, 1926. Since he was vocally opposed to the Cristero War, he obviously was a strong contender to become Primate of Mexico as the rebellion proved ineffective. Relatively young and vigorous at age fifty-three in 1928, Díaz obviously felt that the religious strike had been a failure. If it continued, the Church might lose its voice forever among the people, and only a truce would restore the clergy to some leadership in Mexican society. It was evident that the Church would never regain the position that it had lost under Calles, but it was also clear that it would not do to cut itself off from all contact with the populace as this would be playing into the government's hands. Díaz had . . . argued against violence. Ruiz y Flores had taken a stronger stand, and as the Archbishop of Michoacán he had tried to block the establishment of the League in his diocese in March 1925.

Palomar y Vizcarra recounts the struggle for power that split the hierarchy and lay Catholics into two fundamental groups: those favoring continued war and those favoring peace. The hierarchical leaders who were ranged against the peace moves of Díaz and Ruiz y Flores included, among others, José Mora y del Río, Francisco Orozco y Jiménez, Leopoldo Lara y Torres, Jesús Manríquez y Zárate, José María González y Valencia, and Miguel M. de la Mora. The Apostolic Delegate in Washington apparently sided with the former two bishops and the Pope leaned to their interpretation that the guerrilla war could lead to no successful conclusion, for it could do no practical good for the Church. The latter bishops, however, were not interested in such mundane matters; they found martyrdom for the cause glorious.

President-elect Alvaro Obregón was assassinated by a Catholic fanatic on July 17, 1928. Though the zealot apparently acted upon his own initiative, the government originally took the view that the Church was responsible for the murder. Ironically, according to Ambassador Dwight Morrow who was trying to arrange a truce, Obregón had consulted with Calles on the day before he was assassinated in order to arrange a possible *modus vivendi* between Church and state as soon as he took office on December 1, 1928.

Once the Cristero War was under way, Calles must have been tempted to pursue it to a successful conclusion; but a government can successfully confront only so many major problems at any given time, and early in 1928 Calles had realized the problems facing peaceful transition from his administration to a new Obregón regime. Morrow had persuaded and "pressed" Calles to resolve problems which gave Mexico a bad reputation, and under this friendly push Calles had reoriented his view of government to a conservative one which matched the temper of a time when Wall Street appeared to have found the answer to economic well-being. Thus, Calles not only negotiated with church leaders to establish a truce but also ruled against expropriation of the foreign-held oil industry and drastically cut land distribution to the peasantry.

Interim-President Portes Gil was intent upon renewing the distribution of land beginning December 1, 1928, but he also had to face serious problems. Pressure from the United States against any renewed land reform program, as well as international complications over Mexico's support of the Sandino resistance to United States forces in Nicaragua, troubled diplomatic relations. Domestically, Portes Gil had to appease the Obregón wing of the official family which believed that Calles had ordered Obregón killed in order to prevent him from returning to the presidency. A serious military rebellion erupted in March 1929, which posed a grave problem for the government as rebel army leaders tried to link up with the Cristeros. In May, a "rebellion" by National University students over the substitution of written for oral exams turned into a bloody battle between police and students; the ensuing protest of young intellectuals was soon linked to the tense political atmosphere. The cry went up that Calles and his followers had ruled Mexico too long, and the university became a focus of political opposition to the Revolution. With a heated special presidential election scheduled for November 1929, in which Catholics and other dissidents could effectively protest against a divided Revolutionary Family, Portes Gil was determined to play down the religious problem.

As Church and state each internally faced crisis, it is no wonder that a *modus vivendi* was reached on June 21, 1929. Although the government could not definitively defeat the Cristeros in the western states, neither could the League's forces rouse much spirit of support in other areas of Mexico.

.    .    .

The Cristero conflict began when Church and state relations deteriorated in the early 1920s, and both sides were responsible for the war which broke out in 1926. We may conclude that the Church was testing its limits under the new Constitution and that the state would sooner or later have had to show the Church that it meant to enforce its laws. Voices of moderation in the Church counted for little until the violence of militant Catholics was discredited as harmful to the Church's best interests. When intransigent leaders on both sides gained power, a war was the result. Unity broke down in each camp as the conflict continued, and moderates made peace in the name of Church and state in 1929. Whereas the hierarchy gave up its demands of constitutional revision in order that the clergy could return to the churches, it had to revoke the support that an earlier Primate of Mexico had given the Cristeros. The state conceded little and gained time to consolidate its position in a difficult period.

The result of the armistice meant that the division among lay Catholics and churchmen was to be damaging for decades. The trust of union was shattered by surrender of goals.

It was easy for the revolutionary government to mount a new offensive against the Church during the early 1930s, especially when the Church insisted upon celebrating the quadricentennial of the Virgin of Guadalupe with a giant public celebration on December 12, 1931. The government's plans for establishing sexual and socialistic education in a decade influenced by social experiments in Russia found Church and state again at odds. In the new battle the state held all the cards, for it emerged from the Cristero truce ready and able to continue another round in a long struggle.

# 26

CARLETON BEALS

·

# THE INDIAN WHO SWAYS MEXICO'S DESTINY, JOAQUÍN AMARO*

❧

*By 1930 Mexico's pacification was assured. The Cristero revolt and the abortive military upheaval of 1929 had passed into history; and General Joaquín Amaro, who won much credit for these victories, was free to continue his program, which was designed to create a professional military spirit. The generals were still a major influence in national life, however, and the importance of General Amaro was underscored by Carleton Beals in this dispatch to* The New York Times. *Beals was introduced to the reader in Selection 15.*

There are on record few instances of the rise of a personality to ascendency as remarkable as that of the full-blooded Tarascan Indian, General Joaquín Amaro, who now holds the powerful post of Secretary of War in Mexico. Twenty years ago he was a poor boy, lost in the obscurity of his people. Today he is head of the Mexican military machine. He has organized Mexico's unruly revolutionary forces into

* Carleton Beals, "The Indian Who Sways Mexico's Destiny," *The New York Times,* December 7, 1930. Copyright 1930 by The New York Times Company. Reprinted by permission.

one disciplined body of fifty thousand men. Twenty years ago Amaro wore a red glass bead in his ear as a protecting amulet. Today from the lofty balcony of the National Palace on the vast Plaza de la Constitución he reviews thirty-five thousand troops, equipped and drilled as no troops have ever been trained in Mexico, even under the great Porfirio Díaz. Once Amaro had no shoes on his feet. Today he administers more than seventy million pesos annually. Seventeen years ago he was fighting at the head of a small body of men in the wilds of Guerrero against the usurpations of President Victoriano Huerta. Today he heads the most powerful organization in Mexico.

Fifteen years ago Amaro appeared with his followers by the side of General Alvaro Obregón in Celaya, where the crucial battle was fought that drove Pancho Villa forever north into the Durango cactus and placed Carranza in the presidency. Five years later he again joined with Obregón, this time against Carranza; but, still in his early thirties, he was far from being an outstanding general. In the ten short years since, he has emerged into a commanding position, both politically and militarily. He distinguished himself during the suppression of the De la Huerta revolt in 1923 and 1924. At a ticklish time when the major part of the Army had turned against the government, Amaro held the Puebla lines, preventing the rebels from breaking through to seize the nearby capital. With inferior numbers and inferior equipment, he released a cavalry charge and wedged his troops in behind with such impetus that he swept the rebel columns south into the state of Oaxaca and broke the backbone of the rebellion at the most dangerous moment for the government.

Thus, Amaro built his reputation, and when General Plutarco Calles became President in 1924 he named Amaro Secretary of War—a post that he has held since, under three administrations. Obregón, Villa, Carranza, all of them have gone down to bloody deaths, but Amaro remains—next to General Calles the most powerful personality on the Mexican scene.

.    .    .

He is something of a mystery, a large "X" written over the future of Mexico. Stern, taciturn, secretive, he is not easy to approach. He hoes his row in silence. Rarely is he quoted in the press. He never talks politics, although a political regime has grown up around him. He is shy and suspicious of people whom he does not know. He never boasts or talks about himself. He disclaims all knowledge of anything except military affairs, and when people remind him of his importance he answers with an embarrassed disclaimer, not at all affected. He lives a rigorous, abstemious life, which gives him no time for futile gestures. He does not drink or smoke, and he invariably leaves social gatherings by ten o'clock. In ordinary intercourse he is mild, quiet, gentle, almost deferential. But among Army people he is reputed to be violently direct of speech and does not hesitate to call the toughest, most brutal general by the plainest names when he feels the man has erred.

The day after the last Independence Day parade, I saw Amaro, at the Balbuena Aviation Field, put several generals on the mat for certain remissnesses the previous morning. Those generals were men accustomed to rule, to kill, to fight, to work their will unhampered, but Amaro cursed them out like flunkies. One has to realize the unruly arrogance and jealousy of the military caste in Mexico to appreciate such an episode and its meaning in terms of personal assurance and control. Not by mildness could the Mexican general be dominated, but by stern matching of wits and courage and occasional brutality. Fantastic tales are told of Amaro's cruelty; but unless he is angered or suspicious, his eyes are almost mild, with the black liquid softness of his race. Formerly he had a violent temper, and it has been said he has struck cabinet ministers and generals across the face with his riding crop when they have affronted him. Yet he is slight of build—slight, but handsome and commanding; even more handsome than he was before the accident that lost him an eye.

That accident almost cut short a career. Shortly before

the outbreak of the Escobar revolt in 1929, Amaro, when playing the popular Basque game of *pelota,* was struck in the eye with terrific force by the hard ball. The ball drove into the eye socket with such force as to smash the bones. Amaro was rushed to Rochester; and for a time it was feared that fatal infection would set in; that in any case he would be left totally blind. But one eye was saved; and he returned to take up his duties.

Meantime, the revolt had been put down by Calles, but it was Amaro's discipline, his unflagging efforts to drill and equip the Army, that made it possible to smash the rebellion so soon, even though it was led by the most outstanding of the old-line revolutionary generals.

In quashing the earlier 1927 Gómez-Serrano revolt in less than a week, Calles and Amaro worked together. They installed their headquarters in Chapultepec Castle, where direct wire and radio connections kept them constantly informed. They toiled incessantly for three days and nights without sleep. I recall one scene vividly. Amaro had put his desk out on the *terraza,* which overlooks the wide bowl of the Valley of Mexico. Calles dashed out in his shirtsleeves, his suspenders hanging down, three days' growth of beard on his haggard face, to give some orders. Amaro, though weary under the strain, had somehow managed to retain a trimmer military aspect. But ordinary platitudinous courtesies had broken down.

Facing a deadly situation, the two men made their orders snap and crackle, and their language was good barracks-room vernacular, without any frills. Yet in a lull, Calles gave a humorous turn to some phrase, with that inimitable Mexican sense of humor that is never quite floored by any situation. Not so Amaro, who never lets down the firm exterior texture of his personality, who ever remains an enigma. Even his own relatives and closest friends never attempt familiarities but address him deferentially as "My General."

In 1928, just after the assassination of Obregón, Calles— then about to leave office—instituted the custom of having cabinet members report on the work of their departments to Congress. Amaro sat among the members of the government, a small dark figure in plain khaki uniform, immobile save for a slight movement of his hands—which, even from the box, I could see were tense, mobile, expressive, almost like the slow movement of a cat's tail. He rose and presented his curt address with an almost professorial manner, without the least show of braggadocio or self-importance. And Congress gave him an ovation. Outside were the visible results of his efforts. The granite edifice was surrounded by troops. And inside, though the deputies did not know it, were invisible machine guns, set for any emergency, for it was a ticklish moment. Affairs of state hung in the balance. Ambitious personalities were glowering there in the shadows. Men were present who soon were to plunge the country into new bloodshed.

But outside were the red and black cavalry and the gray and black *Yaqui* guards, long lanes of them through which Calles and the Cabinet had whirled to this rendezvous. Eight years before I had seen those same Yaqui troops march in to take Mexico City for Obregón, whose body had recently been laid to rest, riddled with an assassin's bullets. Those Yaquis had been clad in white "pajamas," and shuffled along in one-thong *guaraches* to the beat of their queer tomtoms. On their heads they wore odd small beribboned straw hats. Eight years later they had become one of the smartest corps of troops in the world. This was largely due to the efforts of Amaro.

Inside the chamber, lined up behind Calles in extravagant full dress uniforms, weighted under gold braid and epaulettes and shivering medals, were all the generals of Mexico, at a moment when Calles was telling Congress that the hour for the end of the rule of Mexico by military chiefs (*caudillos*) had struck. Behind him were men who for more than a decade, some of them for two decades, had held human lives and human property in their hands, whose only law had been their personal caprice, who had marched and countermarched the length and breadth of the land, who had balked at no means to achieve their ends. They had stood men before firing squads; they had razed cities. Many were violent and unruly spirits, accustomed to graft, plunder, the satiation of every human desire and lust. Power had been theirs. Wine, women, and song had been theirs. A number of them I had seen in wild orgies and shooting affrays. Others I had seen, begrimed and weary in campaigns, cursing, laughing, with the typical Mexican mixture of intense purposefulness, good humor, and dare-all courage.

No group of men in the world is so ambitious, so lustful for power, so unmoved by the ordinary Occidental criterions of justice. They are the product of their environment and the Revolution. Most of them came up like whirling clouds from the alkaline dust of Mexico, as strong and hard and cruel as the crags that bore them. To achieve precedence over them, to rise from such ranks, to impose upon them an outside will, to rule and dominate them, to force them into cooperating units of an organization loyal to the state—few men in Mexico have ever accomplished this for any length of time. Today the most powerful military figure in Mexico is the silent little dark Tarascan Indian, who reads congressional messages in a prosy voice and who rules himself with more of an iron hand than even he rules others.

. . .

The constant aim of Amaro has been to weld the various feudal armies of the Revolution, based on personal leadership, into a national institution based on loyalty to the state. At the same time, he was obliged to reduce it in numbers, make war on graft, cut down total expenditures. Also, he had to solve the problem of how to bring the armed peasants under control, so as to insure peace in the rural districts.

To break the vicious tradition of the Army is no easy task. More than probably it has not been completed. But since 1920 Army expenditures have been reduced from more than one hundred thousand pesos to seventy thousand pesos; and the size of the Army has been cut from nearly one hundred thousand men to about fifty thousand. Graft has been greatly reduced. All branches of the service have been improved. The Aviation Department now has airplanes that actually will fly. Rifles are less likely to explode in the hands of the users. The government munition works now manufacture all uniforms, rifles, machine guns, and other army supplies. Most of the rank and file are now literate, and regular army schools are maintained. The National Academy in Popotla—Mexico's West Point—is one of the most modern, best equipped, and organized institutions of its kind anywhere.

Gradually the armed peasants have been brought under control. They have long constituted "the second line" army of Mexico. Most of them are trained fighters, schooled in the guerrilla bands of Villa, Zapata, and other leaders. At any sign of trouble they have been always ready to spring up at a moment's notice. Some years ago I was invited by the Governor of Morelos to the annual commemoration of the death of Zapata and saw ten thousand of them ride by the palace on their lean cayuses. Their huge gray felt sombreros bobbed with the movement of their mounts; sarapes and rifles were slung at the saddle bow. During the recent revolt of Escobar, fifteen thousand of them suddenly sprang up from nowhere and swept across the desert sands of Chihuahua to offer their services to Calles.

The first move of the government was to recognize the local Social Defense Corps under accepted leaders. These voluntary contingents, in a number of crises, have stood valiantly behind the government. Gradually, Amaro has weeded out less reliable elements. He has improved the personnel and the organization of the Social Defense and now has brought it more directly under the Army. The Army now ratifies the regional chiefs; they are supposed to take their orders from the War Department, but they still exercise a considerable autonomy and refuse to be controlled in all matters. Yet, a definite effort has been made to imbue them with a spirit of loyalty to the government, and ultimately they will probably be definitely absorbed into the governmental machinery to form a corps resembling the famous *rurales* of Porfirio Díaz.

# 27

ROBERT E. SCOTT

———•———

# THE FOUNDATION OF
# MEXICO'S OFFICIAL PARTY*

❋

*Spanning the difficult transition in national politics that took place as the decade of the 1920s closed and the years of the 1930s began, the foundation of the National Revolutionary Party (PNR) provided a means of accommodation by which political contenders could share power. The need to rebel in order to capture power passed as the official party increased its efficiency to work out the country's political destiny within the Revolutionary Family. As Jesús Silva Herzog has remarked, military men became accustomed to lucrative positions in the government and to fat contracts for the construction of public works, and they could no longer afford to risk their lives in struggle for power.*

*The PNR, founded in 1929, was reorganized in 1938 as the Party of the Mexican Revolution (PRM, see Selection 39) and again revamped in 1946 as the Party of Institutional Revolution (PRI). The foundation of this evolving official party has been described by Professor Robert E. Scott, a political scientist at the University of Illinois. Scott is the author of*

* Robert E. Scott, *Mexican Government in Transition* (rev. ed.; Urbana: University of Illinois Press, 1964), 122–123. Reprinted by permission of the author and publisher.

*"Budget Making in Mexico,"* Inter-American Economic Affairs, *9, 2 (1955), 3–20; and "Mexico, the Established Revolution,"* in Lucian Pye and Sidney Verba *(eds.)*, Political Culture and Political Development *(Princeton: Princeton University Press, 1965)*, *330–395.*

During March of 1929, in the historic city of Querétaro, where the Constitution of 1917 had been written, the *Partido Nacional Revolucionario* was set up as the accepted agency of the Revolution. Unlike its official successors, the original PNR was not highly centralized; instead it was an amalgam of local political machines and of various agricultural, labor, and other interest associations, backed by the silent but ever-present force of the military. Included were the organizations of the military *caudillos*—Rodríguez in Sonora, Cárdenas in Michoacán, Cedillo in San Luis Potosí, Maximino Avila Camacho in Puebla—and those of the civilian *caciques*—Portes Gil in Tamaulipas, Adalberto Tejeda in Veracruz, and the party of the recently deceased Felipe Carrillo Puerto of Yucatán. Each component in the coalition was to retain its organizational identity but act under the mandate of a National Executive Committee.

To be sure, in making this concession to Calles, the generals had no intention of giving up any of the power they exercised. Their cooperation was, to them, no more than a temporary expedient to carry them through a somewhat clouded political situation. A few local political leaders refused to enter Calles' coalition but in time their political strength withered away, for local machines could not oppose the combined might that the PNR could bring to bear.

The attitude of the leadership of the functional interest associations toward the PNR was no less devious than that of their military brethren. They had no wish to lose control over their followers. Having been in opposition to Calles, the Agrarian Party was an especially hard nut to crack. Nevertheless, with the aid of one of its less intransigent leaders, Aaron Sáenz, and by spending plenty of government money, Calles managed to split the farm party's organization, purge his opponents, and add the *agraristas* to his coalition.

Ironically, Morones' Labor Party, which previously had supported Calles, remained outside of the official fold. Partly because of suspicion of the strong man's motives, partly through lack of encouragement from Calles because public opinion somehow connected the *laboristas* with Obregón's death, Morones did not join the PNR. He and his labor organization have been trying ever since to regain their lost prominence, with little success. Other labor groups of course now flocked to the new party, but they gained few immediate advantages. For the time being, the power factor represented by organized labor, as compared with other factions in the party, was not strong enough to warrant major concessions. Presidents Portes Gil, Ortiz Rubio, and Rodríguez, all of whom served at one period or another during the next presidential term, were not particularly dependent upon labor.

Neither was Calles. Although he had relinquished the office of president, as *jefe máximo* of the revolutionary party he exercised an almost complete control over the increasingly centralized political organization. He continued to think in the personalistic tradition, however, not recognizing that the existence of the PNR had changed the nature of his relationship with his followers. In 1931, for example, Calles put his son Alfredo, who was not yet old enough to hold office legally, into the state legislature of Tamaulipas. He also tried to force amendment of the state constitution of Tamaulipas to reduce the minimum age for gubernatorial candidates, so that he could consolidate his position in the state by imposing Alfredo as governor. Emilio Portes Gil was particularly outraged by this, because Tamaulipas was his own stamping ground. As he put it a few years later, "General Calles was not satisfied that his sons Rodolfo and Plutarco governed Sonora and Nuevo León. He also wanted Tamaulipas under the thumb of the family."

# 28

# CARLOS FUENTES

————•————

# "A HANDFUL OF
# MILLIONAIRES"*

❧

*All men find it possible to defend their actions. There-
fore, Mexico's generals rationalized their power in the
official party as a guarantee of peace, and Mexico's
new class of politicians and bankers have justified
their power as a guarantee of prosperity. In this selection by novelist Carlos Fuentes, banker Federico
Robles explains why corruption is good. This explanation provided by the Marxist Fuentes reveals
the success of Mexico's Revolution in attracting dissident intellectuals to work within an institutional
framework. Fuentes, born in 1928, did not know
Mexico's violent era firsthand, as he was not only too
young to understand much but also grew up in foreign capitals where his father was employed in diplomatic work. Despite the fact that he belongs to a new
generation, Fuentes has not only criticized the Revolution but also has given it much credit. His unstructured technique in* Where the Air is Clear *is designed to reveal unstructured, confused, and complex
urban life and revolutionary change.*

————————

* Reprinted with permission of Farrar, Straus & Giroux, Inc., from
*Where the Air is Clear* by Carlos Fuentes, tr. Sam Hileman. Copyright © 1960 by Carlos Fuentes, 86–88.

"We may be criticized on many counts, . . . and critics say that we of the old guard, a handful of millionaires, have gathered our wealth from the sweat of the nation itself. But when you remember what Mexico was before, things take a different light. Gangs of bandits who never stopped shooting, the economy paralyzed, generals with private armies. No prestige abroad. No faith in industry. The countryside full of fear. Public institutions gone. And it was our lot to try to defend the principles of the Revolution and at the same time make them work toward progress and order and the national good. It was no easy task to reconcile those purposes. To proclaim revolutionary ideals is easy: land reform, labor laws, whatever you please. But we had to face reality and accept the only political truth, compromise. That was the moment of crisis for the Revolution. The moment of decision to build even if it meant staining conscience. To sacrifice ideals for the sake of tangible achievement. And we did it, and well. We had the right to take what we wanted, because of what we had suffered, gone through, to earn it. One man had been forced into the Army, another's mother had been raped, another had had his land stolen. Don Porfirio had given none of us any way up, the door had been closed on all our ambitions. Now our ambition could grab what it cared to. Yes, but always working for the good of the nation, always taking only what was ours and taking it not for ourselves but for the nation."

On his feet in front of the window, Robles spread his hand across the anarchic expanse of Mexico City. "Look outside. There are still millions of illiterates, barefoot Inians, poor people starving to death, farmers who don't have even one miserable acre of their own, factories with no machinery, nor parts, unemployed workers who have to flee to the United States. But there are also millions who can go to schools that we of the Revolution built, millions for whom company stores and hacienda stores are gone forever, and there are some factories in the cities. Millions who, if this were nineteen hundred ten, would be peons are now skilled workers, girls who would be cooks and maids are now typists, there are millions who in only thirty years have moved into the middle class, who own cars and use toothpaste and spend five days a year at Tecalutla or Acapulco. Our plants have given those workers jobs, our commerce has given them time-payment plans and savings accounts. For the first time in Mexican history a stable middle class exists, the surest protection against tyranny and unrest. Men and women who do not want to lose their jobs, their installment-plan furniture, their little cars, for anything in the world. Those people are the one concrete result of the Revolution, . . . and we made them. We laid the foundation for Mexican capitalism. Calles laid it. He did away with the generals, built highways and dams, organized banking. What if we did get our percentage from every highway contract? What if the collective farm directors do steal half the appropriations they are given? Would you prefer that in order to avoid these evils, we had done nothing at all? You want us to have the honesty of angels? I repeat, because of what we went through, we are entitled to everything. Because we were born in dirt-floor shacks, we have the right now to live in mansions with high ceilings and stone walls, with a Rolls-Royce at the door. Only we know what a revolution is. A revolution is fought by flesh and blood men, not by saints, and every revolution ends with the creation of a new privileged class. I assure you that if I had not been a man able to take advantage of his breaks, I would still be scratching corn rows in Michoacán, and just as my father was, I would be satisfied. But the fact is that I got my breaks and I am here, and I am more useful to Mexico as a businessman than as a farmer. And if I hadn't, someone else would have seized what I have seized, stand where I stand now, do what I do. We, too, were of the common people, and our homes and gardens and automobiles are, in a way, the people's triumph. Moreover, this is a land that falls asleep quickly and can wake unexpectedly, and who knows what will happen tomorrow? We have to protect ourselves. To get what we have, we had to gamble. None of today's easy politics. You had to have, first of all, balls, in the second place, balls, and in the third place, balls. To do business, you had to wade into politics up to your neck and to change when the wind changed. There were no North American partners to protect against any eventuality. You gambled everything, and every day. And so we grew powerful with the true Mexican power which does not consist of a show of strength. Today no one tyrannizes Mexicans. They don't need to. Mexicans are tyrannized by what they are. And for thirty years there has been no other tyranny. What we have had to do is very different, to kick the country in the ass and keep kicking it, not give in, never let it go back to sleep. Which has produced, far from upheaval and protest, admiration. In Mexico no one is more admired than a perfect son of a bitch, you know."

# 29

# ABELARDO RODRÍGUEZ

———•———

# ON STRIKES*

❧

*As the world depression engulfed Mexico in the early
1930s, the new class running the government found
itself in a most difficult position. The masses demanded their right to strike, which had been compromised by Luis N. Morones and Calles. Abelardo
Rodríguez, who was to replace Pascual Ortiz Rubio
in the presidency in less than two months, was hap-
pily expanding his economic power from Baja California to the national level, utilizing the Ministry of
Industry and Commerce as his new base of operations. In this situation he called on Mexico's workers
not to strike. Realizing that he had to look for fresh
arguments to prevent strikes, he abandoned the argument that Calles had worn out: because union leaders
held government posts, the interests of the working
class were protected without strikes.*

I wish to stress the state of misery that plagues the country.
Daily, I find my desk piled with complaints full of anguish
from unemployed workers, as well as more or less well-
founded explanations from managers who are closing their
mines or businesses because of the impossibility of supporting them as a consequence of overproduction . . . or foreign protective tariffs. If to these calamitous circumstances

---

\* Translated from Abelardo Rodríguez, "Por hoy son indebidas las
huelgas," *El Nacional,* July 7, 1932.

we add the present drought with its bad harvests and deep repercussions on our entire economic system, it is logical to infer that the strikes in communications services are bound to increase our ills considerably, because the distribution of products will be upset, raising the price of transportation sometimes to a prohibitory level. Then . . . the rate of unemployment will increase, because the moment communications are restricted, the small businessman, the industrialist, the farmer, and so on, will paralyze their enterprises and many will remain jobless who at present find in these activities their daily sustenance. At the moment, the most convenient thing to do is to wait for a change in the order of things. . . . and, as Secretary of Industry, Commerce, and Labor, I have the unavoidable duty to supervise not only the situation of the streetcar operators but also that of the miners, day laborers, and so on, that is, of all the workers. The leaders of the Chamber of Labor of the Federal District must understand that we have an immediate necessity to encourage capital investment that multiplies industry, mining, and agriculture, and that can defeat this state of economic stagnation in which we find ourselves today, thus permitting us to reach our sought-after revolutionary ideal: the raising of our collective economic and social level. We will never reach this goal with reticence and distrust toward our authorities, who are an integral part of a government that is the Revolution itself. We need much cooperation and more understanding in order to prevent the depressing absence of capital, which exists in many northern and southern zones and other parts of the country, from extending all over the Republic. If the members of the [Strike] Committee would travel in those places they would change their tactics radically the moment they discovered the misery that reigns there.

.    .    .

I repeat, as a revolutionary and as an official of a progressive government, I believe the strikes to be just, . . . but in view of the painful situation that prevails in the Republic, they do seem to me to be totally inopportune as long as the situation exists. And I want to conclude by declaring that the President as well as his collaborators are deeply concerned in overcoming the economic depression and achieving the greatest good for the country in general, and for the workers in particular, who are the ones who suffer the most and whose betterment is the main objective of the Revolution.

# 30

# VICENTE LOMBARDO TOLEDANO

———•———

# LETTER OF RESIGNATION
# FROM THE CROM*

✿

*Given rising protest against Luis N. Morones' corrupt
Regional Confederation of Mexican Labor (CROM)
and clamor for more radical action to improve the
lot of the worker, it was clear to such an intellectual
as Vicente Lombardo Toledano that the organization had no future. Thus, he severed his connections
as theoretician of the CROM. As a free agent, he was
in a position to found his own labor movement, and
after one abortive attempt, he would be called in 1936
by Lázaro Cárdenas to organize and unify labor into
one central Workers' Confederation of Mexico
(CTM). Lombardo has frequently been accused of
being a Communist, but he has always claimed to be a
non-Communist Marxist, and he has certainly been
embroiled in bitter battles with most Mexican Communists. Lombardo is author of numerous books and
articles, including, among others, ¿Moscú o Pekín?
La vía mexicana hacia el socialismo (México, D. F.:
Partido Popular Socialista, 1963).*

*Compañero* Morones is against the ideology that I have sustained because he thinks it is a radical one and harmful to

---

\* Translated from Leafar Agetro, *Las luchas proletarias de Veracruz*
(Jalapa: Editorial Barricada, 1942), 197–200.

the labor organization. He has stated that the organization cannot maintain an advanced doctrinary program nor establish itself as a permanent censor of the state and its government and, at the same time, call upon the government to solve its problems, as I have been doing constantly. He has stated that the labor organization cannot hope for its salvation as a social class but instead must work for the improvement of living conditions of all social classes, and that one must not dream of utopias like internationalism.

These assertions, among others, were made as a criticism of my speech, and the manner in which they were emphasized suggests, according to my interpretations . . . that my presence in the CROM is a hindrance to Compañero Morones in his present dealings with the government, which consist of, in his own words, offering anew his cooperation to the government.

·  ·  ·

My experience of twelve years of struggle, my constant studies, and the scientific discipline with which I entered the CROM have led me to the increasingly firm and clear-cut conviction that only knowledge and its commentary and diffusion, as the action program of the proletariat, can provide this class with a sense of social strength and its historical responsibility. Therefore, the CROM must be the permanent judge of the state, of the government, and of its people . . .

I am an enemy of the bourgeois regime and often I am against the government, yet I have friends among government officials, and I make appointments with all of them to ask for strict observance of the law and for the protection of the working class . . .

I will thus continue being a radical Marxist, even though not a Communist, by my own convictions, offspring of my own studies and my own observations of the social panorama of the world. I will continue being an internationalist and shall fight against a chauvinistic nationalism and in sum will continue fighting for the advent of a better life, having liquidated first the current bourgeois system.

I ask you to accept my resignation as Secretary of Education of the Central Committee, a post that I have had for eight years. At the same time I am addressing myself to the Council of the Federation of Unions of the Federal District Union, submitting my resignation to the post of Secretary General of its Executive Committee.

# 31

# EYLER N. SIMPSON

———•———

# CALLES' AGRARIAN
# IDEOLOGY*

❁

*Influenced by Ambassador Morrow and a trip to Europe in 1929, Calles had called for a speedy halt to further land reform in December 1929 and thus caused a crisis in revolutionary ideology. If a major pillar of the Revolution was land reform, then an important prop of the government was removed at a time in which the Callistas could little afford discredit, especially after they had abandoned revolutionary goals in the field of labor. According to Eyler N. Simpson, Calles thought that Mexico was "destroying the large estates and splitting up the land in a lot of little ejido parcels," thus heading "for the same difficulties in which France found herself with her overdivision of the land and her little peasant proprietors unable to take advantage of modern machine methods of agricultural exploitation."*

*By May 1933 the debate over Calles' policies threatened to become unmanageable and the Supreme Chief of the Revolution decided that if his government was to remain in the vanguard of leadership it would have to develop a Six-Year Plan, including*

* Eyler N. Simpson, *The* Ejido, *Mexico's Way Out* (Chapel Hill: University of North Carolina Press, 1937), 441–443. Reprinted by permission of the publisher.

*an agrarian program, to cover the new six-year presidential term beginning in 1934. Calles said:*

It is my opinion that the hour has come to formulate a detailed program of action for the period covered by the next six-year presidential term; a program that must be based on reason, statistics, and the lessons of experience. . . . Thus, for example, in the case of the agrarian problem we must tackle at once the question of the dotation [grant] of *ejidos;* the program of distributing ejido lands to villages must be carefully planned within the law . . . with the aim of achieving its complete realization during the next six years. The breaking up of the large estates will take care of itself. The Government has only to provide the facilities. Since the landlords cannot reestablish the exploitation of the peon—for, if not in its entirety, surely 80 per cent of this [peonage system] will disappear—they will not be able to revive the old methods of agriculture. In irrigation . . . the Federal Government must plan the works which it will be able to construct . . . the States also . . . must make their plans for the building of small irrigation projects. . . . The Ministry of National Economy should set forth, in its turn, plans for the progressive development of national production and exploitation, the establishing of cooperatives, etc. Thus, with each department of the Government cooperating . . . a minimum program of action [will be formulated] scaled to the six-year period and based on concrete facts and our ample experience.

*Eyler N. Simpson was in Mexico during the early 1930s, and his account of agrarian reform ranks with George M. McBride's* The Land Systems of Mexico *(New York: American Geographical Society, 1923) and Nathan Whetten's* Rural Mexico *(Chicago: University of Chicago Press, 1948), classic accounts of different periods of land reform in the Revolution.*

If one may presume on the basis of . . . declarations to summarize in somewhat more informal style what was going on in the mind of the leader . . . of the revolutionary group, one would probably come out with some such statement as this:

Balancing the books after almost eighteen years of experiment and experience, it seems to be pretty clear that the agrarian reform has failed in practically every respect to achieve the results hoped for. This has been due partly to the lack of leadership and capable administration, and partly to the failure to develop any coherent plan of action. In particular the ejido program has not worked out very well: the amount of land distributed per family has been too small to allow the *ejidatarios* to take advantage of modern methods in agriculture; and the process of giving land to villages has been dragged out for too long a period with the result that confidence has been undermined and the feeling of security necessary for stable production lost.

There are several facts about the ejido that might as well be faced: the giving of land to villages is not the only and, in the long run, not the best way of redistributing the agricultural resources of the nation; the ejido conceived as a system of collective or communal landholding cannot be regarded as a desirable system of land tenure or as a suitable basis for the organization of agricultural production; in a word, the ejido is only one aspect of the agrarian reform and a transitory aspect at that.

If, then, production is to be increased, if prosperity is to be restored and if the country's agriculture is to be constituted along modern lines, the following steps should be taken: In the first place, the distribution of ejidos must be finished as soon as possible. All the villages that have a right to receive lands under the law as it now stands must be given land (for, of course, the "solemn promises of the Revolution" should be respected!), but as quickly as may be these village lands must be divided into individually held parcels and the ejidatarios started on the road to becoming independent small farmers. In the second place, emphasis in the agrarian reform must be placed at once on forcing a redistribution of land by limiting the amount that any one individual may own and requiring the excess to be divided up and sold on easy terms. This will not only help the ejidatario to graduate into the *ranchero* class, but will immediately create a large body of small property owners out of the peasants who have not benefited under the ejido program. Once this has been accomplished then all classes must be guaranteed in their rights: big landlords and small landowners alike. Finally, a coordinated plan must be worked out for accomplishing the redistribution of land and achieving the fundamental desideratum of creating a large group of middle class independent farmers and for organizing and improving the whole system of agricultural production through irrigation projects, good roads, banks, and cooperatives.

# 32

GRACIANO SÁNCHEZ

———•———

# THE AGRARIAN REFORM
# MUST CONTINUE*

❋

*At the December 1933 convention in Querétaro, which met to approve Calles' Six-Year Plan, the delegates took control and rewrote the agrarian plank of that document in radical terms. Thus, Calles was dismayed by the results of his convention in Querétaro, much as Venustiano Carranza had been disappointed by the meeting he had called there in 1916 and 1917 to draft a new constitution. Rarely has a chief of the Revolution been overruled at a convention, and it is a strange coincidence that the two major occurrences of this sort took place in Querétaro.*

*Graciano Sánchez spoke for the agrarian wing of the official party in demanding changes in the Six-Year Plan, which could bring success to the program of land distribution. Land reform had enjoyed little success, maintained the long-time agrarian leader, not because it was improperly conceived but because it had been improperly carried out. His catalog of errors won the day and set the stage for Cárdenas' rapid distribution of land. The final act of the convention was to nominate Cárdenas as the official*

---

* Translated from *Memoria de la Segunda Convención Nacional Ordinaria del Partido Nacional Revolucionario efectuado en la Ciudad de Querétaro del 3 al 6 de diciembre de 1933* (México, D. F.: n.p., 1934), 104–113.

*party's candidate for the 1934 to 1940 presiden-*
*tial term.*

The established proceedings in agrarian law have been so complex and defective that we see cases [like the following]: The inhabitants of a village send an application [to acquire land]. The government of the state, aware of those peasants' needs, then provisionally gives them land. The document goes to the agrarian delegation and from there to the National Agrarian Commission. After three years of red tape the National Agrarian Commission decides that the applicants do not fulfill the residence requirement because when provisional possession was granted the peasants had only five months and a half in residence, for example, and the law requires six months (applause). And we ask: Where has this requirement come from? What revolutionary need makes it imperative? Did those who sacrificed their lives for the redemption of the peasants believe that only those born and raised in one place had any right to the land? That attitude is entirely opposed to the spirit of sacrifice of the Mexican revolutionists.

There is another condition: land can only be given to applying peasants when it be available within seven kilometers. And we ask ourselves: "What if there is not any land available within seven kilometers? Are the citizens of this area doomed to live forever naked and in misery?" (applause). We could point out similar situations that show the need to abolish all those unnecessary requirements from the Regulatory Law of Article 27 of the Constitution, which may have been created with good intentions, but which have gravely harmed the peasants.

We have documents with authenticated signatures and all the requirements of irrefutable evidence to prove that there are peasants who are not able to cultivate their lands because they derive no security from their *ejido;* because their plot of land is only one-half or one hectare, and thus they prefer to return to their old condition of peons or wage earners in the nearby haciendas to earn a living; because one hectare of land can barely be of any use, even for teaching school children how to cultivate land.

. . .

Those of us who know the living conditions of the peasantry, because we have dedicated ourselves to attend to their problems, make a very clear and precise classification of those who work the land. The *arrendatario,* who has means to rent a plot of land from the *hacendado,* . . . does so in a dignified manner, because he does not have to submit to any insult or harm from the latifundist. The *aparcero,* who obtains a plot of land from the latifundist, almost invariably has his own tools to cultivate the plot; therefore, he, also, establishes a dignified relationship with the owner. The *jornalero,* the temporary day laborer who does not live in the hacienda, . . . at least owns his own hut and has some dignity left. . . . But the *peón acasillado,* who lives within the wall built to defend the interests of the latifundist, is a slave to his material and moral misery, and is the one forever oppressed, forever insulted. It is necessary for those among us who live in the city to know that the injustice that has made a victim of the peon has not yet disappeared; the peon is abused today, as he has always been throughout the centuries (prolonged applause).

. . . In the old days the peon was handcuffed, he was placed on a stock or hung from the handspike in the sugar mills, he was beaten or tied to the stake in the plantation's corral, facing the sun for as long as the owner of the hacienda pleased. Today the hacendados' tactics . . . consist of corrupting the officials in charge of applying the land reform laws (prolonged applause).

. . .

We must also keep in mind that when the hacendados cannot prevent the application of the law, they resort to an easy way out by dividing their *latifundios* among their wives and children, among their relatives, and sometimes even among false relatives who hardly have a shirt to wear, but who also appear as buyers of these latifundios . . . (applause).

These proceedings, in many occasions, have resulted in many communities waiting as much as six or seven years without achieving a definitive solution for their [agrarian] problem. Can we say frankly that one of the most dear ideals of the Revolution . . . is being carried out? Or are the peasants expected to continue living their miserable lives, being food for the exploiter's greed, whether he be foreigner or not?

# 33

# ARNULFO PÉREZ H.

———◆———

## "GOD DOES NOT EXIST"*

❧

*The Querétaro Convention of 1933 also took up the matter of education, for many delegates felt that the Church remained powerful because the state's educational program was neutral. Arnulfo Pérez H. demanded that the state actively foster "scientific truth" in order to combat the Church's "dogma and superstition." This point of view was one that sparked the amendment of Article 3 of the Constitution of 1917 and created socialist education in 1934.*

*Arnulfo Pérez H., self-styled "Personal Enemy of God," was a rabid anticlerical who represented Tomás Garrido Canabal's state of Tabasco. As Governor of Tabasco and absolute boss of that state after 1922, Garrido closed all the churches during the* Cristero *War and decreed that priests must be married. Religious images were forbidden and large piles of images and books were frequently burned with festive rejoicing by Garrido's red-shirted squads. Even the word* adiós *was suppressed. Such activities prompted Graham Greene to visit the state and write his famous novel,* The Power and the Glory *(1940).*

---

* Translated from *Memoria de la Segunda Convención Nacional Ordinaria del Partido Nacional Revolucionario* . . . (México, D. F.: n.p., 1934), 138–145.

*John W. F. Dulles has summed up Garrido's reign as follows:*

At an exhibition of livestock a fine bull on exhibit would be called "God," a donkey named "Christ," a cow named "The Virgin of Guadalupe," an ox named "The Pope," a hog named "The Archbishop," etc. Such animals often came from "La Florida," experimental stables belonging to the dictator.

Among the children of the dictator was a son named Lenin and a daughter named Zoila Libertad (I am liberty), a name which at one time provoked the saying that the only liberty existing in Tabasco was the daughter of Garrido. Garrido was sometimes accompanied by a nephew named Luzbel (Lucifer).[1]

*Although most delegates to the Querétaro Convention were anticlerical, they did not follow Pérez in his attempt to destroy religion.*

But when we see that the peasant and proletarian masses of Mexico are still under the yoke of religious dogma, when we see vampires in cassocks and miter who continue to be but a scourge to the people, . . . [we see that] to be a revolutionary means . . . to shape minds and build will power to destroy the yoke of superstition and prejudice, to tear down idols, to demolish altars, and to save the child and the worker from the claws of the clergy and from the tentacles of religion.

.    .    .

This is precisely what is being done in Tabasco: idols are being torn down, altars demolished, and temples transformed into schools. The word of the teacher has triumphed over the deceitfulness of the priest in order to form a collective conscience, which attributes its good luck to its own efforts and does not have any other religion but work, nor any God but its own will.

The masses who suffered the tortures of the stock and

1 John W. F. Dulles, *Yesterday in Mexico, A Chronicle of the Revolution, 1919–1936* (Austin: University of Texas Press, 1961), 620. Reprinted by permission of the publisher.

the pains of the whip, those angered masses, who expected everything from divine help, are now tired of believing, tired of imploring, and, instead of raising their hands toward heaven to beg for crumbs of bread, they raise their creative hands, which sow the seeds of liberation; and instead of humbling prayers that implore the Almighty for goodness and mercy, they raise protesting voices . . . which rhyme to sing the virile chant of progress.

It is for this iconoclastic work, for this crusade . . . that the conservative reactionaries insult the government of Tabasco. That is why the reactionary . . . newspaper, *La Prensa,* attacks Tomás Garrido Canabal, destroyer of vices and dogmas; because these reactionaries, incapable of combating us in the fields of battle or in the intellectual plane, can only fight us from the pulpit, from *cantinas,* and from clerical newspaper editorials.

. . .

I declare that there are heroic revolutionaries who bear the scars of battle on their chest, who feel the pain of the underdog and dream of a society where fraternity and justice may reign; but many of them do not dare to break the lying ideology of religion because of a deep respect they have for maternal sentiment.

Close to that picture, another one emerges: a son going to a private school where the clergy is represented by fanatic teachers; there he memorizes the reader of "Saint Michael" and Ripalda's catechism; there he is taught to venerate fetishes; there the virus of religious doctrine is injected into him and instead of making a man out of him, he is made into a slave and a eunuch. When the child goes to secular schools, then the teachers—whether backward or revolutionary—remain neutral and let the clergy snatch away from them the immense treasure, which is a child's mind.

And I ask, gentlemen: Is it fair to let the future generations go astray in the name of tradition or respect for maternal sentiment? If childhood is the foundation of new civilizations, if the future greatness of Mexico lies in its children, let us sacrifice home in defense of childhood and in defense of the revolutionary ideal (applause) and let us modify Article 3 of the Constitution so that the Revolution, turned into a Rationalist School, may be able to combat the clergy, religion, and—let us say it frankly—in order to combat "God!" Yes, gentlemen, the Revolution has the imperative duty of combating that false divinity that is venerated in every temple and that has many altars in the hearts of the people. We must fight this outdated and absurd belief, inspired only by the fear and ignorance of humanity. We must fight "God," the maximum myth from which the greatest lies have been derived to exploit humanity and keep it on its knees throughout the centuries. "God" does not exist. Therefore, we must combat the absurd belief of the masses and we must destroy that belief in the name of truth and love. Once a thinker said: "It was not God who made humanity; it is humanity who invented God" (applause).

Where is that God who has allowed so much injustice and crime? Where is that God who is not moved in the face of the working masses, who has allowed fetters, chains, and yokes to be used on the destitute masses? Where is that God who allows the treasure chests of the leaders to be filled, and permits the clergy to wear diamond crowns, and overlooks the peasant dressed in rags without even a bread crumb to take home?

# 34

JAMES W. WILKIE

———•———

# SEXUAL EDUCATION AND SOCIALIST EDUCATION IN MEXICO—THE EARLY 1930s[*]

❦

*Two educational issues were explosive to Mexican Catholics in the early 1930s. The government's program of sexual education was the forerunner of socialist education and both types of instruction were a threat to tradition. Sexual education was really a misunderstood term, and socialist education was perhaps the only radical action that Calles could still support by 1934. Narciso Bassols introduced the first program in 1933. Calles himself called for radical implementation of the second in 1934, perhaps as much to embroil President-elect Cárdenas in a problem that would prevent his hasty action in implementing radical campaign promises as much as to start a new Church-state battle. Calles' action highlighted the new Article 3 of the Constitution which, by amendment on October 10, 1933, read:*

The education imparted by the State shall be a socialistic one and, in addition to excluding all religious doctrine, shall combat fanaticism and prejudices by organiz-

———————

[*] James W. Wilkie, "Ideological Conflict in the Time of Lázaro Cárdenas" (unpublished M.A. thesis in history, University of California, Berkeley, 1959), 45–59. Reprinted by permission of the author.

ing its instruction and activities in a way that shall permit the creation in youth of an exact and rational concept of the Universe and of social life.

*Such thinking today seems naïve but to some Mexican educators it simply meant authorization to teach such courses as sexual education. To most in the government, however, it gave an opportunity to implant Marxism or to fight the Church. Certainly the new language of Article 3 represented a shift in Mexican thought from the passive to the active state, which would begin to direct national life rather than simply to provide channels for development.*

Narciso Bassols took over the Ministry of Public Education in 1932 for President Rodríguez. He set about reforming the educational system in his two and a half years in office and emphasized the economic aspect of rural education. He met resistance on several sides. The education bureaucracy fought reorganization. The Catholics fought his sexual education program. The Cristero revolt of 1926 had hinged in part on Calles' secularization of primary education. Bassols realized that the Constitution did not specify the type of secondary education to prevail and that it was openly in the hands of the Church. In December 1932 Rodríguez remedied this situation with a presidential decree. The clerical reaction was immediate. The Archbishop of Mexico, Pascual Díaz, ordered all parents to refuse to send their children to the lay secondary schools and threatened excommunication of teachers. He imposed an obligation on them to choose Catholic schools for their children, and if that were impossible, to lay their case before the hierarchy. The weapon that the Catholic hierarchy finally used to force Bassols' resignation, however, was the much publicized sexual education, which they misrepresented to the faithful.

Bassols had followed the suggestion of the Sixth Pan-American Child Welfare Congress held in Lima, Peru, in 1930, which noted that all governments of the Americas should provide physiology and hygiene courses in the school curriculum. In 1933 the Mexican Eugenic Society presented to the Bassols' ministry a list of suggestions by leading physicians of Mexico. Bassols published this list in May to solicit opinions on its recommendations. The suggestions pointed out that some kind of sexual education was necessary because year after year adolescent girls died as a result of criminal abortions or else were burdened for life with unwanted children and venereal disease. And those girls were not only from poor families but often products of "good" middle class homes whose parents had kept them in ignorance. The course adopted for the schools was a direct translation of a standard physiology text in the United States, but Bassols was bitterly attacked. Public demonstration calling for Bassols' resignation was the result of wild gossip against "sex in schools." Tales were told of men teachers seducing their students, practical classroom experiments in sex, and nude models in front of the class. The names of teachers were added to the stories to lend some authenticity to the hysteria. Typical of the fervor against sex education was the following article by one Josefina Santos Coy de Gómez, which appeared in the Catholic paper *La Palabra*:

> I turn to you—mothers of Mexico—and first of all to the wife of the first ruler of our nation . . . You, Señora, whom the public voice has acclaimed a model of mothers . . . will you watch, without indignation, while your little children are being initiated into the mysteries and vulgarities of sex? Well, then, if you are good, raise your protest, together with ours, against those who want to pervert our children's souls.
>
> It fills me with panic even to imagine the grade of perversion to which future humanity will sink after it has been prepared, shamelessly, by such an education; it is terrifying to think that a ten-year-old child will be made to understand the sexual instinct.
>
> In the name of human dignity, we must oppose this abominable project of education. . . . When my little daughter María Teresa turns upon me her limpid eyes which reflect the whiteness of her soul, I feel

the desire to adore her as one adores an angel . . .
and render homage to her innocence . . . and when
I think of the monstrosities that sexual education will
create in children, I think of my ten-year-old daughter and say to myself, it would cause me less pain to
see her lying dead than see her innocence brutally
shattered!

Our grandparents were educated in blessed ignorance of all sexual problems. . . . The highly immoral science which our government is trying to impose upon the country will only create perverts and
candidates for the insane asylum.

Bassols tried to appease the Catholic populace by changing the name of his educational program from "sexual" to
"social," which might indicate that he was either imprudent
or deliberately trying to cause trouble by labeling his program sexual education in the first place, but he was forced
to resign in May 1934. As he withdrew, Bassols pointed out
that sex education was only the whipping boy. The real
issue was socialism in education and clerical agitation for
nullification of the newly proposed reform of Article 3 of
the Constitution.

.　　　.　　　.

[With the Constitution amended to provide for socialist
education,] Calles spoke to the people of Guadalajara on
July 20, 1934:

But the Revolution has not yet ended. The eternal
enemies lie in ambush and are laying plans to nullify
the triumphs of the Revolution. It is necessary that we
enter a new period of the Revolution. I would call this
new period the psychological period of the Revolution. We must now enter and take possession of the
consciences of the young, because they do belong and
should belong to the Revolution.

.　　　.　　　.

It would be a very grave stupidity, it would be a
crime for the men of the Revolution to fail to rescue
the young from the claws of the clericals, from the
claws of the conservatives; and, unfortunately, in

many states of the Republic and even in the capital
of the Republic itself the school is under the direction of clerical and reactionary elements.

We cannot entrust to the hands of our enemies the
future of the country and the future of the Revolution. With every artfulness the reactionaries and the
clericals are saying that the children belong to the
home and the youth to the family. This is selfish
doctrine, because the children and youth belong to
the community; they belong to the collectivity, and it
is the Revolution that has the inescapable duty to
take possession of consciences to drive out prejudices
and to form the new soul of the nation.

Therefore, I call upon all governors throughout the
Republic, on all public authorities, and on all revolutionary elements that we proceed at once to the field
of battle which we must take because children and the
young must belong to the Revolution.

This *"grito de Guadalajara"* in the stronghold and center
of Catholic resistance during the Cristero revolt of the 1920s
. . . had other reasons than that of burdening Cárdenas
with an unsolvable problem to occupy his time. Calles'
speech rode the rising wave of socialist action. Calles knew
he had to lead to keep control of Cárdenas. The anti-
church attack might not only serve to forestall the proletarian Revolution, but to unify the party and gain control of
its alienated factions by utilizing the only deep conviction
common to all revolutionary elements.

# I V
# The Cárdenas Era

*Mexican capitalism is indebted to two men: Calles and Cárdenas. Calles laid the foundation. Cárdenas brought it to life by creating the possibility of a large internal market. He raised wages, gave labor every conceivable guarantee, protected workers so there was nothing for them to agitate about; he established once and for all the policy of Federal investment in public works; he broadened credit, broke up landholdings and on all levels tried to stimulate a vast circulation of stagnant wealth. Those were permanent accomplishments, still living. If Cárdenas hadn't given the labor movement an official character, administrations since would not have been able to work peacefully and increase national production. And above all, Cárdenas ended Mexican feudalism. Mexico might become anything, but never again a kingdom of great absentee landlord estates ruled by a perfectly useless agrarian plutocracy. Plutocracy we may have, but thanks to* this *plutocracy, markets are created and jobs are provided and Mexico moves ahead. The*

*Mexican Revolution has been wise; it understood early that to be effective, the time of militancy had to be brief, private fortunes had to be large. Not one important decision has been left to chance; all that has been done has been done after meditation. Each time the right man has become president. Can you imagine this poor country in the hands of a Vasconcelos or an Almazán or a General Henríquez? It would, to be blunt, be flushed down the drain by the rhetoric.*

---

*"Múgica was a man with a one-track mind, and that was the mind of a revolutionary, a destructor; he was not a man with any capacity to rule, administer, plan, or organize. This, on one hand. And on the other, it seems to me that people have not realized that there are two predominant elements in Cárdenas' government. First, the launching of agrarian reform, understanding it simply as carrying out distribution of lands to the limit; and from this point of view, one can say that Cárdenas' revolutionary activity is purely negative or destructive. Second, people forget that it was Cárdenas who initiated the policy of industrial development in the nation, and this policy required an attitude which was conservative and constructive, and not revolutionary, demagogic, Marxist, or destructive.*

*"Maybe it would be convenient to find out . . . if Cárdenas did not attribute more importance to industrial development than to agrarian reform, understanding the latter as destruction of the great properties. Or,*

*it is very possible that Cárdenas believed that since he had already destroyed the great properties, . . . the nation could then dedicate itself to carry out something constructive such as industrial development."*

---

Translated from Daniel Cosío Villegas; James W. Wilkie and Edna Monzón de Wilkie, *Oral History Interviews with Daniel Cosío Villegas*, Mexico City, January 26, 1965.

# CHRONOLOGY OF
# THE CÁRDENAS ERA

———————•———————

1935  Cárdenas encourages Mexico's proletariat to organize and to strike for improved conditions; land distribution is carried out on an extensive scale; Calles opposes such "excesses" as threats to governmental stability.

1936  The Mexican Confederation of Labor (CTM) is founded to back Cárdenas against Calles and the CROM; Cárdenas expels Calles from Mexico; cotton land in La Laguna is expropriated.

1937  Catholic laymen organize the *Sinarquista* movement against the Mexican Revolution; nationalization of major railroads takes place and expropriation of henequen plantations of Yucatán is undertaken; strikes begin in the oil fields.

1938  Cárdenas expropriates the foreign-owned oil companies and puts down Saturnino Cedillo's rebellion; The PNR is reorganized as a Mexican popular front and becomes the Party of the Mexican Revolution (PRM).

1939  The National Action Party (PAN) is founded to oppose the PRM.

1940  Manuel Avila Camacho wins presidential election and carries nation into a new era.

# 35

# JOHN W. F. DULLES

———•———

# STRIKES UNDER CÁRDENAS*

❧

*Despite the Church-state struggle over socialist educa-
tion, President Lázaro Cárdenas was not deterred
from encouraging radical action to undertake the proletarian phase of the Revolution. Unlike Franklin D.
Roosevelt, Cárdenas' attempt to "pack the Supreme
Court" in Mexico had no trouble, and he could proceed with his plans to forge a new society. In 1934
Cárdenas had the term of office of justices of the Supreme Court changed from life-tenure to a six-year
period coinciding with the presidential term, thus
bringing an entirely new court into office under his direct political control. Supreme Court Justice Xavier
Icaza reflected Cárdenas' views that socialist education
was closely related to the proletarian struggle in
which the masses would be educated so as to learn
how to fight for their rights, and he stated Cárdenas'
philosophy of the role of the state and the courts
when he said in* El nuevo derecho obrero de México
(*1936*):

The interpretation of labor law in favor of the worker
is a technical matter. Labor law is essentially protectionist
as it tries to balance the lack of equality between manage-

---

* John W. F. Dulles, *Yesterday in Mexico, A Chronicle of the Revolution, 1919–1936* (Austin: University of Texas Press, 1961), 629–
631 and 637–638. Reprinted by permission of the publisher.

ment and labor. It puts the weight of the state in favor of the latter in order to prevent abuse by the capitalist, owner and deforciant of the means of production.

*This definition of the capitalist as a "deforciant" re-vealed that the new government viewed the worker as deprived of his rights in Marxist terms.*

*As John W. F. Dulles shows, Calles did not like the strikes that threatened Mexico's economic de-velopment. Son of the late John Foster Dulles, the author of this selection lived in Mexico for many years where he was representative of several mining firms.*

What the workers started late in December 1934, against the El Aguila Petroleum Company turned into a series of strikes and demands. The El Aguila strike which took place on January 7 touched off other strikes, such as that of the Veracruz electricians, who cut off the port's electricity; when it was settled El Aguila's workers thanked their com-panions. But on February 4 the workers started another strike against El Aguila, and at the same time demanded payments from both the Huasteca and El Aguila oil com-panies in compensation for conditions in the past. For ex-ample, El Aguila was asked to pay half a million pesos for overtime from the years 1906 to 1933. Meanwhile gasoline became scarce.

In February the city of Puebla found itself subject to a general strike. On February 12 the taxi drivers of Mexico City went on a strike, which was settled favorably for them. Many of the chauffeurs appear to have been striking soon again and dividing themselves into two conflicting groups. Some of them, annoyed at the president of a conciliation and arbitration board, threatened him, and in addition de-stroyed the furniture in the board's office.

· · ·

The railroad workers, who went on strike on March 7, were backed by the Mexico City streetcar workers in a strike of their own. On March 21 President Cárdenas agreed to act as arbiter in the case of the railroad strike, which was finally ended when it was three weeks old.

. . .

The Mexico City streetcar strike continued after the end of the railroad strike. The company said that it was losing 26,000 pesos daily, and not only rejected the workers' demands but refused to talk about paying salaries lost during the strike. However, with the end of the streetcar strike on May 6, the company was ordered to pay over half a million pesos in salaries lost during the strike; the company's property was attached to assure this payment.

In April 1935, a general strike in Puebla, this time throughout the state, was occasioned by one labor group's opposing another. The Tampico electricians backed up the Huasteca Petroleum Company workers by paralyzing most of Tampico's activity. Then in turn the Tampico strikers were supported by strikes by the power plant workers of Celaya, Uruapan, León, Mérida, San Luis Potosí, and elsewhere, including parts of Jalisco. Conversations between the sugar workers and the sugar company owners broke off abruptly when representatives of the latter group became offended at remarks by the workers.

It was June 1935. There were strikes by the telephone company employees, the bus drivers, the employees of the movie houses, and the workers at the paper factory, San Rafael y Progreso Industrial. The phone strike was brought to an end after several weeks, and the government stepped in to terminate the paper strike. As paper had become scarce and costly, the government, later in the year, invested half a million pesos in a new company which was to import paper and regulate its price.

According to the official statistics, those who proclaimed the occurrence of 1,200 strikes were exaggerating. It can be easily seen, however, that the effects of the Federal Labor Law and of the attitude of the Cárdenas administration were considerable:

|      | *Number of strikes* | *Strikers involved* |                          |
| ---- | ------------------- | ------------------- | ------------------------ |
| 1929 | 14                  | 3,473               |                          |
| 1930 | 15                  | 3,718               |                          |
| 1931 | 11                  | 227                 |                          |
| 1932 | 56                  | 3,574               | (not a complete recording) |
| 1933 | 13                  | 1,084               | (not a complete recording) |
| 1934 | 202                 | 14,685              |                          |
| 1935 | 642                 | 145,212             |                          |

[With strikes increasing rapidly, Calles released a statement to the press on June 12, 1935, implicitly challenging Cárdenas to end the labor turmoil or face the same consequences as Ortiz Rubio had faced in 1932—forced resignation from the presidency. Calles said:]

What is happening now is exactly what happened during the period of President Ortiz Rubio. One group called itself *Ortizrubista* and another *Callista*. At that time, as soon as I found out what was going on, I tried, personally and through my friends, to stop it; but the perverse elements were stronger and carried on to the end, with what results you know. At this very moment this same personalistic movement is being carried on frankly and openly in the Chamber of Deputies and I could tell you the names of those who are promoting it. All those men who are trying to divide us are engaged in perfidious work. The recent history of our politics has taught us, with plenty of examples, that personalistic divisions lead only to final disaster. Therefore in the legislative chambers, the unjustified categories of Cardenistas and Callistas should be suppressed. When the division into groups based on persons begins, first the deputies, then the senators, governors, cabinet ministers, and, finally, the Army, take sides.

·　　·　　·

For six months the nation has been shaken by constant strikes, many of them entirely unjustified, the labor organizations in many cases showing themselves to be ungrateful for what they have already received.

These strikes hurt capital much less than they hurt the government, because they close the sources of prosperity. Thus the good intentions and untiring work of the President are constantly obstructed, and far from taking advantage of the present moments, so favorable for Mexico, we are going backward, always retrogressing; it is unfair for the workers to cause this harm to a government headed by an honest citizen and a sincere friend of the workers like General Cárdenas. They have no right to create difficulties for him and obstruct his progress. I know the history of all the organizations, from their birth; I know their leaders, the old leaders and the new leaders. I know that they are not in agreement among themselves . . . I know what they are capable of, and I can affirm that in these agitations there are vigilant appetites, very dangerous to unprepared people and organizations. They are provoking, and playing with, the economic life of the nation, without respect for the generosity and frankly pro-labor position of the President . . . In a nation where the government protects them, helps them, and surrounds them with guarantees, to disturb the march of economic construction is not only ingratitude, but is treason. These organizations represent no force but themselves. I know them. In the hour of crisis, of danger, you will not see a one of them coming to the rescue, and it is we, the soldiers of the Revolution, who have to defend the cause. And we cannot stand tranquilly by while they, in order to defend bastard interests, are compromising Mexico's opportunities. They don't even know enough to select cases that are appropriate for their strikes. They declare a strike on the Streetcar Company which is in bankruptcy, which is losing money.

# 36

# NATHANIEL AND SYLVIA WEYL

———•———

# RISE OF THE CONFEDERATION OF MEXICAN WORKERS (CTM)*

❧

*In the emerging struggle between Plutarco Elías Calles and Cárdenas, the President did not resign as expected, but mobilized to defend his position. Cárdenas' main source of strength was the organization of a unified labor central led by Vicente Lombardo Toledano. With this new militant power concentrated in the Federal District, the Army was no longer free to dictate the outcome of such a crisis, and Calles was forced into voluntary exile on July 20, 1935.*

*The Weyls visited Mexico in the late 1930s to report on the development of Cárdenas' program. According to his later admission, Nathaniel Weyl was a Communist when he wrote his book on Mexico. Subsequently, he was employed as an economist with the United States Federal Reserve System and held posts in the Board of Economic Warfare and Department of Commerce during World War II. In 1960 he wrote* Red Star Over Cuba (*New York: Devin-Adair, 1961*) *to denounce Fidel Castro as a Communist.*

---

* Nathaniel and Sylvia Weyl, *The Reconquest of Mexico; The Years of Lázaro Cárdenas* (New York: Oxford University Press, 1939), 235–238. Reprinted by permission of the authors.

By 1934, the Mexican trade-union movement had become a chaos of bickering factions. While the people hungered, politicians promised the New Jerusalem and used the evanescent labor federations they created as the building blocks of power. The Regional Confederation of Mexican Labor (CROM) had originally organized the working class of Mexico. Acquiring unqualified government support during the Calles presidency, the CROM leadership became corrupt and control was vested in the self-appointed "action group" of Luis Morones' friends. After its fall from official favor, the CROM lost its power, but retained its vices. "Self-defense against the Red menace" became the battle standard of a narrow and embittered factionalism. The lavish entertainments given by Morones, the leader's diamonds and his far-flung property holdings contributed to working class disillusionment with trade unionism. If the CROM had stolen while it organized, some of its successors merely stole. Anarchist moods and the distrust of any and every leadership gained strength in the minds of Mexico's workers.

This heritage of autocracy and internecine warfare was to be swept aside by Vicente Lombardo Toledano, probably the outstanding revolutionary theorist of Mexico. The son of a ruined Puebla copper magnate, Lombardo went to the National University to drink the weak tea of Bergsonian idealism and absorb Carlyle's philosophy of heroes and history. At twenty-three, he entered the field of labor education, becoming Secretary of the Mexican People's University. Three years later, while government secretary of the Mexico City district, he risked sudden death by cleaning up prostitution, then controlled and exploited by the lawless "generals of the Revolution." At twenty-eight, he became Director of the National Preparatory School, but his decision to espouse the cause of labor cut short his academic career.

Lombardo Toledano brought a rare scholarship and an unusual breadth of historic perspective to the tasks of labor leadership. Author of the standard book on the Mexican labor movement, he has also written on ethics, metaphysics, education, geography, the Mexican agrarian question, and dialectical materialism. He is a cold, analytic orator, who destroys his antagonists with the arrows of irony. He has the honor of being the most heartily hated man in Mexico. He is detested by the professional politicians because he has principles, and loathed by the pedants of the National University because he has placed his knowledge at the service of the disinherited.

Lombardo Toledano was schooled in the CROM's ruthless tactics of trade-union organization, but in 1933 he withdrew from the parent body to form his own labor federation. This schism was not government engineered, and Lombardo and his associates were at first skeptical of Cárdenas' promises and were prone to analyze the Mexican situation in terms of a cycle of revolutions that would eventually sweep labor into power. Inflexible in their theoretical views, they tended to draw historic parallels between Cárdenas and Kerensky. In a floor debate at a labor convention in December 1934, Lombardo Toledano declared:

> It is not a question of incorporating workers' representatives into the state, but of recognizing the power of the working class organized against the state . . . The root of the controversy is that the comrades who oppose the motion uphold the anarchist ideology and believe that all power, merely because it is power, corrupts. I believe the opposite, for I believe that we must arrive at the dictatorship of the proletariat.

But the point of view of Lombardo Toledano and the labor movement he led was to change. By his actions, Cárdenas convinced labor of his revolutionary integrity, while the rise of fascism in Europe compelled a revaluation of labor strategy and tactics on an international scale.

The 1935 revolt of Calles and the foreign business groups which looked to him for leadership against the advance of organized labor precipitated unification of the working class movement. When Calles threw down the gauntlet to the Cárdenas regime, a Committee for Proletarian Defense was formed on the initiative of the powerful Mexico City Electricians Union. The declared object of the committee was to defend the civil liberties of the people, with general strike, if necessary, and to thwart "the efforts of the representatives of the bourgeoisie to . . . inaugurate a period of repression of the revolutionary demonstrations of the worker and peasant masses of the nation." A pact of solidarity was signed which left each constituent body autonomous, but obliged all to cooperate in the battle against reemerging reactionary forces.

The Confederation of Mexican Workers (CTM) was the permanent organizational expression of the unity achieved in the struggle against Calles . . . and other reactionary forces. The new labor federation was multiform in structure. Its basic units were the big industrial unions in the railroads, the mines, the power houses, the oil fields, the printing shops, and the sugar fields. The conservative wing comprised the Mexico City and Puebla regional federations of shop unions, bureaucratically run, and led by men whose financial standards were not always above suspicion. The third group was a welter of small factory and craft unions which were gradually welded into state labor federations. The CTM also included large groups of agricultural workers and *ejidatarios,* small artisans, self-employed professionals, intellectual workers, and the powerful teachers' union.

# 37

ALBERT L. MICHAELS

———————•———————

# THE CÁRDENAS-CALLES
# BREAK*

❊

*In view of the conflict over land policy in the early
1930s, it was surprising that the labor issue was to
decide Mexico's future under Cárdenas, for the President was first and foremost an exponent of land reform. Because of the wave of strikes that shook Mexico after Cárdenas' assumption of office, however,
labor problems initiated a political crisis.*

*Although many writers have interpreted the Cár-
denas-Calles break in purely personalistic terms, it is
clear that the two men stood for different national
policies and represented very different ideological out-
looks. This selection seeks to explore the reasons for
the end to the long Cárdenas-Calles friendship by examining the background of these ideological differences.*

Lázaro Cárdenas and Plutarco Elías Calles had much in
common. They had fought side by side in the Revolution
and in the civil war against Pancho Villa. As Calles rose to
power, Cárdenas faithfully backed him against all opposi-

* Albert L. Michaels, "Mexican Politics and Nationalism from
Calles to Cárdenas" (unpublished Ph.D. thesis in history, University
of Pennsylvania, Philadelphia, 1966), revised, 74–77. Reprinted by
permission of the author.

tion. As a reward for this loyalty, Calles oversaw Cárdenas' appointment to several important national posts in the late 1920s and the early 1930s. The two men were good friends, yet it was inevitable that they part as enemies.

In 1934 Lázaro Cárdenas was young and vigorous and he wanted to govern in fact as well as name. Furthermore, he and his supporters wanted power for themselves. They knew Calles would have to go before they could have real power. As Frank Tannenbaum has noted: "Traditionally speaking, the President of Mexico must be able to do everything or he will be unable to do anything he wants."

By 1933 Mexico was tired of *Callismo*. The Catholics had been placed in a tight position and were desperate. The *campesinos* feared they would never own the land that had been promised them. The workers were chafing under the dictatorship of Morones and his moratorium on strikes. The younger politicians wanted the positions of authority so long held by Calles' friends. Furthermore, Calles' ideas were out of date; his capitalism and individualism, which were a heritage from the prevalent liberalism of the nineteenth century, had been temporarily discredited all over the world. Even across the northern frontier President Roosevelt was experimenting with social reform. It was only natural for the Mexican to want a "New Deal" of his own. In the Six-Year Plan Calles attempted to meet the demands of the new generation, but this effort came too late. The radicals no longer trusted him; a vacuum had been created that sooner or later would have to be filled.

General Cárdenas came from the poor, overpopulated state of Michoacán. He grew up in a region with a tradition of Indian collectivism and a centuries-old struggle of the poor for a right to live. This background made him particularly open to Marxist theories based on collectivism and the struggle of poor against rich. He had gone into the country and had seen that the poor needed immediate help. It was, therefore, not surprising that he expressed a popular nationalism based on class warfare with immediate benefits to the oppressed classes. General Calles came from the richer, sparsely populated state of Sonora with its tradition of mining and small ranching. In Sonora, the enemy had been the man across the border in the United States rather than a countryman of a different class. The Northerner was proud of his white blood and skeptical of the Indian's ability to become the equal of the Spanish-descended white. Cárdenas, on the other hand, loved the Indian and named his son Cuauhtémoc after the Aztec hero. As Cárdenas readily accepted collectivism and class warfare, Calles opted for a nationalism of individualism and class harmony. He believed in a measured economic development benefiting all classes equally. He thought that by giving free rein to the man of ambition and initiative, individuals could develop the economy as the Spaniard had developed the North. Once economic development was underway, the rewards would trickle down to all classes. Both of these ideas of collectivism and individualism were enshrined in the Constitution of 1917. Calles extracted the latter ideal and attempted to mold Mexico in its image; Cárdenas extracted the former and tried to build a collectivistic Mexico. Both men had the same aim, the development of Mexico for the Mexicans, but they were trying to use different ideological tools to achieve this object. Calles and Cárdenas represented different nationalisms; they were bound to clash, and it was this clash, as much as political rivalry, that led to the split of June 1935, followed by Calles' self-exile.

When Calles returned to Mexico after six months in order to reestablish his position, he found himself in difficulties which finally resulted in his deportation by the Cárdenas government on April 10, 1936.

# 38

# REV. JOSEPH LEDIT, S. J.

———•———

# SINARQUISMO VICTORY
# IN TABASCO*

❧

*Although Cárdenas controlled the political sphere after Calles' expulsion in 1936, he faced mounting opposition from Catholics. Beginning in 1937 lay Catholics again began to organize after the disastrous* Cristero *War. Rejecting the violence of the Cristeros, they turned to nonviolent protest to redress their grievances. Led by Salvador Abascal, chief of a movement called the "Base," the defense of the Church won victories during early 1937 in Veracruz and Tabasco. This success led to the foundation of the National* Sinarquista *Union on May 23, 1937.* Sinarquismo *was postulated as the antithesis of "anarchism" and thus called for a Mexico "without anarchy" or a country "with order."*

*The Sinarquista impact on Mexico was important in that it capitalized to a large extent on discontent in rural areas among peasants who had not received land or who had lost their land. Because Sinarquismo was organized on principles related to Franco's movement in Spain, the Mexican left realized with first-hand experience that a Popular Front would be nec-*

———————————

* Rev. Joseph Ledit, S.J., *Rise of the Downtrodden*, translated by the author and Anthony Santacruz (New York: Society of St. Paul, 1959), 106–109. Reprinted by permission of the author.

*essary in order to combat the threat of fascism in Mexico, as in Europe.*

*In this selection from* Le front des pauvres *(1954), Rev. Joseph Ledit, S.J., who first visited Mexico in 1943, describes Abascal's program in organizing Tabasco, the stronghold of anticlericalism.*

Then it was that Salvador Abascal came to Tabasco in the name of the "Base," to organize the religious liberation. He had a precedent to guide himself by. In February 1937, at Orizaba (Veracruz), when people were assisting in a private house at a Mass which was illegal, the soldiers broke in and killed a young girl by the name of Teresa. The entire population of the city rose and took possession of the churches that had been closed until that time. Abascal brought from his city of Morelia, Michoacán, two schoolteachers. These girls opened a rural school at a distance of some sixty kilometers (or forty miles) from Villahermosa. At the cost of very much hardship, and almost continually at the peril of his life, Abascal visited the ranches where he found not a few faithful Catholics. He organized reunions of parents at the rural school. Finally, he prepared the march on Tabasco, which was to take place on the night of May 11, 1938, the 12th of each month being consecrated to Our Lady of Guadalupe. He insisted that all come completely disarmed. At Tabasco more than elsewhere, this was heroic. Then, for the first time, the technique of pacific massive protest was put into practice. Meanwhile, the "Base" organized throughout Mexico a campaign of support. The press was mobilized and telegrams were prepared to flood at the proper moment the presidential palace.

The mobilization was made at the sound of native drums, which resounded in eerie fashion in the tropical jungle! Many farmers, who had come from a very great distance, had walked the entire day under a torrid sun, on country roads. At eleven o'clock at night a first group of 400 persons left Tamulté for Villahermosa, but when they entered the city, about midnight, they found close to a thousand companions who had come from another direction, and who had managed to elude the vigilance of the military placed to watch over the wading points of the river. Altogether, shouting *Viva Cristo Rey,* they declared their readiness to die rather than to abandon the struggle. The growing crowd finally stopped at the *Zócalo,* the pretty square in the center of the city, in front of the Governor's palace. They acclaimed Christ the King, listened to the fiery Abascal, and waited for the Vice Governor to appear because the Governor was away. When the Vice Governor failed to show himself, Abascal proclaimed that if he abandoned his post they did not need him any more. Then all went to what had been the Church of the Immaculate Conception, cleared the rubbish and camped there. Two young women, who had brought a Mexican flag with a picture of Our Lady of Guadalupe in the center, put it where the altar had once been, and began reciting the rosary. During the rest of the night, all sang hymns.

About six o'clock in the morning, someone brought along carpenters who started building a little temporary chapel. The crowd aimed at taking possession of the church, illegally stolen from the people and destroyed. Then, having learned that another thousand farmers were stopped by the police, Abascal got together a group of comrades and went to liberate them. In moments like that, he was irresistible. All returned together to the Immaculate Conception. About ten in the morning, there were some ten thousand people there. They sent telegrams to President Cárdenas and to the newspapers, and Mexico City supported the action at Tabasco unanimously. A group of ladies from Tabasco residing in Mexico City immediately asked for an audience of President Cárdenas. The organization and coordination were perfect.

By May 13 the Governor had returned as fast as he could. He sent orders to disperse to the crowd and distributed a manifesto making the same request. The Secretary of the Interior sent from Mexico City orders for the same purpose, but the crowd at Tabasco decided, as an answer, to make a silent procession through the streets of Tabasco at five o'clock in the afternoon. This time, fifteen thousand people paraded. It was the answer of the people to the politicians!

On May 14, 1938, at seven o'clock in the morning, the first Mass was celebrated at Tabasco after the long years of persecution. Since the church was not yet rebuilt, the ceremony took place under the hot, tropical sky. The soldiers who were on guard took off their caps during the Mass, and gave at the collection which was for the reconstruction of the church. They were not bad fellows! Immediately after Mass, small groups brought along bricks, cement, bamboo poles, and the walls started to go up. Everybody worked so merrily and rapidly that somebody observed that angels had come down from heaven to help the builders. Abascal wanted the authorities to behold some concrete facts. Materials were brought on men's backs, so as to cut down expenses; and small groups went to get them so as to avoid incidents with the soldiers.

On the following day, Sunday, there were two Masses with sermons, just as in the most regular parishes. In the afternoon, five young ladies began to teach catechism to the children. Then, the rosary was recited as the practice is throughout Mexico on Sunday afternoon after the catechism. Since it was the month of May, four hundred little girls, all dressed in white, came to "offer flowers" to Our Lady. All this had been improvised. It had been decided that religious life would unfold normally, as if nothing whatsoever had ever happened, through the will of the people. Meanwhile, the threats of the government were ceaselessly repeated, but the answer was always the same: "We will go away when full and entire religious liberty is guaranteed."

On May 30, at ten o'clock in the morning, the Governor surrounded the church with soldiers. Four thousand Catholics were within, and they had brought together enough to eat to face the siege! In the evening, at 5:30, orders were given, and the soldiers fired on the unarmed multitude. Many fired in the air. Still, there were three dead, three grievously wounded, and three with minor wounds. The bullets whistled over the heads of the crowd and Abascal, like a solemn archangel, faced the bullets. Nobody answered the fire, and the soldiers realized that they were murderers. They stopped firing! Father Hidalgo came at once in surplice and stole to assist the wounded and the dying. A few hours later, it was heard that a group of armed peasants were coming from Tamulté to avenge their comrades. Abascal sent word that they were to leave their arms, and come completely disarmed. They obeyed at once. Discipline was perfect.

All Mexico thrilled at the formidable news that the bulwark of Godless revolution had crumbled under the impact of a weaponless multitude. Then the President, General Lázaro Cárdenas, realized that the Galilean had conquered once more.

# 39

NATHANIEL AND SYLVIA WEYL

———————•———————

# MEXICO'S POPULAR FRONT—THE PARTY OF THE MEXICAN REVOLUTION (PRM)*

❧

*Organization of the Party of the Mexican Revolution (PRM) in 1938 overlapped with events leading to the expropriation of the oil industry by Cárdenas. The President knew that if his programs were to be successful, he would have to mobilize mass support going much beyond his base of power in the CTM. With a threat from the* Sinarquista *movement at hand and confrontation with the foreign owners of Mexico's oil leading to a crisis in late 1937, Cárdenas called for the rejuvenation of the country's official party.*

*To some observers, reorganization of the official party along sector lines then fashionable in Italy suggested that Cárdenas was influenced by fascism; others saw this development as a consequence of the Popular Front movement championed by Mexican Communists. Although the Weyls believed that the new PRM could not be characterized as a fascist importation to Mexico because Mussolini had borrowed*

---

* Nathaniel and Sylvia Weyl, *The Reconquest of Mexico; The Years of Lázaro Cárdenas* (New York: Oxford University Press, 1939), 344–349. Reprinted by permission of the authors.

the corporative theory of functional representation from guild socialism and the anarcho-syndicalist theories of Georges Sorel, it seems that Cárdenas was looking to Mussolini's successful organization of political life and not to idealized theories. Cárdenas was a man of his epoch, and the times were influenced by Marxist and fascist thought. Ironically, he was not adverse to borrowing from Mussolini in order to structure a Mexican Popular Front-oriented official party capable of combating Mexico's Fascists.

Cárdenas was intent upon devising a scheme in which competing power groups would hold each other in check within the official party while giving the President of Mexico final decision-making authority on national policy. The CTM, under Lombardo Toledano, prevented the military from arbitrarily interfering in politics but itself threatened to challenge the power of the Chief Executive. In fact, Cárdenas had to move decisively to prevent Lombardo from organizing peasant branches of the CTM. On June 27, 1935, Cárdenas had called for the organization of one unified peasant confederation, but he was forced to warn the CTM in 1936 that urban and rural labor were so different that it was necessary that the government organize the peasants in order to conduct agrarian reform properly. The CTM did not give up hope of controlling the peasants until the National Confederation of Peasants was formally constituted on August 29, 1938.

Oil expropriation came on March 18, 1938, and the Party of the Mexican Revolution was formed March 30, 1938. Cárdenas' control of the political situation was assured by the new PRM, and expropriation of the oil gave the masses a banner to follow with pride.

Although Mexico's masses were to gain a position in the official party, Cárdenas also arranged for the economic elite to be heard from outside the party when he organized chambers of commerce and industry with obligatory membership. Contrary to some views, Cárdenas did not seek political democracy, he sought social democracy through political discipline.

*In sum, Cárdenas used moderately authoritarian means in order to develop better social conditions for Mexico's masses. The development of the PRM, however, meant that the masses could no longer be ignored politically. Although presidents might manipulate party sectors, they would have to fulfill the PRM's promises to the people or face revolt in party ranks.*

*The authors of this selection were introduced in Selection 36.*

It was not until almost two years after his inauguration as President that Cárdenas attempted to transform the party machine into a vehicle which would express the people's will. The President faced the urgent task of consolidating left-wing power. He needed a disciplined battle organization, not a laboratory for democratic experimentation.

.  .  .

The Spanish civil war had just begun and the Blum government was in power in France. Enthusiasm for the new popular-front tactics swept the labor movement of Mexico. At its foundation congress, the CTM had pledged itself to work for the establishment of a Mexican People's Front in close cooperation with the Communist Party. Although in some regions the people's front alliances were supported by the dominant labor organizations, the revolutionary youth groups, and the United Front for the Rights of Women, they were often merely shadow organizations.

Hardly had the new executive committee of the PNR [taken office] when it issued an historic manifesto to the workers of Mexico. "The new democracy to which the National Revolutionary Party aspires," it declared, "is one in which organized laborers and peasants shall exert a growing influence . . ." All Mexican workers and peasants automatically became members of the PNR with the right to vote in its primaries, provided they were organized and that their organizations were revolutionary. The party pledged itself to treat all labor and peasant groups impartially and announced that it "would favor a policy on the part of the proletarian groups of entering into agreements among themselves, rather than creating political rifts during elections." The metamorphosis of the Calles machine into the Cárdenas functional party had already begun.

The Mexican people responded enthusiastically to this invitation. The component organizations of the popular front poured their members into the ranks of the PNR, gradually supplanting the old bureaucracy. After profound soul searching, the CTM urged its members to vote exclusively for PNR candidates in the July 1937 elections. Workers' blocs, responsible to the CTM which had elected them, emerged in the new state legislatures and the national Congress.

Close advisers of Cárdenas were impressed with the example of France and favored a broad coalition of the mass organizations of the nation in a Mexican people's front. Lombardo Toledano proposed a popular-front alliance between the CTM, the government peasant confederation, the Communist Party, and the National Revolutionary Party.

Cárdenas was sympathetic to the plan. In an interview with the American author, Joseph Freeman, he expressed the hope that his successor would be elected by a Mexican people's front. The new European strategy coincided with the President's determination to unite the nation behind a single revolutionary leadership. The plan, however, collapsed because the National Revolutionary Party high command stood adamant for the exclusion of the Communist Party.

Instead of coalescing existing organizations, the President decided to broaden the National Revolutionary Party from an organ of workers' and peasants' democracy into one that included every force supporting his revolutionary program. In March 1938, the PNR was transformed into the Party of the Mexican Revolution (PRM). Four autonomous sections—Labor, Peasant, Popular, and Army— were fused into a single political entity.

A more auspicious time could not have been chosen for the launching of the new organization. The expropriation of the oil industry a few weeks previously had united the people in support of Cárdenas and his defiance of foreign imperialism. National unity had to be maintained if the Republic was to be piloted through the crisis.

The Government had recognized that the Army must be brought into politics openly to obviate the constant illegal intervention of the military and its perilous strategy of conspiracy, *putsch,* and insurrection. It was hoped that the PRM could transform the military machine into a civilized political instrument. Through its participation in the political life of the nation, the Army might be taught the social and economic aspects of the Mexican Revolution.

Another reason for the change was that effective transformation of the PNR had been impeded by its source of funds. The organization was supported by a check-off on the salaries of government employees, whereas the workers and peasants contributed nothing. State governors held the purse strings of the regional organizations. The shifting of the economic control of the party obviously could not be accomplished without broadening the membership of the organization.

At the foundation congress of the PRM, the four sectors agreed to participate in electoral politics solely through the medium of the Party of the Mexican Revolution. The labor and peasant organizations retained autonomy in their social and economic activities and agreed not to solicit membership outside the classes they represented. The Popular Sector, which had not yet been created, was to retain the same organizational independence. The military were to function as citizens within the PRM, not as official representatives of the Army, and the general and soldier were awarded equal political rights.

The declaration of principles and the program of action adopted by the PRM declared that its most fundamental task was "the preparation of the people for the establishment of a workers' democracy as a step toward socialism." While advocating cooperation with the democratic powers in the destruction of fascism, the party reaffirmed the anti-imperialist position of the Mexican Revolution. The congress pledged the party to collaborate with the Cárdenas government and support a legislative program to better the economic conditions of the social groups it represented.

Membership in the PRM is confined to those members of its constituent bodies who are Mexican citizens with full legal rights. Dealers in alcohol and drugs, members of religious cults, and members of organizations that oppose the party's principles are excluded.

Thus the Party of the Mexican Revolution is not an organization of the elite, such as the Communist Party of the Soviet Union, the Italian Fascist Party, and the German NSDAP. It is essentially a coalition of existing organizations, and its power to discipline and expel individual members is only effective as a means of forcing professional politicians to toe the line and of maintaining unity within its parliamentary fraction. The PRM, moreover, lacks a coherent body of doctrine that could serve as the articles of faith of its membership. The bulk of its members are within the party because of a decision taken by the leadership of their organizations. Hence they feel little responsibility toward it and cannot always be persuaded to carry out its mandates. Its only cohesive force is the prestige of Cárdenas and the willingness of the Mexican people to fight for the preservation of the harvest of the Revolution.

The PRM is a functional organization which marshals its members in terms of their economic relationship to society. The basis of representation is not residence, but class and occupation. All voting in the party primaries takes place within the four sectors. In the central offices of the party on the Paseo de la Reforma, there is almost continuous horse trading among the sector leaders for control of elective offices. Once this delicate task has been accomplished, each sector elects the candidates assigned to it. If the party assigns a public office to one of the sectors, the other three are excluded from voting in the primaries. Regardless of which group names its candidate, the entire membership of the party is obligated to support him in the constitutional elections.

Within each sector, the members vote in the customary meeting places of their organizations. A representative from the National Executive Committee of the PRM supervises all party primaries, receives complaints concerning fraudulent practice, and watches the tallying of votes. In the case of the military section, the Ministry of National Defense submits a slate of precandidates that the soldiers vote on in their barracks. The party statutes provide that the military vote with the Popular Sector, but the Army authorities apparently prefer to segregate the soldiery from the civilian populace.

The primary elections to choose a candidate for the presidency of Mexico are to follow a different procedure. The local organizations of each sector will vote for the various presidential aspirants. Each national sector will then cast its one vote for its plurality candidate. In the unlikely event of deadlock between the four sectors, the matter will presumably be thrown in the lap of the party convention.

# 40

# WILLIAM CAMERON TOWNSEND

•

# CÁRDENAS EXPROPRIATES THE FOREIGN-OWNED OIL INDUSTRY*

❧

*Cárdenas' expropriation of the oil industry on March 18, 1938, came as a great shock to observers who did not understand that the President was attempting to bring economic, as well as political and social problems under executive control. Frank Kluckholn of* The New York Times, *for example, had written that Cárdenas was more interested in agrarian policy than oil problems and that Mexico was dependent on oil-production taxes. He believed that these factors would prevent expropriation. In addition, it appeared that Mexico's lack of technicians, together with an inability to compete in the monopolized world oil market, would make expropriation virtually impossible. This analysis overlooked the fact that the oil companies in effect refused to accept Cárdenas' program when they rejected the Supreme Court's award handed down in favor of increased benefits for striking workers. Although the United States government contemplated suspension of silver*

---

* William Cameron Townsend, *Lázaro Cárdenas, Mexican Democrat* (Ann Arbor, Mich.: George Wahr, 1952), 256–259. Reprinted by permission of the author.

*purchases to bring about a reversal of expropriation,
the silver lobby in Washington, D.C., realized that
Cárdenas might also nationalize American mines.
Thus, silver purchases were restored within a short
time. The oil companies complained to the world that
they had been "legally robbed," but without help
from the United States government they already had
lost any hope of regaining their properties.*

*In this selection, William Cameron Townsend re-
counts the expropriation and analyzes its meaning.
Townsend has been one of Cárdenas' closest foreign
friends since 1935, and he was greatly helped by Cárdenas in his project to teach Indians to read in their
native language. As a nonsectarian missionary from
the United States, Townsend has spent most of his
adult life helping Indian tribes of Latin America.*

The companies expected the government to place their
properties in a receivership which would have given them
time to work. The government, hampered by the economic
problems that the companies could have created had they
been permitted to keep their fingers in the pie, would have
found it impossible to have run the business successfully.
The companies were in a better position to withstand a long
drawn-out struggle than Mexico was. They thought, too,
that by prolonging the conflict they would be able to profit
from divided opinion among the Mexicans themselves and
would be able to build up anti-Mexican opinion in the
United States.

President Cárdenas, however, realized that every moment
of delay made the companies more powerful in their position and placed the government more at their mercy. He
determined to take from them their power to cripple the
nation from within. Without serving notice to anyone, not
even to solicitous Ambassador Daniels who might have
been able to bring the companies to their senses had he
been able to warn them how serious their situation had become, he went before the microphone on March 18, 1938,
and announced his decree of expropriation against the seventeen oil companies. Speaking to the nation, he said:

A total halt or even a limited production of petroleum would cause in a short time a crisis which would endanger not only our progress but also the peace of the nation. Banks and commerce would be paralyzed, public works of general interest would find their completion impossible, and the very existence of the government would be gravely imperiled because when the state loses its economic power it loses also its political power, producing chaos.

It is evident that the problem which the oil companies have placed before the executive power of the nation by their refusal to obey the decree of the highest judicial tribunal is not the simple one of executing the judgment of a court, but rather it is an acute situation which drastically demands a solution. The social interests of the laboring classes of all the industries of the country demand it. It is to the public interest of Mexicans and even of those aliens who live in the Republic and who need peace first and afterward petroleum with which to continue their productive activities. It is the sovereignty of the nation which is thwarted through the maneuvers of foreign capitalists who, forgetting that they have formed themselves into Mexican companies, now attempt to elude the mandates and avoid the obligations placed upon them by the authorities of this country.

The attitude of the oil companies is premeditated and their decision has been too deliberately thought out to permit the government to resort to any means less final, or adopt a stand less severe [than expropriation] . . . I call upon the whole nation to furnish such moral and physical support as may be needed to face the consequences that may result from a decision which we would neither have wished nor sought had it depended on ourselves alone.

The people did respond with their full support. The President's bold stroke appealed to their patriotism and they became united as I have never seen them before or since. A great manifestation of confidence and support took place in the capital five days later, and it was my privilege to observe from a point of vantage that spontaneous mobilization of feeling on the part of the Mexican people.

The notes I made right on the spot will describe it:

> I sit writing in a large room on the second floor of the National Palace which forms one side of the *Plaza de la Constitución* (*El Zócalo*). Here at crucial times throughout many centuries events of utmost importance in the history of Mexico have taken place. On a balcony nearby stands President Lázaro Cárdenas accompanied by members of his cabinet and scores of other officials watching the greatest popular demonstration which has taken place in this land during recent years.
>
> The broad plaza, flanked on our right by the anciently solemn but stately cathedral, and on the left by the more modern Municipal Palace, is thronged with thousands of people, while thousands more march by beneath the President's balcony in a steady stream which will continue for hours and then flow on out into history as Mexico's second Declaration of Independence.
>
> Just above where President Cárdenas stands waving a frequent recognition to the acclaims of the laborers and students as they march before him, there hangs the very bell which Hidalgo the priest rang one hundred and twenty-eight years ago in the far-off town of Dolores, announcing the intention of a handful of patriots to fight for the political independence of Mexico from Spain.
>
> Last Friday, March 18, President Cárdenas figuratively rang the bell for economic independence by declaring that his government would not bow before the oil interests, principally British and Dutch, in their defiance of the Supreme Court which had found the demands of their employees for better wages and working conditions to be just. The impasse which resulted when the companies balked left the President no other alternative than to take over most of the oil industry.
>
> Consternation has resulted in financial circles. The foreign colony here in Mexico City is decidedly parti-

san to the oil interests, fearing that what has been done will serve as a precedent for the confiscation of their own investments. Some declare their intention of selling out while they can and returning to their respective countries, though others say that they are making such large profits they will remain as long as they can buy more trinkets and can go more places with the same number of dollars.

President Cárdenas, in an effort to calm industry in its very reasonable fear of further confiscation, published a statement yesterday calling the attention of the public to the emergency conditions under which the expropriation law was resorted to in the case of the oil industry, and promising that it will not be applied to other enterprises. On the contrary, he promised that they will be given every encouragement possible.

The Bank of Mexico has had to redeem ten million *pesos'* worth of its bills with silver coin during the past few days, but the run seems to be over and plans have been formulated to mint fifty million more silver pesos so that there will be ample coin in circulation if the lack of confidence in bank bills should continue.

I stop writing long enough to step out onto a balcony and watch the Communist section march by. It consists of just a handful of demonstrators sandwiched in the multitude. They carry a large red banner which reads, "The Communist Party of Mexico," and a white and red one which says something about "On with the International Revolution." It is noteworthy today that the red and black emblems, which had almost supplanted the Mexican flag in parades here a few years ago, are less in evidence, while the national colors of green, white, and red are seen everywhere.

Labor unions, peasant leagues, and syndicates of schoolteachers and other federal employees have called a halt, temporarily at least, in their almost incessant petitioning for rights. The majority of the people have forgotten for the moment to complain against the rising cost of living, injustices, and this, that, and everything, in order to join in the nation-wide rally to the support of their daring leader.

Perhaps the Mexican Revolution has passed into a new phase as regards the psychological basis of its program. For a number of years past it has endeavored to teach the masses, long trained to subserviency, to rebel against all imposition and to demand their rights at every step. Very little was said about duty. The pendulum swung so far in that direction, especially during the first two years of the administration of General Cárdenas, who democratically insists that the only citizenry which can be properly and enduringly developed is one which is free and realizes that it is free, that at times chaos threatened not only laborers but also in the ranks of the school-teachers and other government employees. Many observers wondered how a sense of duty would ever be instilled into them. The emergency of today, however, may perform the necessary miracle.

Two hundred thousand people are parading, carrying banners which express their approbation in terms such as these: "Down with imperialism," "The laborers desire the economic independence of Mexico," "General Cárdenas, you are the only one who has had the courage to defend our rights," and "President Cárdenas, we are with you in the enthusiasm of today and we will be with you in the struggle of tomorrow" (the economic struggle which will be necessary for Mexico to pay for the expropriated property).

The President, of course, must realize that he has bitten off a chunk which will require all his exceptional energy and that of his colleagues to chew to a point of semidigestion during the remaining three years of his administration. Everyone knows the government has been spending every *centavo* it could lay its hands on to promote development projects among the peasants where returns will be very slow to materialize. They know that for three months it has been hard put to meet its minimum obligations, due largely, it claims, to deliberate efforts on the part of the oil companies to embarrass it financially. How, then, can it hope to pay the large sum required to reimburse the companies even over the ten-year period which the expropriation law permits and at the same time meet the demands of the laborers?

Perhaps the rebirth of patriotism which is in evidence today will prove to be the solution of the situation. Not only the laborers, but the thinking citizenry in general realize that the honor of the nation is now at stake, and a do-or-die attitude seems to have been aroused. Both labor unions and government employees have declared in printed statements a willingness to tighten up their belts ten notches if necessary and sacrifice until Mexico has met the obligation with which she has saddled herself.

A united and duty-conscious Mexico *can* refund the oil companies. The industry which has been 90 percent foreign-controlled, something which we would never permit in the United States, will then be placed at the service of the nation. The living conditions of the laborers will be improved, and further exploitation will be directed by the consideration of national expediency rather than by the whims of foreign interests.

# 41

# E. DAVID CRONON

———•———

# OIL COMPANY REACTION*

❧

*The campaign launched by American oil companies to vilify Cárdenas' action soon reached scandalous proportions. Speeding up their own presses and "subsidizing" national magazines in the United States, American companies portrayed themselves as robbed by bandits who were masquerading as government leaders, in spite of the fact that Cárdenas promised full settlement of claims. Some companies were not so much worried about money but about the precedent that Cárdenas had set for other nations where American oil interests were in operation. With regard to money, Standard Oil of New Jersey claimed its holdings in Mexico to be worth over $400,000,000. In 1941, however, the New Jersey company accepted the award of a joint Mexican-American expert commission that, using "standard American valuation based upon prudent investment theory," appraised their holdings at $18,391,641, including interest from the date of expropriation. Thus, Jersey Standard's original bargaining figure was reduced by about 95 percent. E. David Cronon quotes American appraisers who noted:*

———————————

* E. David Cronon, *Josephus Daniels in Mexico* (Madison: University of Wisconsin Press, 1960), 208–211 and 269. Reprinted with permission of the copyright owners, the Regents of the University of Wisconsin.

We were pretty embarrassed at times. We insisted that Standard Oil had invested $400 million in their properties, only to have the Mexicans bring out the books of the oil company which plainly showed that they had put in much, much less.

*Attempts to prevent sale of Mexico's oil by the American and European companies affected in the expropriation virtually forced Cárdenas to export to the Axis powers during the period from 1938 to 1939. Cárdenas was loath to deal with fascist countries as he was the champion of Republican Spain in its battle against Franco. Repeatedly he stated that Mexico would prefer to sell to the democracies, but by the end of 1938, for example, Germany accounted for about one-third of Mexico's oil exports. Because the outbreak of war in Europe was imminent, and there was much fear in the United States concerning fascist infiltration and the rise of* Sinarquismo *in Mexico, the boycott of Mexican oil ordered by American oil companies may be considered as an unfortunate drama on the eve of World War II.*

*E. David Cronon is professor of history at the University of Wisconsin.*

Vain or not, the oil companies were doing everything possible to make President Cárdenas' position untenable. Immediately after the expropriation they launched a boycott of Mexican oil based upon their control of most of the world's tanker fleet and their obvious capacity to retaliate against independent tanker operators. By legal action they sought to tie up Mexican oil shipments abroad. They also persuaded a number of American manufacturers to refuse Mexico's prepaid cash orders for equipment needed to operate the oil industry. By 1940 this boycott was even being applied to American export firms suspected of supplying Mexico. When Westinghouse closed down its Mexican branch in 1939, [Ambassador] Daniels reported that the local company representative believed the move was the result of pressure by Rockefeller and power interests.

The companies' boycott of Mexican oil was helped by

quiet support from the State Department. In 1939, for example, Secretary Hull blocked the purchase of Mexican fuel oil by American ships on a naval cruise, explaining in a policy directive: "This department as a policy matter of considerable importance would not consider it desirable for any branch of the United States government to purchase Mexican petroleum products at the present time." The State Department continued this ban on government purchases of Mexican oil until early 1942, some months after the general diplomatic settlement with Mexico. Moreover, it encouraged Latin American governments to take a similar stand against Mexican oil. Even when they were low bidders, American suppliers who offered Mexican oil were unable to get U.S. government contracts. When one such firm protested, it was told by the State Department's legal adviser that Mexico must not thus "reap the fruits of this wrongful act." The Sinclair interests discovered to their surprise and great unhappiness that acceptance of a settlement with Mexico in 1940 did not necessarily remove the taint from their oil. Jersey Standard quickly objected when Sinclair underbid it on a large Navy contract in the fall of 1940, and received State Department help in getting the Sinclair bid rejected. The Department also frowned on private operations in Mexican oil. An official advised the T.A.D. Jones Company of New Haven, when it sought approval of a profitable import deal, that it was "fishing in troubled waters." It seemed hardly a coincidence, too, that the representative year used by the department to set import quotas for foreign oil was 1939, when because of the boycott Mexican imports were at a minimum.

The oil interests also went to considerable pains to mobilize American public opinion. Jersey Standard's company magazine, *The Lamp,* began portraying Mexico as a strifetorn land of revolutionaries and brigands. Through their service stations, the companies warned American tourists against undertaking a trip into Mexico. Motorists were advised that there was danger of an uprising, their personal property might be in jeopardy, travel by car was unpleasant and hazardous, and even the Mexican railroads were unsafe. Wide publicity was given to the claim that Mexican gasoline was dangerously inferior. Its octane rating was alleged to be only 48, barely adequate to operate an automobile engine at minimum power.

Standard Oil of New Jersey made a special effort to publicize the companies' side of the dispute, sending a public relations expert to make the rounds of leading newspapers and magazines. At least one reporter, Seward R. Sheldon of the *Cleveland Press,* was offered an all-expense trip to Mexico if he would write a series of articles to "put the people right." Sheldon declined the invitation, but others went to Mexico to write highly partisan reports. For example, newspaper publisher Henry J. Allen, a former Republican governor of Kansas, toured Mexico briefly in the summer of 1938, and returned with a series of articles charging that Cárdenas was a dedicated Communist who was determined to establish a Soviet Mexico. One news service refused to handle the Allen articles as too obviously propaganda, but they were ultimately syndicated by the New York *Herald Tribune,* excerpted in the *Reader's Digest,* and sent out in pamphlet form by the Committee on Mexican Relations, an obscure group financed by Jersey Standard. After having thus qualified as an expert on Mexican affairs, Allen traveled about the United States demanding that the administration abandon the Good Neighbor Policy and force Mexico to return the oil properties.

Perhaps the most ambitious attempt to promote the cause of the oil interests came in July 1938, when the *Atlantic Monthly* published a special issue entitled "Trouble below the Border." Like the Allen articles, this was a thoroughly procompany analysis of the controversy, designed to persuade its readers that Mexico was sliding into dangerous chaos as a result of radical leadership. Daniels called it "rotten oil propaganda," a view that was reinforced after he learned . . . that the issue had been paid for by the companies. When the *Nation* exposed the source of the oil used to lubricate the *Atlantic*'s presses for this particular run, the magazine's embarrassed publisher could only retort lamely, "Well, we have our racket and you have yours." *Collier's* published a highly partisan article repeating company claims that Mexico's oil industry was rapidly breaking down under incompetent government direction, and charging that to Mexicans the term expropriate was "a polite, international word for 'steal.' " But when Mexico submitted an article in reply, *Collier's* refused to print it.

Writers who tried to be more objective in their reporting sometimes found it difficult to get their material into print, at least without significant editing. Anita Brenner, well qualified by years of residence in Mexico, did a balanced and informative article for *Fortune,* but after Daniels compared her original draft with the published version he predicted, "she will not recognize her own baby." Himself a journalist for more than half a century, Daniels winced at such threats to the integrity of his profession. . . . In view of the companies' careful efforts to mold public opinion, it was hardly surprising that a detailed survey of American publications in 1939—paid for by Standard Oil of New Jersey—showed that the press was overwhelmingly on the side of the oil interests in their dispute with Mexico.

# 42

VIRGINIA PREWETT

———————•———————

# PROBLEMS OF THE
# CÁRDENAS GOVERNMENT*

❧

*Cárdenas' expropriation of the oil industry appeared to unite Mexico, and for several glorious months the President rode a wide crest of national acclaim. But, influenced by the harsh reality of problems provoked by agrarian reform, the unity behind oil policy soon gave way to fear that Mexico had gone too far on too many fronts. Also, the approach of a presidential election in 1940 meant the drawing of political lines. Although Cárdenas abandoned his struggle with the Church over socialist education in order to push his land and oil programs, as well as to create national harmony necessary for development of the new PRM, his political position deteriorated rapidly.*

*Cárdenas was widely accused of being a Communist or of turning his government over to Communists because of the state's role in expropriating and distributing land long before the oil issue arose. His creation of thousands of new* ejidatarios *made enemies of persons who believed that a homestead law would have been more realistic. Because the ejidatario does not own his land, and the village may reapportion it, some observers have felt that he lacks the incentive*

———————————————

* From the book, *Reportage on Mexico,* by Virginia Prewett. Copyright, 1941, by Virginia Prewett. Reprinted by permission of E.P. Dutton & Co., Inc., 142–147 and 151–152.

*to invest time and money or take production risks. To overcome problems of production generated by distribution of land among many small ejidos, Cárdenas experimented in La Laguna, for example, with "collective ejidos." By expropriating and distributing three-fourths of the irrigable land in La Laguna on October 6, 1936, the President settled a general strike of peasants against landowners in the region, an area of 1,500,000 hectares in southwestern Coahuila and northeastern Durango. This area was devoted to market production of cotton and wheat instead of subsistence agriculture; it was turned over to some 38,000 heads of families organized into about 300 ejidos. These ejido members worked the land collectively instead of cultivating individual plots as in the case of regular ejidos. Because management of all ejidos was elective, economic expediency was often sacrificed to political decisions, particularly in the new collective ejidos.*

*In this selection, Virginia Prewett, a newspaper reporter with firsthand experience in Mexico, describes problems facing the Cárdenas government after the oil expropriation. Special attention is given to the subject of land reform.*

At the time when the controversy between the oil companies and labor was reaching its climax and it was becoming increasingly evident to those on the inside that Cárdenas and [Lombardo] Toledano were sweeping on toward expropriation, there arose in the minds of some of the men around Cárdenas a doubt as to the wisdom of undertaking such a step when the effects of his other social reforms were being strongly felt in the national economy. One of them was General Francisco Múgica, [who] was co-author and chief proponent of both the agrarian and labor clauses of the 1917 Constitution. He was older than Cárdenas, had known him since he was a young officer, and called him by his nickname, Trompudo (Snouty), to his face. As a cabinet member—he was Minister of Communications—Múgica expressed his doubts, but his objections were overridden.

Agricultural production in Mexico is divided into two main divisions, the subsistence crops, such as corn, beans, sugar, rice; and the commercial export crops, henequén, bananas, coffee, chicle. The lands producing subsistence crops were the first to be divided into *ejidos* under Cárdenas' land distribution program and production of these crops had shown a progressive decrease from the first harvest. In 1937 and 1938, when the commercial agricultural crops had begun to be affected, a downward trend was noticeable in the yield from these crops.

It would have been a miracle if the Cárdenas program had been a success overnight—it would have been a miracle if what he undertook to do, with the means he had to do it with, had been a success in a generation. After 1937 and increasingly after the harvests of 1938, it began to be seen that all was not going smoothly with the agrarian program, and this, combined with the effect of other government policies instituted by Cárdenas, was to affect the political situation within the country very deeply. In his annual message to Congress near the end of the year 1938, Cárdenas reported that 1,570,507 peasants had received 22,343,501 hectares of land. Statistics have not been compiled to show how many of the people affected were family heads nor what the average size of their families was, but the greater majority of them undoubtedly were heads of families and thus the number of people directly involved in Mexico's land experiment is far greater than these figures indicate.

The causes of the difficulties that the land program encountered during its first few years of life are various. The *New York Journal of Commerce,* in its issue of August 27, 1940, carried an article that summed up what may be called the official version, the one that you get by research in Mexico City. The article said:

> In many parts of the Republic, peasants had long been accustomed to cultivate plots of two acres or so of their own, in addition to working on the hacienda fields. When given a plot of ten acres or more in the

ejido, after the expropriation of the haciendas, many peasants have refused to change their mode of life. They would plow and plant only sufficient land to provide the foodstuffs they need, neglecting to cultivate the balance of the land allotted to them so that large fields are found lying idle and unused, thus causing a decline in total output of farm products. Abandonment of farm machinery, which had been in use on many estates, and less efficient cultivation methods have contributed to this result.

Marketing of agricultural products has fallen off more than production. Numerous peasants, left to their own resources, have consumed a larger portion of their produce, or have refrained from planting as much as formerly when they worked on the hacienda, because they feel they have no need for added cash income. Also there have been complaints that the proceeds of produce marketed through the ejidos have failed to get back to the individual peasants in whole or in part.

A detailed history of how each agricultural industry of Mexico was affected by the agrarian reform would fill volumes, for the Cárdenas program introduced new and profoundly disturbing factors into the raising, producing, and marketing process of every product of the national soil.

I will give one or two examples by way of illustration. Hog production, for instance, declined under the Six-Year Plan; the causes were intricately bound up with the land distribution. Before large-scale expropriations, most Mexican rural families kept a pig or two that either foraged for themselves or lived off scraps or waste grain. The commercial production of hogs was confined to large farms where food was raised for them on a regular stock-farm basis. When these large farms were broken up into small units and turned over to the peasants, they tended to continue their habit of raising one or two hogs for family use. The corn shortage that followed land expropriation caused a rise in corn prices, which discouraged those who might have been enterprising enough to undertake hog raising for

the market even on a small scale. Another factor introduced by the Six-Year Program was that of better secondary roads. In the old days, when corn was abundant, and
roads were so bad the only way it could be taken out was
on a mule, a burro, or a human back, it was found more
profitable and more practical to feed corn to hogs and drive
them out to market. With the coming of better roads and
higher corn prices, it was more profitable to ship corn out
by wagon or truck than to feed it to hogs. This caused a
considerable decline in the custom of raising small herds.

Hog production represents the extreme of individual enterprise. Sugar raising, one of Mexico's largest agricultural
industries, represents the other end of the scale, the highly
collectivized industry. Sugar lands were expropriated,
turned over to peasants who were organized into peasant
cooperatives that supplied cane to mills operated by labor
cooperatives. I have already mentioned the rivalries that
arose between workers and peasants; another factor also
discouraged the development of this industry. The sugar
that the peasant and worker cooperatives produced was
marketed through a semiofficial government agency; as
prices rose, the government, through this semimonopoly,
kept the price of sugar at a steady level, at the same time
encouraging distribution through a system of equalized
freight rates on the government-controlled railroads. By
this means the consumption of sugar was greatly increased.
With the price held steady, there was not sufficient incentive to the producers to expand their production, and they
did not do so. Disturbances within the bosom of the cooperatives have actually led to a decrease in production.
(Mexico, in 1940, found itself faced with the certainty that
it would have to import sugar for the year 1941.)

                    .        .        .

Within a year after Cárdenas had made for himself an
enduring place in the history of Mexico's great by unloos-
ing the "claws of imperialism" from their grip on Mexico's
oil, Mexico's difficulties were becoming serious.

The agrarian program was limping badly. The industrial worker cooperatives became involved in political squabbles that became more important than the success of the collective effort; that is what they mean when they say that efficiency went down under worker management. A chart prepared by the department of Economic Studies of the Bank of Mexico and published in a *Memoria* of the Mexican Chamber of Commerce and Industry, shows that the volume of production in general, of mining products, of electric energy, and of manufactured products, all of which had been on a gentle rise from the bottom in the depression year of 1932, leveled off in 1937; charts from other official sources show a sharp downward drop beginning with 1938. With agricultural production down, mining production and sales down, with oil production and sales down, Mexico's export surplus declined till only the silver sales kept it from having an adverse balance of payments. The National Railways, mainly dependent on mining, lost revenue. The government's tax receipts fell; tax yield from mining went down with production; a third of the yield from the oil industry went to the government, but the volume of oil sales was down and prices lower. The worker-owned industrial and agricultural cooperatives were, of course, tax free. The annual budgetary deficit, mounting since 1936, jumped from 15,625,000 pesos in 1937 to 58,666,000 in 1938. Issuance of paper money and coins with a silver content that represented only a fraction of their face value was accelerated.

The cost of living went steadily up. By the summer of 1939, its index, taking 1934 as 100, had reached 160. Wages, though they had been increased—from 25 to 33 percent in major industries still owned by private capital, less in the worker-owned factories—were not keeping pace with living costs. Real earnings were down.

The national economy was squeezed between falling exports and rising imports; the people between rising living costs and wages that did not keep pace.

This was the situation that Mexico had to face in the spring and summer of 1939 . . . and along with it, the solution of a problem that has shaken Mexico like an earthquake time and time again, the question of the presidential succession.

# 43

# JOSÉ VASCONCELOS

———————•———————

# MEXICO'S FUTURE*

❧

*By 1939 many Mexicans felt uneasy about the use
of state power under Cárdenas, in part because the
writings of intellectuals like José Vasconcelos were
raising many questions about the nature of Mexico's
experience. In this selection from* What Is the Revolution? *(1937), Vasconcelos looked into the future
to characterize Mexico as it might be presented in
a presidential speech in 1950, given his view of the
course of Cárdenas' government. Vasconcelos correctly saw that in nationalized industry, strikes cannot be permitted by the government, as they threaten
the authority of the state. Indeed, within two years
after oil expropriation Cárdenas told Mexican labor
that since the state was a major employer it could no
longer allow labor turmoil, because strikes unpatriot-
ically threaten the very Revolution itself.*

*Prior to his unsuccessful bid for the presidency in
1929, Vasconcelos gained fame as Alvaro Obregón's
Minister of Education during the early 1920s. In
his* La raza cósmica: Misión de la raza iberoameri-
cana *(Paris: Agencia Mundial de Librería, 1925), he
had pictured Mexico's future as rooted in the mixture
of Spanish and Indian bloods, which would give the
country a hybrid vigor. With the prospect of Indian
power in the 1930s, Vasconcelos found himself to be*

———————————

* Translated from José Vasconcelos, *¿Qué es la Revolución?* (México, D. F.: Ediciones Botas, 1937), 135–138.

*a conservative Catholic who now favored the heritage
of Spanish blood and who looked to Spain's leadership under Franco to restore the cultural glory of
Hispanic peoples. He feared the cultural and economic domination of Latin America by the United
States, claiming that Washington was corrupting the
Catholic unity of* Latin America *in order to create a
bastard* Pan American *union of Protestant peoples.*

*During the 1930s Vasconcelos wrote a four-
volume account of his life, which has been published
in several editions. A translated abridgment,* A Mexican Ulysses *(Bloomington: Indiana University Press,
1963), gives a fine one-volume version in English of
this autobiography. Vasconcelos' autobiography offers
revealing insight into the life of a Mexican intellectual
during the course of the Revolution, and it may be
profitably read by all students of the Mexican Revolution in order to understand how one man became
hopelessly embittered.*

Government officials of high rank formerly called themselves socialists; but, when their term of office expired they
left power with their pockets full, with gold deposits in foreign countries and [with] houses, plantations, and cattle
ranches.

Now that those agrarian properties that belonged to
Mexican reactionaries have been socialized, we can say that
. . . today all landholdings, all industries, belong to the
banking sector whose intelligent management resides for
the most part in New York and Washington. . . . This explains why our Secretary of the Treasury is on such intimate terms with the Treasury Department of the United
States, and why he spends so much time abroad. From
abroad we receive, with the light of new ideas, the necessary norms for correct orientation of our economy. Only
those large agrarian enterprises governed by special status
. . . are able to escape this beneficial subordination.

In the new estates wages are much higher than those paid
on the very same properties when they belonged to retro-
grade Spaniards and Mexican reactionaries. The torpid

Spaniards by no means could have granted pay raises, because they used only coins of gold and silver. Now we pay wages with paper money, and the silver and gold are conveniently sent abroad for safety. While this is going on, the larger industries, duly socialized and managed by international bankers, are free of strikes and riots, which are not justified anymore because, on one hand, management no longer exists to which such demands could be directed, and on the other hand, strikes belong to the capitalistic epoch, not to our advanced era. Today, in spite of rumors circulated by a few retired nationalists, it is the International Banking Council that ultimately decides, without appeal, what is to be considered an adequate wage for workers as well as how they should use their paid vacation and leisure time.

The total elimination of the capitalistic class has brought us the added advantage that there is no one to clutter our minds with anachronistic concepts of country, language, and religion. A single culture from North to South, from Canada to Guatemala, spreads its benefits on a liberated population. The fight between Protestants and Catholics (the roots of the old conflict between Mexico and the United States) has been eliminated and we confidently expect that the happy transformation experienced by modern Mexico will serve as a good example to the countries to the South, which are still drowned by the spectre of Catholicism, of regionalism, and of that which is Spanish.

## 44

## MANUEL GÓMEZ MORÍN

•

# THE FOUNDING
# OF THE NATIONAL ACTION
# PARTY (PAN)*

❧

*A rising tide of protest against the Cárdenas govern-
ment culminated in the presidential campaign of
1939 and 1940. The foundation of the National
Action Party (PAN) on September 14, 1939, under
the leadership of Manuel Gómez Morín, marked the
formulation of the first effective political opposition
to the official party. The PAN, whose initials spell
"bread" in Spanish, has gained increasingly wider
support since 1939.*

*Although the PAN has been called a "clerical
party" and the "political embodiment of traditional
conservatism" in Mexico, these epithets constitute
dangerous half-truths. The PAN has been in harmony
with the Church on educational policy and the need
for economic and social order as the basis of a
healthful and happy society, but it has disassociated
itself from Catholic Action and has not been an arm*

* Translated from James W. Wilkie and Edna Monzón de Wilkie,
*México visto en el siglo XX; Entrevistas de Historia Oral: Ramón
Beteta, Marte R. Gómez, Manuel Gómez Morín, Vicente Lombardo
Toledano, Miguel Palomar y Vizcarra, Emilio Portes Gil, Jesús Silva
Herzog* (México, D.F.: Instituto Mexicano de Investigaciones Eco-
nómicas, 1969), 176–178. Reprinted by permission.

*of the Church hierarchy. Yet, its members often have held prominent positions in many lay Catholic organizations. In 1939 leaders of the PAN felt that Cárdenas' programs were needlessly destructive of individual initiative, and they rejected the idea that the state should extensively direct social and economic change. In their view, Cárdenas seemed to be disrupting traditional society to socialize misery rather than to create a Mexico in which with hard work one might enjoy the fruits of capitalism.*

*Emergence of the PAN as a political force coincided with the world's realization that capitalism had not died in the world depression of 1929. Experiments with state action had obviously not resolved the problems with which capitalism had failed to cope, and it was easy for the PAN to take advantage of this awareness. Because many professional men supported the PAN, irrespective of religious persuasion, the party soon earned the name "club of bankers." Here again another half-truth gained currency, for the party gained strength from many elements of society in addition to those who wished to defend the right of property.*

*Gómez Morín was an adviser to the government on agrarian credit and monetary matters during the 1920s, while he maintained his private law practice. He has since specialized in corporation law and in arranging joint Mexican-American business ventures. Among his writings, the reports he submitted to the PAN are readily available in* Díez años de México: Informes del Jefe de Acción Nacional (*México, D.F.: Editorial Jus, 1950*).

*Manuel Gómez Morín:* The situation in Mexico by 1938 had become intolerable, with an imminent threat of the loss of all liberty. At this time we started to have meetings here in Mexico City and in the different states of the country because we anticipated another big threat, namely, Almazán, another general, who had appeared as a candidate for the presidency. We knew that Almazán could not win peacefully, as Cárdenas would never turn over power to him unless he revolted, and in the end that would have amounted to having just another general as President. To continue under the same political system was not only absurd but unbearable. Must we sink lower and lower? At that time we thought of revising the whole political framework, because the base of Mexico's problem is in the lack of citizenship. In Mexico, we had never been trained to be citizens, we lacked a background in citizenship. First, we experienced the colonial days when there was no alternative but to obey and say nothing; then followed the days of independence with civil strife; then the years of foreign wars and intervention. Thus, we never had the chance to organize our democracy. . . .

*James W. Wilkie:* Then came the *Porfiriato.*

*Manuel Gómez Morín:* Yes, there were thirty years of the Porfiriato, which did not create a civic spirit. After Díaz we had the rule of Madero, brief as a flash of lightning. Then came the Revolution with its military leaders. We had to recognize the need for the creation of a civic conscience, a civic organization. Thus, we decided to organize the party.

I began in 1938 by making a tour of the whole country to form the initial groups. By 1939 we were able to call our first national convention, where we adopted a platform and established the statutes of the party and a program of minimum action. Our program was small and practical, it was not a one-year or a ten-year program. We would have to organize and define it as we went, based on acquired experience as we studied it and put it into practice. We well knew that it was a program to be presented to public opinion . . . and not for us to carry out. We know that it will take many years before we can come to power so that we can achieve the realization of a complete program. However, we have always been of the opinion that government policy comes from outside the government as well as from within, provided there is a strong political force that has sufficient backing from the public to enable it to present alternative measures to the government for its adoption. Moreover, we had confidence and faith in the rationality of politics—perhaps somewhat naïvely, but then, in the end it may turn out to be justified in that our continuous arguments someday will make an impact on the public and its responsible officials.

To think that the solution to the agrarian problem consists of merely distributing land among the peasants is absurd! At the present time we have at least 4 million heads of family on the land, and among them there are about 6 million male adults. From where will arable land come to fill their needs? The agrarian problem has to have a different solution; it should be approached with a greater sense of humility. Agrarian problems are not solved by government decrees!

*James W. Wilkie:* After the expropriation of the petroleum industry by Cárdenas in 1938, Cárdenas had to consolidate his political position by moderating his radicalism. He called for an end to strikes, especially because many would now be against the government, and he could not permit that situation. Cárdenas reorganized the official party, and inside the party a pact had been made by some state governors in order to prevent Múgica from becoming the next President. By that time, according to reports, the problem with the clergy and the Catholic Church had eased, especially after the expropriation took place when Cárdenas was no longer able to put up a fight on all fronts.

.    .    .

Do you believe the intolerable conditions threatening all liberty persisted in 1939, and that with the changes that I have just mentioned, the situation worsened to the point where it was necessary to call for civic action?

*Manuel Gómez Morín:* I believe so. If in 1939 there had not been a political solution to the state of anxiety in Mexico, we would have had a tremendous revolution. Perhaps it is erroneous to say "fortunately," but fortunately, popular unrest was directed toward a legal change in government.

Most of the people thought Almazán could make that change. We didn't think so, and the day after the frustrated elections, we said:

"We must carry on our civic efforts; we must fight on, but only to solve the real problems of Mexico!"

*James W. Wilkie:* Didn't the National Action Party side with Almazán?

*Manuel Gómez Morín: Acción Nacional* entered the campaign on the side of Almazán, but in a very conditional form. Almazán was "the other one," the only possible candidate in opposition to the official candidate. The word was passed around:

"The official party already has named its candidate, and Almazán is the only one running against him. Let us not divide the opposition."

Many of our members suggested that Acción Nacional not make any decision at this stage about which candidate to support. To do that, however, would have meant that we were not really a political party, but just an academy, an institution for the study of political science—something we did not want to be. We desired to create a genuinely active political party.

*James W. Wilkie:* And that takes many years.

*Manuel Gómez Morín:* It takes many years, and even at the outset the group must be ready to enter the fight, either to take the defeats or the victories; but it must remain in contact with the other political forces.

*James W. Wilkie:* But isn't it rather difficult to attract people to the party when there are so few probabilities of its coming to power? Don't people join a political party for the opportunities of earning positions in the government?

*Manuel Gómez Morín:* It is miraculous that the party continues to exist after twenty-five years without a single presidential victory; but there we are, and every year we increase our membership.

*James W. Wilkie:* Yes, that is extraordinary.

*Manuel Gómez Morín:* It is an extraordinary effort. There is no political precedent for this in Mexico. No other opposition party has lasted for twenty-five years, fighting continuously against the party in power with its slanderous charges, monopoly of the press, and general economic repression.

# 45

## BETTY KIRK

# ELECTION DAY, 1940[*]

❊

*In spite of stiff opposition to the official party in the election campaign of 1939 and 1940, Cárdenas' "Unknown Soldier"—General Manuel Avila Camacho— won the presidency on July 7, 1940. Many party regulars were embittered that General Francisco J. Múgica, the Constitutionalist of 1917 and a leader of the Mexican left, had not been nominated as Cárdenas' logical successor, but Múgica's radicalism and unstable personality apparently frightened even Cárdenas. In the charged atmosphere of war in Europe, the United States was apprehensive that any political miscalculation by the PRM in Mexico might result in a civil war comparable to the Spanish experience from 1936 to 1939, and Washington was happy to see that Avila Camacho assumed no radical poses. Avila Camacho stated shortly after his election, "I am a believer," and thus quieted many of Mexico's Catholics who might have supported a rebellion by the defeated opposition candidate General Juan Andreu Almazán. President Franklin D. Roosevelt sent Vice President-elect Henry A. Wallace to attend Avila Camacho's inauguration and Juan Andreu Almazán realized that rebellion was hopeless.*

*Cárdenas must be given much credit for provid-*

---

\* From *Covering the Mexican Front,* by Betty Kirk. Copyright 1942 by the University of Oklahoma Press. 239–244.

*ing a successful transition in which the PRM main-
tained control of presidential power in 1940, for
after the radicalism of his government he found strong
opposition. The official party triumphed because its
new organization allowed the masses to participate
with more vigor and faith in the government than ever
before. Although it is evident in Betty Kirk's dispatch
from Mexico City that the official candidate lost the
capital, it seems probable that the opposition candidate lost the countryside. Because the official party
could not admit that it lost in the capital without
fanning revolt, official figures gave Avila Camacho
72 percent of the vote in Mexico City compared to 93
percent in the country as a whole.*

*Betty Kirk covered the Cárdenas years as an Amer-
ican journalist.*

Violence reached its climax on July 7, election day. I
kept a play-by-play diary of the frenzied events. This diary,
which follows, tells the story as it unfolded.

6 A.M.—Awakened early to the tolling of church bells
calling the faithful to early Mass. Today Generals Almazán
and Avila Camacho will fight it out at the polls. President
Cárdenas has promised a free election. There has never
been one before. 6:45—María, my maid, calls and says she
can't come today. There are no buses. The CTM has ordered its union to transport only voters to the polls. 7:45—
Jack O'Brine of the *Herald Tribune* called to say he and Ed
Morgan of the United Press are on the way to pick me up.
We're working together today in a network that they have
flung over the city. We're all to cover Avila Camacho's vot-
ing. Jack and Ed go on to Almazán and I'm to return to the
United Press offices and help in handling the phones. We
take along with us Jerry Flamm, a big lanky boy from San
Francisco who's one of our leg men, covering Avila Cama-
cho headquarters. 7:50—On the way downstairs I asked
Felipe, the porter, who he's voting for. "Almazán!" Outside
I encounter my news dealer. He too is voting "Almazán!"
Last night my taxi driver answered, "Almazán!"

8 A.M.—Arrival Avila Camacho headquarters. Ben

Meyer of Associated Press, Jellenik of *PM*, Harry Block of *The Nation*, Jack Glenn of *March of Time*, Bob Capa of *Life*, Wayne Thomas from *The Chicago Tribune*, and many other special correspondents are gathering. 8:45— We leave for Avila Camacho's house. The street is flanked on both sides with the cars of politicos and press. We loiter outside the gates with more of our fraternity. Army officers go in and out. 9 A.M.—General Avila Camacho is scheduled to vote now but he doesn't appear. We wait in the bright sunlight. 9:45—The doors swing open. General Avila Camacho appears [and] halts for pictures, smiles sweetly. He has a friendly manner. Everyone dashes for cars. About seventy-five cars take off, including politicos and press.

10 A.M.—We park two blocks away from Constanza 610, where Avila Camacho is voting. As we rush down the hill an army officer ten feet ahead is beating a civilian on the head and shoulders with his fist. The civilian flees angrily up the hill. Jellenik says the civilian tried to stop him and tell him a tale of chicanery at the polls when the army man drove him off. We can't get inside the gate, which is filled with politicos and their henchmen. Avila Camacho votes, leaves for his headquarters. 10:15—We go back up the hill. Decide to investigate the report of wounded in the house around the corner. When they find we're foreign correspondents they let us in. Dr. Francisco Montaño Luna, wearing a Red Cross arm band, explains what happened. The Mexican electoral law provides that whatever party arrives at the polls first has the right to open them and elect the day's officials. The *Almazanistas* opened this poll at nine o'clock. One hundred were collected to vote when a horde of *Avilacamachistas* arrived and seized the polls. They drove the Almazanistas off by clubbing them on the head with pistol butts. We were introduced to *Ingeniero* Gonzalo Aceves, his brother Alfonso, and his son Albert, and inspected the bandages on their heads with the blood oozing through. Dr. Montaño Luna had his hand smashed when he tried to intercept a pistol butt. 10:30—Jellenik

and Harry Block want to investigate the story at the polls. On the way back we meet an angry crowd of citizens, men and women, residents of the neighborhood. They tell the same story. "We can't vote! This is our democracy!" The polls are almost deserted now. Jellenik and Block call my attention to an Almazanista who is being permitted to vote. They say it's a sign of social justice. The man votes and we walk out the gate with him. He turns, grinning: "They told me there weren't any ballots until you came up. Because you're the foreign press they let me vote."

10:55—Back in the United Press office working with Quesada at the phones. Jerry calls in from Avila Camacho headquarters. General Jara has just announced: "We've got it in the bag!" 11 A.M.—Jack O'Brine calls in that Almazán voted at 10:15 at polls in a neighboring feed store. 11:15— A United Press leg man reports that President Cárdenas tried to vote at Juan Escutía 35 but couldn't because an Avila Camacho general had seized and closed the polls to prevent eight hundred Almazanistas from voting. Cárdenas waited half an hour, couldn't vote, left for a tour of the polls. While he was waiting the people clamored: "We want Almazán! You promised us a free election! *¡Viva el General Cárdenas!*" 11:30—Report two wounded at Convento de Vizcaínes in battle for the polls. First opened by Avila-camachistas. Seized by Almazanistas. Truckload of soldiers arrived and restored to Avilacamachistas. Two seriously wounded. All reports now are of battles for the polls.

12 N.—Redmont, another of the day's leg men, reports rioting in front of the Labor newspaper *El Popular.* An Almazanista shouted *"¡Viva Almazán!"* while passing. Someone started shooting. Bricks, stones flying. The Almazanista killed, his windows and tires riddled. A battle is on. Redmont is dodging bricks as he phones. 12:15—Ed Morgan phones from the cable office. He reports the *El Popular* battle is a wow. Alejandro Carrillo, director of *El Popular* and right-hand man to Lombardo Toledano, mixes in the street fighting, retires. 12:15—Redmont reports increased fighting. Bricks, pistols, machine guns being used. 12:30—

A North American, Edward Mallen, reported shot in the stomach. Was bystander at riot in front of Palace of Fine Arts. Five minutes later two United States and one Brazilian student here on vacation reported shot. . . . 1:20—United Press leg man reports a senator and former diplomat shot a woman in the leg at the polls at Durango 131. 1:25—Jerry reports that fifty men armed with clubs and machine guns have left for the post office. 1:30—Red Cross reports forty injured up to one o'clock, three dead. New riot reported breaking out at Jardín de Santo Domingo. We don't have a man there. 1:45—Tampico reports election quiet. Afterward an Almazán parade past the bakers' union started a riot. Three wounded. Army exerting pressure for Avila Camacho. 1:50—A new report comes in on Cárdenas' attempt to vote this morning. The crowd surrounded him, pleading, "We want Almazán." Cárdenas replied: "It appears that all are Almazanistas here. Vote for him and if he wins he'll be the President." Cárdenas everywhere greeted with *vivas*.

2 P.M.—The post office is now the center. Four dead, unknown number wounded. . . . 2:30—Jerry reports four men leaving with machine guns. 2:30 to 4—There is a lull. Time out for lunch. The telephones are quiet. A United Press leg man comes in with the story that an army colonel led twelve *pistoleros* who attacked Almazán voters in the polls at Monte Himalaya.

.  .  .

4:05—Morgan reports big crowd of Almazanistas collecting in Cinco de Mayo, one of the main streets leading into the Zócalo, where the National Palace is located. Redmont also reports this crowd rapidly growing. The lull is broken. 4:30—*Almazán headquarters report that Almazán will lead the Cinco de Mayo crowd onto the Zócalo*. The news drops like a bomb in our office. Dead silence. A Mexican speaks: "It's suicide!" 4:35—New reports from Cinco de Mayo. Hundreds gathering. The sky is overcast, threatening rain. The crowd attempts to seize XEFO, the broadcasting station of *El Nacional,* the government newspaper.

4:40—One reported dead from Cinco de Mayo. Our tally to date, 24 dead in the city, 150 wounded. From Puebla, 10 reported dead, making a total of 17 from the States. 4:45—Almazán decides not to lead the march on the Zócalo. Asks his followers to go home, await further orders. (An unconfirmed rumor says Cárdenas asked him to do this.) It's raining now. Neither orders from the General nor the rain have any effect. Ten thousand are reported in Cinco de Mayo. 5 P.M.—The Cinco de Mayo crowd is moving on the Zócalo. Redmont reports the Zócalo is an armed camp. Troops and police form a ring inside it and have barricaded every entrance a block away. No one is permitted to pass within their lines. 5:30 to 6—The crowd arrives at the Zócalo. They attempt to break through police and troop lines. The soldiers are ordered to fire. Reports come in that it's a shambles.

6:30—Redmont reports nine ambulances full leaving the Zócalo, but our count gives only six dead, seven wounded. 6:30 to 7—There's a quiet spell. Then word comes in that President Cárdenas himself went among the mob to quiet them. Again, as all during the morning, the people appealed to him: "We want Almazán, give us Almazán, we're tired of these Communists and thieves!" And Cárdenas' answer was: "If he was elected, he'll be the next President." As always the magnetic spell which he exercises over the people had its effect. He promised them free elections. They fought all day to vote. The decision, which means the count of unstuffed boxes, is now in his hands. Believing in him, the people went home. Their last shouts were: *"¡Viva Cárdenas! ¡Viva Almazán!"*

# 46

## VALENTÍN CAMPA

———•———

# A COMMUNIST'S
# VIEW OF CÁRDENAS*

✤

*With all the charges and countercharges about com-
munism during the period from 1934 to 1940, many
observers have felt that President Cárdenas was a
Communist. However, Valentín Campa, a long-time
member and director of the Mexican Communist
Party, saw Cárdenas as a bourgeois leader of first
rank. Writing with fifteen years of perspective after
1940, he presented a view of Cárdenas that has been
little heard in the United States.*

*Campa is currently serving a long prison term for
"social dissolution" as a result of his role in the series
of strikes that swept Mexico when President Adolfo
López Mateos took office in 1958. Nevertheless,
Campa's columns continued to appear in the Marxist
news magazine* Política (*Mexico City*) *with a Lecum-
berri Prison dateline.*

The appearance of General Lázaro Cárdenas as a presidential candidate of the official party (PNR) under the control

---

* Translated from Valentín Campa, "El cardenismo en la Revolución
Mexicana," *Problemas agrícolas e industriales de México*, Número
3, Vol. VII (1955), 227–230. Reprinted by permission of the publisher.

of Calles . . . was due to the following fundamental factors:

1. When the campaign for the presidential election was initiated in 1932, Mexico was undergoing a cyclic capitalistic crisis of overproduction as a result of the 1929 crash on the New York Stock Exchange. This crisis was felt with greatest intensity in Mexico during the years from 1930 to 1932.

Calles' policies had increased the dependence of Mexico on the imperialistic countries. . . . On this account Calles ordered the burning of sugar cane fields. The same was being done in Cuba, only on a larger scale. In the United States, Roosevelt was ordering the slaughtering of millions of pigs, assigning subsidies to farmers as long as the meat was buried in the ground, while millions of unemployed workers were starving. In Brazil entire shiploads of coffee were dumped overboard, and sometimes it was used as fuel. In Mexico, industry and commerce discharged more than one-third of their laborers and office workers.

The middle bourgeoisie, which developed during the progressive period of the Calles government, was losing its holdings rapidly. Many of the bourgeoisie were generals and politicians of the government itself, and they watched with hatred how only Calles and his associates (Abelardo L. Rodríguez, Aaron Saénz) prospered in their business ventures amid the panorama of ruin and desolation. It is a known fact that when these cyclical crises occur, the larger capitalists, instead of losing money, increase their holdings at the expense of the bourgeoisie who are forced to mortgage their businesses and go bankrupt.

That middle bourgeoisie of the PNR, ruined by the cyclical crisis, had been irritated by the capitalistic pretensions of Calles and Co., and they became aware of the great indignation registered among laborers, and the urban middle class. Cárdenas represented the feelings of the middle bourgeoisie of the PNR, at first presenting his campaign platform with great ability, and then with great clarity, proposing a platform that favored not only the middle bourgeoisie but all the people of Mexico, and his candidacy became a landslide within the PNR. Calles, confident at first that he could control Cárdenas, accepted the platform.

2. The second important factor in the appearance of Cárdenas as the candidate of the PNR, with a program that would give impetus to the Revolution, was the fact that he adopted in his program practically all of the original objectives of the Revolution.

From the beginning of the land distribution program until 1934, only 7.5 million hectares of land had been distributed among 780,000 *ejidatarios,* while there were 90 million hectares of land still in the hands of big landowners and 2.5 million farm workers without land. Basically, feudalism was still present in Mexico, preventing economic improvement for vast sectors of the people.

*Callismo* had surrendered to imperialism, and the imperialists were in control of most of industry and most of large landholdings, exporting their enormous profits extracted from the Mexican people who lived in complete misery. Foreign investment increased in Mexico, displacing the precarious investments of the national bourgeoisie; industrialists from imperialistic countries saturated our market with their goods, ruining not only our weak bourgeoisie dependent on the manufacturing industry, but our craftsmen as well.

The working class was the object of a many-sided exploitation, especially by foreign capitalists. Employers, professionals, and the trading petit bourgeoisie all became the victims of acute impoverishment.

This general situation, product of the frustration of the program of the Mexican Revolution, worsened with the effects of the economic crisis previously mentioned.

An increase in capital investment was brought about under Cárdenas in the following way: farm workers were given land to increase their purchasing power, and the petroleum industry was nationalized to put an end to the bleeding of profits exported by foreign companies. The new role of the national railways, and investment in the construction of dams, highways, and other public works gave strong momentum to capitalistic development.

It was during the Cárdenas period that economic forces, which previously had been kept idle, were put to work. With them, production output and capital resources increased considerably; however, the impact of those forces was not felt so much during the Cárdenas regime as during those regimes that came after Cárdenas.

Development of the national economy caused many of the petit bourgeoisie to become middle bourgeoisie, and many of the capitalists to become great capitalists. The capital of the *Porfiristas* (including that of the clergy) went into circulation, and it increased also.

All economic development during the Cárdenas regime, including farming, was capitalistic. The bourgeoisie of the manufacturing industry was consolidated, as was the bourgeoisie of commercial enterprises; also a new banking bourgeoisie began to form.

Cárdenas' government officials were unable to put a stop to the increase in the number of capitalistic enterprises. Instead, they took advantage of them. From the ranks of the Cárdenas government sprouted such new millionaires as Maximino and Manuel Avila Camacho, Miguel Alemán, Eduardo Suárez, Ramón Beteta, and many others.

. . . These gentlemen, who at first had belonged to the petit bourgeoisie, were converted into potentates who, in the last two years of the Cárdenas government were the ones who decided who was to be the next President. . . .

At the end of the Cárdenas presidential period a false theory was spread, even among the workers' movement, that emphasized the need to halt the revolutionary program in order to consolidate its accomplishments, thus hiding designs for a backward and counterrevolutionary epoch. We shall point out two of the negative measures adopted by the Cárdenas government during the last days of its regime:

1. The creation of the ill-fated Office of Small Property, protector of the agrarian bourgeoisie and enemy of the peasants.
2. The promulgation of a law regulating the work of bank employees in violation of Article 123 of the Constitution, a proof of the government's interest in rapidly creating a banking bourgeoisie.

The new bourgeoisie created during the Cárdenas administration imposed a capitalistic outlook on the government. It was able to block any presidential possibilities of General Francisco J. Múgica, a Jacobin who never accumulated any capital. Múgica represented the middle bourgeoisie who were interested in establishing an alliance with the peasants and with the industrial workers for the defense and progress of the Mexican Revolution. This naturally did not suit those of the established bourgeoisie.

Ever since its foundation, the PRM was an official party that faithfully carried out all the policies of the Cárdenas government, with all its successes, with all its errors, with all its retrogressions. It was organized in such a fashion that it would not permit the integration of a popular front . . . with the Communist Party representing the working class, . . . allied to the government party but remaining essentially independent. The merging of the CTM into the PRM meant the placing of the union movement under the orders of the government; it created the dangerous situation of handling unions as if they were political pressure groups, confusing the working class and sidetracking it from its main objective—the creation of a great party of its own.

# 47

ALBERT L. MICHAELS

—————•—————

# A SUMMARY OF
# THE CÁRDENAS EPOCH*

❧

*Certainly the communist view offers some interest-
ing points, but in order to understand the impact of
Cárdenas on Mexico it is necessary to turn to more
balanced and scholarly interpretation. Perhaps Cárdenas' land program changed the course of Mexico's
history more than any single factor:*

Regarding the matter of land distribution, Cárdenas
crushed the strength of *latifundia* by signing resolutions
to break up 20,136,936 hectares of land and to give it to
the rural masses. This meant that in six years 10.2 per
cent of the country's continental area was designated for
eventual distribution, an average of 279,680 hectares per
month. This was rapid work, compared even to Porfirio
Díaz's creation of the *latifundia,* for Díaz's average was
only 132,139 hectares per month. Cárdenas' activity was
truly astounding, and it is no wonder that conservative
elements raised active opposition to such a policy. When
Cárdenas came into power previous presidential resolutions had pledged only about 6 per cent of Mexico's area
for distribution, and when Cárdenas left office 16 per

* Albert L. Michaels, "Mexican Politics and Nationalism from Calles
to Cárdenas" (unpublished Ph.D. thesis in history, University of
Pennsylvania, Philadelphia, 1966), revised 374–380. Reprinted by permission of the author.

cent had been marked for rearrangement into small holdings. . . .

Land reform psychologically affected Mexican life.
After Cárdenas, Mexico was definitively committed to
land redistribution; investment in land, the traditional pattern, was no longer feasible, for land might be taken
over at any time—paid off in government notes of ques-
tionable value. Even if landholdings were within the
legal limits of small property protected by law, in the rush
to distribute lands, legal formalities might be overlooked.
Also, one could never tell when the maximum size of
legal holdings might be reduced. On the one hand, in-
vestors had to look for new sources of investment, and
industry and commerce gained as agricultural investment declined. On the other hand, the recipients of parcels of land could take pride in owning their plot of
ground. No longer were they required to work for someone else. If this meant subsistence agriculture based on
*minifundio* in most cases, it also meant a change in the
way the peasant comported himself. He was no longer
an unequal, inferior being.[1]

*Although Professor Sanford Mosk has stated that
Mexico's Industrial Revolution began in the early
1940s, his statistical analysis has been reinterpreted
by Professor James W. Wilkie to show that "the basis
for rapid industrialization was firmly established when
Cárdenas left office. In fact, the volume of manufacturing production increased about as fast during the
Cárdenas era as it did during the Avila Camacho
epoch."* [2]

The Cárdenas epoch ended the phase of upheaval in the
Revolution and prepared the country for a twenty-year period of economic revolution, from 1940 to 1960. Since
1960 Mexico has entered into yet another stage of its Revolution in which the goals of the political phase (1910–

[1] James W. Wilkie, *The Mexican Revolution: Federal Expenditure
and Social Change Since 1910* (Berkeley and Los Angeles: University
of California Press, 1967), 76.

[2] Compare *Ibid.,* 264–265, and Sanford Mosk, *Industrial Revolution in Mexico* (Berkeley and Los Angeles: University of California
Press, 1950), vii and 120.

1930), social period (1930–1940), and economic era (1940–1960) are joined to create "balanced Revolution."

*In this final selection, Albert L. Michaels presents a broad synthesis of the many factors influencing history during the Cárdenas years.*

During the 1933 presidential campaign, Lázaro Cárdenas had defined the nation as "a territory whose natural wealth the people enjoy in common." In his six-year term Cárdenas conscientiously sought to make Mexico fit this definition. To a large degree he succeeded; his popular government divided much of the land, expropriated the oil holdings, and infused Mexican labor with a new sense of purpose. More important still, he encouraged both the urban and rural proletariat to form strong organizations, which theoretically could defend their rights no matter who the President might be. Furthermore, Cárdenas improved education, gave the Army a national identity, and established a truce with Mexico's Catholics. In 1940 Mexico was more closely integrated for the masses than it had ever been in all its previous history. Yet in 1940, for reasons that he has never explained, Cárdenas turned over the government to Manuel Avila Camacho, a soldier who stressed the importance of economic improvement over social improvement. There were several considerations that might have influenced this strange choice.

James W. Wilkie in his study of the Mexican federal budget and its effect on social change gives the following description of the results of Cárdenas' policies:

Cárdenas himself seized the opportunity that the crisis in political revolution presented to undertake the social restructure of Mexico. He not only definitively reoriented the economy away from the agricultural hacienda system, he also proposed to change the educational system and swiftly to integrate the Mexican people into a nation, a program which had been delayed since Mexico's independence in 1821. We have seen that his programs had little practical effect on the life of the common man, who remained illiterate, shoeless, isolated, underfed, and without sewage disposal. A large number still could not speak Spanish by the time Cárdenas left office.

Cárdenas may have come to understand this by the end of his term; he certainly was no longer the unsophisticated popular nationalist who had entered office late in 1934. Like his predecessors, he may have come to the conclusion that Mexico had to develop wealth before it could achieve socialism. As Daniel Cosío Villegas once suggested to me: "Cárdenas had destroyed many things; perhaps he believed it was time to begin rebuilding."

The world situation no doubt also influenced Cárdenas' choice of Manuel Avila Camacho. Cárdenas, a Marxist-oriented politician, always had hated and feared the world fascist movement. Mexico was one of the few nations to support actively the Spanish Republic against German and Italian aggression. The Cárdenas government officially protested fascist attacks on Austria, Albania, China, Poland, Belgium, and Norway. In 1938, in the midst of the oil crisis, Cárdenas secretly proposed to President Roosevelt that Mexico and the United States should support an economic boycott against aggressor nations, even though such a move would have ruined Mexico's German oil market. Later, in November 1940, Cárdenas stopped all oil exports to Japan. In the late 1930s, the Mexican government always made it clear that its sympathies lay with the Western Allies, and against Hitler and Mussolini.

In regard to presidential politics, Cárdenas must have felt that if a radical leftist like Francisco J. Múgica was to become president, the weak ties holding Mexico together might break, thus bringing on a civil war, such as Spain had experienced. If such a conflict developed, Mexico's middle classes and even the Army might be driven into the arms of cryptofascist groups like the *Sinarquistas*. On the other hand, a moderate soldier like Avila Camacho would certainly have a better chance of uniting all Mexicans

against the totalitarian threat than would have an intransigent radical like Múgica.

Unrest engendered by the world depression of 1929
greatly altered the fate of the official party's ideology. The
economic crash of 1929 had destroyed faith in the laissez-
faire capitalism, which had created prosperity in the United
States. As a result even the newly rich like Calles and President Abelardo Rodríguez declared themselves in favor of
strong state intervention in the economy. Seeking to keep
political power and meet the economic crisis of the early
1930s, they decided that they could no longer justify gradual economic development within the capitalistic system.
Lacking the mass appeal to meet the restlessness of the
Mexican people, the *Callistas* turned to a more dynamic
leader, Lázaro Cárdenas, who, to almost everyone's surprise, actually believed that the nation would only become
united and peaceful if Mexico's wealth belonged to all of
the people. Cárdenas strived to generate immediate social
justice, and the Mexican proletariat responded to his program by giving him the mass support that he needed to
supersede Calles.

The new concept of the nation rapidly spread to sectors
previously hostile to the nationalism of the revolutionary
government. The extreme left, heretofore internationalist,
cooperated with the government. Justifying their position,
the leftists, led by Vicente Lombardo Toledano, explained
that nationalism was necessary in the struggle of an under-
developed country against colonialism; however, they
hoped that the necessity of having a nation would disappear
in the coming world revolution. Even the Catholic right,
which had previously opposed radical reform, took up popular nationalism. Authoritarian-minded Catholics flocked
to the rabidly nationalistic Sinarquista movement, which
promised to integrate the nation by halting class warfare.
Both the extreme right and the extreme left had seen that
they would have to espouse popular nationalism if they
were to survive.

In 1939 political considerations again altered the face of the Mexican government's program. Faced with economic crisis and the rise of fascism, Cárdenas emphasized the unification of all Mexican classes over immediate justice for the proletarian class. In 1940 he presided over a campaign in which his hand-picked candidate abandoned the radical ideas that had inspired him in 1933. Cárdenas pursued this new policy, not because he had betrayed the Revolution, but because he was a pragmatic Mexican nationalist.

# V

# Conclusion

*Each new epoch demands a rebirth of ideas. The clamor of the entire Republic now demands the material and spiritual consolidation of our social conquests in a prosperous and powerful economy. It demands an era of construction, of abundant life, of economic expansion.*

---

Manuel Avila Camacho, Inaugural Address; translated and quoted by Betty Kirk, *Covering the Mexican Front* (Norman: University of Oklahoma Press, 1942), 330.

*The principal problem that modern Mexico will have to solve, at whatever cost, is the total transformation of the present situation with regard to its wealth and income. . . .*

*At the present moment, Mexico is in a state of social and economic transformation. In the past the majority of the Mexican people lacked economic opportunities, and the development of individual initiative on their part was impossible because the means of production were controlled and monopolized. . . .*

*The new distribution of the sources of production will in time create a condition unknown in the past; a truly rich Mexico, the wealth of which will be due to productive efforts freed from all the obstacles that formerly obstructed them.*

---

Federico Bach, "The Distribution of Wealth in Mexico," *The Annals of the American Academy of Political and Social Science,* 208 (1940), 77.

# 48

# HOWARD F. CLINE

———•———

# MEXICO'S
# TRANSITION IN 1940[*]

❧

*After three decades of upheaval, Mexico clamored
for stability and economic development. Howard F.
Cline, introduced in Selection 12, has written that
Mexico successfully entered into a new stage of Institutional Revolution in 1940, and his comments provide a fitting conclusion to our synthesized history of
Mexico's years of upheaval after 1910.*

The threat of the Second World War was beginning to
loom over the hemisphere when President Cárdenas completed his crucial six-year term in 1940. To his successor,
Manuel Avila Camacho (1940–1946), fell the task of consolidating the Cárdenas gains. Camacho attempted to heal
the splits and divisions created under Cárdenas, which had
been held in check during his rule largely because of his
personal prestige and the almost adulatory support he received from peasants, laborers, and above all, the armed
forces. Many Mexicans claim that the Revolution ended in
1940 when Cárdenas, faithful to its basic political principle—"effective suffrage, no reelection"—stepped aside.

———

[*] From *Mexico: Revolution to Evolution, 1940–1960* by Howard
F. Cline, published by Oxford University Press in 1962 for the Royal
Institute of International Affairs, 34 and 231–233.

But most believe that the Revolution is greater than one man, and continues, transformed but still vital as a result of Mexico's participation in the Second World War and the changes it engendered.

Certainly the history of modern Mexico and of the Revolution has taken a different course since 1940. Quietly but efficiently President Avila Camacho brought about some degree of national unity, while making Mexico an effective member of the United Nations after it had declared war on the Axis. Thus 1940 marks a significant watershed in the course of recent Mexican history.

.     .     .

The Institutional Revolution differs significantly from earlier periods since 1910. One of the clearest and most important of these distinctions lies in its economic policies.

Although the earlier phases of the Revolution pioneered in political and social realms, they seldom strayed in the economic field far from the orthodox lines of the day. The years from 1910 through the middle 1920s were primarily concerned with political problems: the creation of political stability was a paramount goal. Their economic programs were not successful. With a Mexican record of default on bonds and other obligations as a result of the Militant Revolution, and with xenophobia at a high pitch, there was small incentive to domestic or foreign investment. Few local sources had creative capital. World-wide depression snuffed out the very small beginnings of economic development, initiated after political tranquillity had been precariously achieved, chiefly through the single-party mechanism invented in 1929.

The years of Lázaro Cárdenas were concerned essentially with social rather than economic matters. But many actions in his times had important economic implications. For example, nationalization policies in railways, agricultural holdings, and above all, petroleum, were socially and politically, not economically, motivated. These actions, all probably necessary and psychologically sound, gave Mexicans a new sense of national identity and freedom to determine their own fate, a spirit nearly unique in the Latin American community. Foreign control of the basic elements of economic life were thus erased, clearing the ground for the next phase. That was to build a national economic system which should provide for the heirs of the Revolution the long-promised material benefits, within the revolutionary framework of institutions constructed since 1910.

The Second World War provided a suitable transition period. The time was ripe, and opportunity was at hand. International credit and prestige had been reestablished, when Mexico placed important material and human contributions behind the Allied war effort. Emphasis shifted from redividing the small resources to increasing the productive capacity of Mexico.

Pressures of war clearly revealed the inability of this rudimentary, semicolonial economic system to support its people. Pulverized into small and uneconomical land plots, agriculture showed its painful inadequacies. The shutting off of manufactured exports by Mexico's traditional suppliers similarly highlighted the small and poorly organized national industrial plant. Creaking and inefficient communications were temporarily patched with outside aid to carry goods, especially critical minerals, for the arsenals of democracy, but their real weakness was fully exposed. These and other considerations made a policy shift imperative.

The new directions, begun under President Manuel Avila Camacho, preserved but modified many older programs; emphasis changed as major new departures were fostered. Economic rather than social criteria measured agrarian recommendations: enlarged land units were distributed within the *ejido* or communal systems, and new stress was placed on increasing the amount of productive land. The policy also encouraged the coexistence of small- and medium-size private holdings by giving them equal financial and technical assistance, not long before restricted only to the communal system.

A main keynote of the new departure was industrialization. Widely debated as to desirability, weight of circumstances brought a definite decision: Mexico must industrialize to progress. The birthday of the Institutional Revolution is 21 April 1941, when the first Law of Manufacturing Industries became effective. It provided tax exemptions to Mexican industries, especially new ones and those thought necessary for further stimulation of Mexican manufactures.

A new generation of businesslike Mexicans, whom the late Sanford Mosk has labelled the "New Group," worked out a coherent and attractive broad plan for an industrialized Mexico, to be coupled with a renovated agricultural Mexico. Their social and industrial programs became the base of new government economic thinking. The larger part of their plan appears in modified form in the charter of modern Mexican industrialism, the "Law for the Development of New and Necessary Industries" (February 1946), still in force.

The New Group program thus fully adopted in 1946 and subsequently elaborated by the Institutional Revolution, aims to raise the standards of living of all Mexicans. For these benefits they were and are expected to accept certain burdens: inflation; disciplined and peaceful labor; the premiss that rural and urban industrialization will outrank agrarian reform as the main focus of the Revolution until the two phases are balanced.

# BIBLIOGRAPHIC ESSAY

———————•———————

In offering a selective guide to additional reading while suggesting the need for further research on the Revolution between 1910 and 1940, we have necessarily omitted many works which we would like to mention. It is not our purpose to present an exhaustive general bibliography or to repeat the fine bibliographic essays in, for example, Stanley R. Ross, *Is the Mexican Revolution Dead?* (New York: Knopf, 1966); Frank R. Brandenburg, *The Making of Modern Mexico* (Englewood Cliffs, N.J.: Prentice-Hall, 1964); and Howard F. Cline, *The United States and Mexico* (Cambridge, Mass.: Harvard University Press, 1953, 1963).

Syntheses of the Revolution to 1940 can be found in differing types of works. The best scholarly account is provided in the pages of the above-mentioned work by Cline. Important interpretations of the Revolution at three different stages are set forth in Frank Tannenbaum's studies: *The Mexican Agrarian Revolution* (Washington, D.C.: Brookings Institution, 1929), *Peace by Revolution, An Interpretation of Mexico* (New York: Columbia University Press, 1933), and *Mexico: the Struggle for Peace and Bread* (New York: Columbia University Press, 1950). Photographic history of the Revolution has been provided by Anita Brenner and George R. Leighton, *The Wind which Swept Mexico* (New York: Harper & Row, 1943); and Gustavo Casasola, *Historia gráfica de la Revolución Mexicana, 1910–1960* (4 vols.; México, D.F.: Editorial Trillas, 1960).

The era of discontent prior to the Revolution is well described by several works. An important analysis of the Porfirio Díaz regime and sources of discontent in 1908 and 1909 is the famous work by Andrés Molina Enríquez, *Los grandes problemas nacionales* (México, D.F.: Imprenta Carranza e

Hijos, 1909). The Liberal Party, the Flores Magón movement, and the labor precursors of the Revolution are examined in both American and Mexican works. Lowell Blaisdell, *The Desert Revolution* (Madison: University of Wisconsin Press, 1962), concentrates on the Magón attempt to seize Baja California in 1911. The classic Mexican work on the early labor movement is Rosendo Salazar, *Las pugnas de la gleba* (México, D.F.: Editorial Avante, 1922). A recent work is James Cockcroft, *Intellectual Precursors of the Mexican Revolution, 1900–1913* (Austin: University of Texas Press, 1968). Readers interested in this era will also want to consult Lyle C. Brown's important article, "The Mexican Liberals and Their Struggle Against the Díaz Dictatorship, 1900–1906," *Antología MCC, 1956* (México, D.F.: Mexico City College Press, 1956), 317–362. We still await a definitive study of the Flores Magón brothers and a full analysis of the Mexican labor movement's role in the famous strikes at Río Branco and Cananea.

Francisco I. Madero, the Revolution's first President and its foremost martyr, has been well covered by two studies in English: Charles Cumberland, *The Mexican Revolution: Genesis Under Madero* (Austin: University of Texas Press, 1952); and Stanley R. Ross, *Francisco I. Madero, Apostle of Mexican Democracy* (New York: Columbia University Press, 1955). Unfortunately, there are few objective biographies of other leading figures in the early Revolution. Almost alone is Michael Meyer's study, *Pascual Orozco* (Lincoln: University of Nebraska Press, 1967). Although hampered by lack of primary sources and biographical information on Orozco himself, Meyer does an excellent job of rehabilitating the much-maligned Chihuahua *caudillo*.

Pancho Villa, the Mexican perhaps most familiar to North American readers, has a vast bibliography, but no definitive biography in any language. Several eyewitness accounts give lucid (and lurid) pictures of the Villa movement. Among the most readable is John Reed, *Insurgent Mexico* (1914), which we have edited with introduction and notes for a new edition (New York: Simon and Schuster, 1969). Other books include Patrick O'Hea, *Reminiscences of the Mexican Revolution* (México, D.F.: Editorial Fornier, S.A., 1966); and Louis Stevens, *Here Comes Pancho Villa* (Philadelphia: Lippincott, 1930). Fortunately, Martín Luis Guzman's two fine works on Villa have been translated into English: *The Eagle and the Serpent,* translated by Harriet de Onís (New York: Dolphin Books, 1965) and *The Memoirs of Pancho Villa,* translated by V. H. Taylor (Austin: University of Texas Press, 1965). The best of many polemical Mexican works on Villa has been written by Federico Cervantes M., *Francisco Villa y la Revolución* (México, D.F.: Ediciones Alonzo, 1960).

Equally famous to North Americans is the southern agrarian leader, Emiliano Zapata. A lively account in English of his Revolution is by a New Orleans newspaperman, Harry Dunn, *The Crimson Jester: Zapata of Mexico* (quoted in Selection 11). Another description is Edgecombe Pinchon's novelistic work, *Zapata, the Unconquerable* (New York: Doubleday, 1941). Less favorable views of the *Zapatista* movement and the Revolution in Cuernavaca can be found in Rosa E. King, *Tempest Over Mexico* (Boston: Little, Brown, 1935). A book, published by John Womack, Jr., *Zapata and the Mexican Revolution* (New York: Knopf, 1969), gives one of the best treatments to date of this controversial leader. Mexican sources on Zapata include Jesús Sotelo Inclán, *Raíz y razón de Zapata* (México, D.F.: Editorial Etnos, 1943). Also, the book by Gildardo Magaña, *Emiliano Zapata y el agrarismo en México* (5 vols.; México, D.F.: various publishers, 1934–1946) contains much valuable primary source material on the life and ideology of Zapata.

Most of the material on the civil war that engulfed Mexico after Madero's death is in Spanish. Unfortunately this material is very partisan in nature. A revisionary study of the usurper Victoriano Huerta, who was obviously not as evil as his detractors have tried to paint him, is badly needed. The first English attempt to vindicate Huerta is a study by William Sherman and Richard Greenleaf, *Victoriano Huerta, A Reappraisal* (México, D.F.: University of the Americas Press, 1960), which is based largely on secondary sources. A much less polemical study of Huerta, although limited to the years before Madero's death, is George Rausch, "The Early Career of Victoriano Huerta," *The Americas,* 21, (1964) 136–145. Contemporary accounts of the era are provided in two books by Edith O'Shaughnessy, *A Diplomat's Wife in Mexico* (New York: Harper & Row, 1916), and *Intimate Pages of Mexican History* (New York: Doubleday, 1920).

There is only a spotty coverage on the confused fighting preceding the victory of Venustiano Carranza in 1915. Professor Robert E. Quirk has ably examined the rivalry between Villa and Carranza and the climax of this rivalry at the Convention of Aguascalientes in his study, *The Mexican Revolution, 1914–1915* (Bloomington: University of Indiana Press, 1960). The same time period is also described by I. Thord-Gray, an English soldier of fortune who served with Carranza, in *Gringo Rebel* (Coral Gables, Fla.: University of Miami Press, 1960).

Carranza's top general and later President, Alvaro Obregón, has left his memoirs of those years in his autobiographical *Ocho mil kilómetros en campaña* (3rd ed.; México, D.F.: Fondo de Cultura Económica, 1960). Those interested in a month by month chronological approach can consult Alfonso Taracena, *Mi vida en el vértigo de la Revolución Mexicana* (México, D.F.: Editorial Jus, 1950). Those who do not read Spanish may sample the flavor of this complicated period by reading the novels of Mariano Azuela, *The Underdogs,* translated by E. Munguía, Jr. (New York: New American Library, 1962), and *Two Novels of Mexico: The Flies, the Bosses,* translated by L. B. Simpson (Berkeley and Los Angeles: University of California Press, 1956). Carlos Fuentes, *The Death of Artemio Cruz,* translated by Sam Hileman (New York: Farrar, Straus & Giroux, 1964), gives the reader an excellent idea of some moral problems in the conflict.

In 1917 the victorious Carranza called a convention at Querétaro to draft a new Mexican constitution. Although the resulting charter is one of Latin America's most important documents, there is no published scholarly study of the convention and the men who drafted the Constitution. The best work in any language is an unpublished M.A. thesis by E. Victor Niemeyer, Jr., "The Mexican Constitutional Convention of 1917" (University of Texas, Austin, 1951). Felix Palavicini has told the *Carrancista* side in his *Historia de la Constitución de 1917* (2 vols.: México, D.F.: n.p., 1938). Juan de Dios Bojórquez (pseudonym, Djed Bórquez) has detailed the same events from the point of view of the more radical followers of Obregón in his *Crónica del constituyente* (México, D.F.: Ediciones Botas, 1938). Those who wish to compare the Constitution of 1917 with the Constitution of 1857 may examine the book by H. M. Branch, *The Mexican Constitution of 1917 Compared with the Constitution of 1857* (Philadelphia: American Academy of Political and Social Science, 1917).

Many scholars see Woodrow Wilson's meddling in Mexican affairs as the major cause of Carranza's victory over Huerta and Villa. The best study of this issue is to be found in Cline's aforementioned *The United States and Mexico,* but more detailed analyses of aspects of this problem are covered in Robert E. Quirk's prize-winning study of the United States' occupation of Veracruz, *An Affair of Honor* (Lexington: University of Kentucky Press, 1962); and Clarence C. Clendenen, *The United States and Pancho Villa* (Ithaca, N.Y.: Cornell University Press, 1961).

There is no scholarly monograph on the government of Carranza or a biography of the man himself. His government is only touched upon in two general studies of the 1920s: Ernest Gruening, *Mexico and Its Heritage* (New York: Appleton-Century-Crofts, 1928) and John W. F. Dulles, *Yesterday in Mexico, A Chronicle of the Revolution, 1919–1936* (Austin: University of Texas Press, 1961). The controversial death of Carranza is described by Ramón Beteta in *Camino a Tlaxcalantongo* (México, D.F.: Fondo de Cultura Económica, 1961).

The period in Mexican history between 1912 and 1921 is one of the most neglected in recent Mexican history. There are no objective biographies in any language of Angeles, Múgica, Blanco, or Cabrera, for example. For the enterprising scholar there are innumerable topics that await investigation, including, among others: the Constitutional Convention of 1917, the military history of the civil war, the conservatives and their attempt to stem the revolutionary tide, the early Mexican labor movement, and the Mexican railroad system and the Revolution.

The period following Carranza's overthrow is even more neglected, if that is possible, than the civil war. A groundbreaking although completely narrative study of Carranza's successors can be found in Dulles' magnificently detailed chronicle of the years between 1921 and 1935, cited above. The only published biography of Obregón in English is the hagiographical *President Obregón: A World Reformer,* by E. J. Dillon (London: Hutchison, 1923). A slight improvement, although based mostly on secondary sources, is Donald D. Johnson's unpublished Ph.D. dissertation, "Alvaro Obregón and the Mexican Revolution" (University of Southern California, Los Angeles, 1946). All the existing works in Spanish are polemical accounts by supporters of the one-armed general or his enemies.

Obregón's successor, General Plutarco Elías Calles, also lacks objective studies or biographies. Those who have an interest in his philosophy while he was President may consult the book of speeches translated by R. H. Murray, *Mexico Before the World* (New York: Academy Press, 1927). Eyler N. Simpson, *The Ejido, Mexico's Way Out* (Chapel Hill: University of North Carolina Press, 1937), gives a complete picture of Calles' agrarian policy and the laws he sponsored.

The best way to approach the 1921 to 1934 period is through a series of monographs on individual problems. So much has been written on the government's disputes with the Catholic Church, that we can only mention the most objective of these. The best study so far is the unpublished Ph.D. dissertation in history by Robert E. Quirk, "The Mexican Revolution and the Catholic Church, 1910–1929: An Ideological Study" (Harvard University, Cambridge, Mass., 1951). More limited in scope but also refreshingly objective among Mexican works on the religious issue is a new study by Alicia Olivera Sedano, *Aspectos del conflicto religioso de 1926 a 1929* (México, D.F.: Instituto Nacional de Antropología e Historia, 1966). The only other unimpassioned discussion of this issue can be found in the appropriate chapters of John Lloyd Mecham, *Church and State in Latin America* (rev. ed.; Chapel Hill: University of North Carolina Press, 1966). Although much has been written on the *Cristeros,* the *Sinarquistas* have almost been ignored. The Sinarquista movement is described during its formative years in Albert L. Michaels, "Fascism and Sinarquismo: Popular Nationalism Against the Mexican Revolution," *A Journal of Church and State,* 8 (1966), 234–250; and Nathan L. Whetten, *Rural Mexico* (Chicago: University of Chicago Press, 1948), Chap. 20. An important neglected source is Salvador Abascal, "Por qué fundé la Colonia Sinarquista María Auxiliadora; Historia del Sinarquismo en México," *Mañana* (May 20– October 28, 1944, serialized).

Regarding labor, Marjorie Ruth Clark has published a scholarly study of the Mexican labor movement: *Organized Labor in Mexico* (Chapel Hill: University of North Carolina Press, 1934). Additional information on the Mexican labor movement during the Northern Dynasty can be gleaned from two highly partisan Mexican sources, Rosendo Salazar, *Historia de las luchas proletarias de México* (México, D.F.: Editorial Avante,

1939); and Luis Araiza, *Historia del movimiento obrero mexicano* (México, D.F.: Editorial Cuauhtémoc, 1965).

Information on the political struggles of the 1920s and early 1930s is extremely incomplete and usually can only be found in highly polemical sources. Ex-president Emilio Portes Gil has written two informative volumes on his role in the events of this period: *Quince años de política mexicana* (México, D.F.: Ediciones Botas, 1941), and *Autobiográfia de la Revolución Mexicana* (México, D.F.: Instituto Mexicano de Cultura, 1964). Also extremely useful is a book by ex-minister of agriculture Marte R. Gómez, *La reforma agraria de México: Su crisis durante el período 1928–1934* (México, D.F.: Manuel Porrúa, 1964). The presidential campaign of José Vasconcelos in 1929 has been ably described by the novelist Mauricio Magdaleno in his *Las palabras perdidas* (México, D.F.: Fondo de Cultura Económica, 1956). Earlier, Magdaleno had pilloried the corrupt politicians of the Revolution in his famous novel, *El resplandor,* translated into English by Anita Brenner under the title of *Sunburst* (New York: Viking, 1944). José Vasconcelos also gives a highly partisan account of this period in his autobiography *Ulises criollo,* which has appeared in many editions (see Selection 43). The best source for the rebellions against Obregón and Calles is Dulles' book, *Yesterday in Mexico,* but there are two good accounts of the 1923 De la Huerta rebellion by Mexican authors: Alonso Capetillo, *La rebelión sin cabeza* (México, D.F: Imprenta Botas, 1925); and Luis Monroy Duran, *El último caudillo* (México, D.F.: José S. Rodríguez, 1924). The memoirs of ex-Presidents Pascual Ortiz Rubio and Adolfo de la Huerta have also appeared in Mexico but both are quite disappointing. Somewhat more informative is an apologia by the private secretary of Abelardo Rodríguez. In this work, *El Presidente Rodríguez, 1932–1934* (México, D.F.: Editorial Cultura, 1933), Francisco Javier Gaxiola, Jr., gives some excellent background information on the rise of Lázaro Cárdenas to the presidency in 1933.

We do not have the plethora of English accounts for the 1920s that exist for the first decade of the Revolution. However, two books by the North American Carleton Beals give us a good idea of what life was like under the Northern Dynasty: *Mexican Maze* (Philadelphia: Lippincott, 1931) is largely impressionistic, and *Glass Houses: Ten Years of Free-Lancing* (Philadelphia: Lippincott, 1938) is autobiographical. The latter offers some valuable material on the origins of the Mexican Communist Party.

There are many books on the diplomatic relations between Mexico and the United States in those years, but all are dated. Also lacking is a book on the important ambassadorship of Morgan banker Dwight W. Morrow, although the subject has been ably handled by Stanley R. Ross in two periodical articles, "Dwight Morrow and the Mexican Revolution," *Hispanic American Historical Review*, 38 (1958), 506–528, and "Dwight Morrow: Ambassador to Mexico," *The Americas*, 14 (1958), 272–290. Harold Nicolson, *Dwight Morrow* (New York: Harcourt, Brace & World, 1935) is based on Morrow's papers but adds little to our knowledge of the Ambassador's Mexican policy which is developed in only one chapter. Of Morrow's predecessor James R. Sheffield we know virtually nothing except that his arrogant attitude thoroughly alienated the Mexicans and apparently brought the two nations to the verge of war.

In 1933 the Mexican presidency was assumed by General Cárdenas who then proceeded to carry out the social reforms that his predecessors had only promised. Although every Mexicanist realizes the importance of Cárdenas' presidency, very little has been published on that topic. In English there are two extremely biased studies of the subject: William Cameron Townsend, *Lázaro Cárdenas: Mexican Democrat* (Ann Arbor, Mich.: George Wahr, 1952); and Nathaniel and Sylvia Weyl, *The Reconquest of Mexico: The Years of Lázaro Cárdenas* (New York: Oxford University Press, 1939). Both are in the class of Dillon's sycophantic study of Obregón. Most helpful in understanding this complex period are acounts of Americans living and working in Mexico. Among the best are Virginia Prewett, *Reportage on Mexico* (New York: Dutton, 1941); Betty Kirk, *Covering the Mexican Front* (Norman: University of Oklahoma Press, 1942); J. H. Plenn, *Mexico Marches* (Indianapolis: Bobbs-Merrill, 1939); and Verna Carleton Millan, *Mexico Reborn* (Boston: Houghton Mifflin, 1939). Mexican studies of Cárdenas all suffer from the partisanship of the individual authors.

The most useful polemics by the detractors of Cárdenas are Victoriano Anguiano Equihua, *Lázaro Cárdenas: su feudo y la política nacional* (México, D.F.: Editorial Eréndira, 1951); and Carlos Alvear Acevedo, *Lázaro Cárdenas* (México, D.F.:

Editorial Jus, 1961). Helpful works by Cárdenas' supporters are Silvano Barba González, *Lázaro Cárdenas,* which is volume IV in the series *La lucha por la tierra* (4 vols.; México, D.F.: Editorial Magisterio, 1964); and Roberto Blanco Moheno, *El Cardenismo* (México, D.F.: Libro-Mex, 1963).

More balanced than the published sources are three unpublished works: James W. Wilkie, "Ideological Conflict in the Time of Lázaro Cárdenas" (unpublished M.A. thesis in history, University of California, Berkeley, 1959), of which an excerpt is reproduced in Selection 34; Lyle C. Brown, "General Lázaro Cárdenas and Mexican Presidential Politics: A Study in the Acquisition and Manipulation of Political Power" (unpublished Ph.D. thesis in political science, University of Texas, Austin, 1964); and Albert L. Michaels, "Mexican Politics and Nationalism from Calles to Cárdenas" (unpublished Ph.D. thesis in history, University of Pennsylvania, Philadelphia, 1966), (see Selection 37).

There are some works of varying degrees of competence on various aspects of Cárdenas' presidency. The best is a study of the labor movement by Joe C. Ashby, *Organized Labor and the Mexican Revolution Under Lázaro Cárdenas* (Chapel Hill: University of North Carolina Press, 1967). Robert Paul Millon's recent study, *Mexican Marxist: Vicente Lombardo Toledano* (Chapel Hill: University of North Carolina Press, 1966), suffers from the worshipful attitude of the author toward his subject. Although the issue is treated in more general studies of Mexican education, the few studies of Mexican socialist education under Cárdenas include an article by Lyle C. Brown, "Mexican Church-State Relations, 1933–1940," *A Journal of Church and State,* 6 (1964), 207–222; and an unpublished Ph.D. thesis by Harry John Carlson, "The Impact of the Cárdenas Administration on Mexican Education," (University of Arizona, Tucson, 1964). The military during the Cárdenas epoch has been analyzed briefly by Edwin Lieuwen in *Arms and Politics in Latin America* (New York: Praeger, 1961), Chap. 4. Also see, Lieuwen's book on *Mexican Militarism: The Political Rise and Fall of the Revolutionary Army, 1910–1940* (Albuquerque: University of New Mexico Press, 1968).

The problem of Cárdenas' successor and the extremely controversial election of 1940 has been largely ignored by scholars. A unique academic study of the election is found in an unpublished M.A. thesis by Shirley E. Stone, "The Mexican Presidential Elections of 1940 as Seen Through the Press of the Capital" (Columbia University, New York, 1949). Other works that give some insight into the *ambiente* of the late 1930s are by Salvador Novo, *La Vida en México en el período presidencial de Lázaro Cárdenas* (México, D.F.: Empresas Editoriales, 1964); Armando de María y Campos', *Múgica, crónica biográfica* (México, D.F.: Compañia de Ediciones Populares, 1939); and Magdalena Mondragón, *Cuando la Revolución se cortó las alas* (México, D.F.: Costa-Amic, 1966).

Diplomatic relations with the United States can be studied through E. David Cronon, *Josephus Daniels in Mexico* (Madison: University of Wisconsin Press, 1960); and the memoirs of our able ambassador Josephus Daniels, *Shirt-Sleeve Diplomat* (Chapel Hill: University of North Carolina Press, 1947). The Mexican view of the oil controversy is eloquently presented by Jesús Silva Herzog in *La expropiación del petróleo en México* (México, D.F.: Cuadernos Americanos, 1963). An excellent study of the "Good Neighbor Policy" of Franklin D. Roosevelt and its effect upon United States–Mexican relations is Bryce Wood, *The Making of the Good Neighbor Policy* (New York: Columbia University Press, 1961).

The problem of the land has been studied by many men at different times; yet we still lack a clear statistical statement on the subject. The best works on the land problem in different epochs are George M. McBride, *The Land Systems of Mexico* (New York: American Geographical Society, 1923); Eyler N. Simpson, *The Ejido, Mexico's Way Out* (discussed above); Nathan L. Whetten, *Rural Mexico* (mentioned above); and Tom Gill, *Land Hunger in Mexico* (Washington, D.C.: C. L. Pack Forestry Foundation, 1951). Many Mexicans have also tackled this still controversial issue, the most useful being Andrés Molina Enríquez, *La revolución agraria 1910–1920* (5 vols., México, D.F.: Talleres Gráficos del Museo Nacional de Arquelogía, Historia y Etnografía, 1937); and more recently, Jesús Silva Herzog, *El agrarismo mexicano y la reforma agraria, exposición y crítica* (México, D.F.: Fondo de Cultura Económica, 1959).

Many scholars have worked on the Mexican revolutionary government's attempts to democratize and modernize Mexico's educational system. The three books that give the most insight into programs since the 1920s are George F. Knellner, *The Education of the Mexican Nation* (New York: Columbia University Press, 1951); George I. Sánchez, *The Development of Higher Education in Mexico* (New York: Columbia University Press, 1944); and Ramón E. Ruiz, *Mexico, the Challenge of Poverty and Illiteracy* (San Marino, Calif.: Huntington Library, 1963).

Discussion of the bibliography of the early stages of the Revolution would be incomplete without mentioning the work that has been done on the revolutionary artists and the folk songs or *corridos* that have sprung from the Revolution. In 1929 Anita Brenner, always a shrewd observer, caught the spirit of the new school of artists in *Idols Behind Altars* (New York: Payson and Clarke, 1929). There have been many books on individual artists, one of the best being Bertram D. Wolfe, *Diego Rivera, His Life and Times* (New York: Stein and Day, 1963). Merle Simmons, *The Mexican Corrido as a Source of Interpretative Study of Modern Mexico* (Bloomington: Indiana University Press, 1957), is indispensable for those interested in the music and politics of the Revolution. In Spanish there are many compilations of revolutionary ballads, the most valuable being Jesús Romero Flores, *Anales históricos de la Revolución Mexicana,* of which Volume V is of *Sus Corridos* (5 vols.; México, D.F.: Ediciones El Nacional, 1941); and Armando María y Campos' two-volume work, *La Revolución Mexicana a través de los corridos populares* (México, D.F.: Biblioteca del Instituto Nacional del Estudios Históricos de la Revolución Mexicana, 1962).

Another very important type of study to emerge from the Revolution has concerned the Mexican national character. Fortunately, the two most famous works have been translated into English: Samuel Ramos, *Profile of Man and Culture in Mexico,* translated by Peter G. Earle (Austin: University of Texas Press, 1962); and Octavio Paz, *The Labyrinth of Solitude,* translated by Lysander Kemp (New York: Grove Press, 1961). Those who wish to consult further should read John Leddy Phelan, "México y lo mexicano," *Hispanic American Historical Review,* 36 (1956), 309–318; and Frederick C. Turner, *The Dynamics of Mexican Nationalism* (Chapel Hill: University of North Carolina Press, 1968).

Related to both the social and psychological changes wrought by the Revolution is the Mexican novel of the Revolution. The most comprehensive studies of this subject are by John S. Brushwood, *Mexico in its Novel; A Nation's Search for Identity*

(Austin: University of Texas Press, 1966); and F. Morton Rand, *Los novelistas de la Revolución Mexicana* (México, D.F.: Editorial Cultura, 1949).

The oral history of the Revolution is being tape-recorded in interviews with Mexican leaders by the Wilkies. A first volume has been published: James W. Wilkie and Edna Monzón de Wilkie, *México visto en el siglo XX; Entrevistas de Historia Oral: Ramón Beteta, Marte R. Gómez, Manuel Gómez Morín, Vicente Lombardo Toledano, Miguel Palomar y Vizcarra, Emilio Portes Gil, Jesús Silva Herzog* (México, D.F.: Instituto Mexicano de Investigaciones Económicas, 1969).

Overviews of the Revolution in relation to the entire span of Mexican history are provided by Hudson Strode, *Timeless Mexico* (New York: Harcourt, Brace & World, 1944); Henry Bamford Parks, *A History of Mexico* (rev. ed.; Boston: Houghton Mifflin, 1950); and Lesley B. Simpson, *Many Mexicos* (rev. ed.; Berkeley and Los Angeles: University of California Press, 1966). Simpson is the master of summing up a man's life or an era of history in a single, pithy adjective and his book is very good reading indeed, if overly pessimistic about Mexico's future. An embittered Catholic view, which is also very readable, is found in Joseph H. L. Schlarman, *Mexico, A Land of Volcanoes* (Milwaukee: Bruce, 1950). The most recent study is by Charles C. Cumberland, *Mexico, the Struggle for Modernity* (New York: Oxford University Press, 1968).

Writings on Mexico have been based on political studies because economic analysis generally has not been available. Except for such works as, for example, Edwin Walter Kemmerer, *Inflation and Revolution, Mexico's Experience of 1912–1917* (Princeton, N.J.: Princeton University Press, 1940); and Edgar Turlington, *Mexico and Her Foreign Creditors* (New York: Columbia University Press, 1930), historical assessment of Mexico's economic development prior to 1940 has been largely neglected. This situation has recently been remedied by such works as Raymond Vernon, *The Dilemma of Mexico's Economic Development: The Roles of the Private and Public Sectors* (quoted in Selection 1); and William P. Glade, Jr., and Charles W. Anderson, *The Political Economy of Mexico* (Madison: University of Wisconsin Press, 1963). In addition, a book by Clark W. Reynolds of the Stanford University Food Research Institute, now nearing completion, will provide the basic statistical data for analyzing *The Mexican Economy: Twentieth Century Structure and Growth.*

Social aspects of Mexican life prior to 1940 have been statistically developed in relation to economic policy in James W. Wilkie, *The Mexican Revolution: Federal Expenditure and Social Change Since 1910* (Berkeley and Los Angeles: University of California Press, 1967), but otherwise such social analysis is almost nonexistent. Some references to social developments between 1910 and 1940 are discussed by José Iturriaga, *La estructura social y cultural de México* (México, D.F.: Fondo de Cultura Económica, 1951); and Julio Durán Ochoa, *Población* (México, D.F.: Fondo de Cultura Económica, 1955), but the subject is basically open to investigation.

Political aspects of social and economic life are discussed in books by Pablo Gonzáles Casanova, *La Democracia en México* (México, D.F.: Ediciones Era, 1965), and *México, 50 años de Revolución* (4 vols.; México, D.F.: Fondo de Cultura Económica, 1960–1962), I. *La economía,* II. *La vida social,* III. *La política,* IV. *La cultura.*

Although there is much good reading on Mexico, it is apparent that historical interpretation cannot be firmly based until some basic work is completed on the nature and course of the Mexican Revolution during its phase of upheaval. The success that Mexico has enjoyed since 1940 (a success not recognized until the 1950s and 1960s) is rooted in the dramatic changes and events that we have chronicled in the foregoing pages. If modern Mexico is to be fully understood, the years from 1910 to 1940 must be more closely examined from many points of view.

# BIBLIOGRAPHIC INDEX
# OF AUTHORS QUOTED

———•———

Arabic numerals refer to Selections 1–48
Roman numerals refer to prefatory notes in Parts I–V

## A Note on the Type

The text of this book was set on the Linotype in a face called TIMES ROMAN, designed by Stanley Morison for The Times (London), and first introduced by that newspaper in 1932.

Among typographers and designers of the twentieth century, Stanley Morison has been a strong forming influence, as typographical advisor to the English Monotype Corporation, as a director of two distinguished English publishing houses, and as a writer of sensibility, erudition, and keen practical sense.

*Composed and bound by*
*H. Wolff Book Mfg. Co., New York, N.Y.*
*Printed by*
*Halliday Lithograph Corp.,*
*West Hanover, Mass.*

*Designed by*
*Anthea Lingeman*

BORZOI BOOKS ON LATIN AMERICA

*Under the General Editorship of Lewis Hanke,*
UNIVERSITY OF MASSACHUSETTS, AMHERST

*\* Also available in a hardbound edition.*

THE MONROE DOCTRINE *
ITS MODERN SIGNIFICANCE
*Edited by* Donald Marquand Dozer

A DOCUMENTARY HISTORY OF BRAZIL *
*Edited by* E. Bradford Burns

BACKGROUND TO REVOLUTION *
THE DEVELOPMENT OF MODERN CUBA
*Edited by* Robert Freeman Smith

IS THE MEXICAN REVOLUTION DEAD? *
*Edited by* Stanley R. Ross

FOREIGN INVESTMENT IN LATIN AMERICA *
*Edited by* Marvin Bernstein

WHY PERON CAME TO POWER *
*Edited by* Joseph R. Barager

MARXISM IN LATIN AMERICA *
*Edited by* Luis E. Aguilar

A CENTURY OF BRAZILIAN HISTORY SINCE 1865 *
*Edited by* Richard Graham

REVOLUTION IN MEXICO: YEARS OF UPHEAVAL,
1910–1940 *
*Edited by* James W. Wilkie and Albert L. Michaels

*Forthcoming:*
THE LIBERATOR, SIMON BOLIVAR,
MAN AND IMAGE *
*Edited by* David Bushnell

*\* Also available in a hardbound edition.*